THE BLOGGING REVOLUTION

THE**BLOGGING** REVOLUTION

ANTONY**LOEWENSTEIN**

MELBOURNE
UNIVERSITY
PRESS

MELBOURNE UNIVERSITY PRESS
An imprint of Melbourne University Publishing Limited
187   Grattan Street, Carlton, Victoria 3053, Australia
mup-info@unimelb.edu.au
www.mup.com.au

First published 2008
Text © Antony Loewenstein 2008
Design and typography © Melbourne University Publishing Ltd 2008

Every attempt has been made to locate the copyright holders for material quoted in this book. Any person or organisation that may have been overlooked or misattributed may contact the publisher.

Cover design by Andrew Budge, Designland
Text design by Alice Graphics
Typeset by Midland Typesetters, Australia
Printed in Australia by Griffin Press, SA

National Library of Australia Cataloguing-in-Publication entry

Loewenstein, Antony.

The blogging revolution / Antony Loewenstein.

9780522854909 (pbk)

Bibliography.

Blogs—Political aspects.
Blogs—Social aspects.
Freedom of speech.

323.443

To imprisoned dissidents everywhere

Contents

Introduction

Getting on the Blogging Bandwagon

Bloggers are not exactly journalists, which is a mistake many people make. They expect us to be dispassionate and unemotional about topics such as occupation and war. That objective lack of emotion is impossible because a blog in itself stems from passion—the need to sit for hours at one's computer, slouched over the keyboard, trying to communicate ideas, thoughts, fears and frustrations to the world.

Iraqi blogger Riverbend, 2006[1]

I T WAS AN INCONGRUOUS situation. I had just arrived in Tehran in early June 2007 and found myself in a cramped, one-star hotel room watching the only English language satellite channel, the BBC. The anchor crossed live to a speech being given by United States President George W Bush in Prague.[2] The pro-democracy conference, organised by former Czech president Václav Havel and ex-Soviet dissident Natan Sharansky[3], aimed to promote Bush's 'freedom agenda' and express solidarity with dissidents the world over. Initially I wasn't interested in hearing what I expected to be a typically disjointed and deluded talk by the US president, but the other Iranian-state channels offered only local news in Farsi (Iran's national language) and a children's program that looked like Muslim *Teletubbies*.

I was soon transfixed by Bush's rhetoric. As he addressed democracy activists from seventeen countries across five continents, such as Burma, Sudan, Zimbabwe and Cuba, he argued that 'the most powerful weapon in the struggle against extremism is not bullets or bombs—it is the universal appeal of freedom'. He continued: 'The policy of tolerating tyranny is a moral and strategic failure ... [and] the United States is committed to the advance of freedom and democracy as the great alternatives to repression and radicalism.' Bush believed that saluting and supporting dissidents around the world, men and women who battled petty dictatorships or autocracies, would 'achieve human rights'. That these autocracies

1

were often Washington-backed was a truth conveniently overlooked by the president.

It was perversely enjoyable to be hearing the speech, directed primarily towards the Iranian mullahs, in the heart of Bush's 'Axis of Evil'. I listened to the entire talk, regularly interrupted by applause, and was left wondering why I was oddly fascinated, in spite of Bush's rampant militarism. Stripped of history and context, Bush's words resonated with me. The struggle for human rights and freedom was often paid lip-service by Western media increasingly obsessed with localism. I wasn't under any illusion about Bush and his policies or a Western world that talked loftily about democracy then rejected election outcomes in blighted lands such as Palestine. Bush and his ideological bedfellows seemed to understand the threat and use of force to impose or support only regimes that welcomed Washington's dictates. It was therefore unsurprising that America's reputation in the world since September 11, 2001 had never been lower.[4]

This shattering of established myths about America's largesse and benevolence—which deteriorated sharply during the Bush years, despite many previous administrations acting with equal self interest—convinced me to investigate the reality of life in nations that had been affected, isolated or embraced by Washington. I wanted to travel in an unembedded way and meet people who were writing, blogging and using the internet to communicate to their fellow citizens and the world. As I travelled in 2007 to Iran and Egypt, Syria and Saudi Arabia, Cuba and China, I heard the same message: that democracy, the rule of law and free media would come in spite of America rather than because of it.[5]

The internet is arguably the greatest tool since the invention of the printing press to facilitate democratic change, although the medium is barely at the beginning of its potential.[6] But I didn't embark on these journeys with the idea that the web was transforming nations into pale imitations of the West. Far too often, Western commentators arrogantly presume that people living in repressive regimes want our help and crave a lifestyle and outlook comparable to our own. Nothing could be further from the truth, but the reasons are more complex than I had presumed before I started this book.

I started working professionally as a journalist in the early part of the decade, then wrote for the *Sydney Morning Herald* online during the beginning of the 2003 Iraq War and its immediate aftermath. I remember talking to a senior editor at the *Sydney Morning Herald* in the months before the Iraq invasion. I asked her why the paper had featured virtually no Arab or Iraqi voices, either for or against the impending war. 'Oh, I never thought of that,' she replied. If Western voices were the only ones important enough to be validated by column inches, the implication was that Arabs' opinions were somehow untrustworthy or predictable.

It was impossible at this time not to be drawn to international blogs and analysis. My disillusionment with the mainstream media coverage in Australia—its endless swallowing of John Howard's spin on Iraq's supposed weapons of mass destruction (WMD) and praise for the 'vision' of the Bush administration—inevitably led me there. September 11 had caused division around the world but there was also a crisis of confidence in the Western media elite, which had been haemorrhaging audiences and credibility. The vast majority of Western journalists became cheerleaders for the war, not critical sceptics. Blogs from across the Middle East therefore became an essential insight into the minds of people my country was about to help 'liberate'. Years later, with up to one million Iraqis murdered and millions of internally and externally displaced refugees, our media still mostly refuse to examine the 'why' and 'how'.

New York Times executive editor Bill Keller complained in a speech in late 2007 that the real threat to the industry was a 'loss of faith, a failure of resolve on the part of the people who make newspapers'.[7] He wasn't incorrect, but he seemed unwilling to understand the reasons why the internet often seemed far more responsive and inclusive than a major newspaper.[8]

In 2004, PBS host Jim Lehrer told MSNBC's Chris Matthews why he thought the media had failed spectacularly in predicting the chaos in Iraq. It was an example of supreme delusion, though not unusual for journalists who, in the words of Matthews, were not 'supposed to be too aggressively critical of a country at combat, especially when it's your own'.[9] Asked why the media had failed to provide 'critical analysis' before the invasion:

Lehrer: 'The word *occupation* … was never mentioned in the run-up to the war. It was 'liberation'. This was a war of liberation, not a war of occupation. So, as a consequence, those of us in journalism never even looked at the issue of occupation.'
Matthews: 'Because?'
Lehrer: 'Because it just didn't occur to us. We weren't smart enough to do it. I agree. I think it was a dereliction of our [*sic*]—in retrospective [*sic*].'

Seeing this attitude repeated hundreds of times in Australia before the war, I craved critical thinking. Blogs offered context, criticism and cynicism and challenged the top-down approach of corporate media. 'Journals of record', such as the *New York Times* and the *Washington Post*, were simply failing in their duty—unless, of course, one believes (as I increasingly do) that the mainstream media rarely holds the powerful to account and instead sees its role, with notable exceptions, as reinforcing and defending the status quo defined by corporate-invested realities. I had once naively thought that journalists were inherently sceptical about power. I was wrong.

This was unintentionally highlighted in early 2008 by a revealing statement from former MSNBC host Tucker Carlson. After Samantha Power, then-advisor to Democratic presidential hopeful Barack Obama, was forced to resign after calling Hillary Clinton a 'monster', Carlson interviewed the journalist from the *Scotsman* who obtained Power's comment. Carlson interrogated Gerri Peev because she dared to include Power's incriminating quote after being asked to keep it 'off the record'. 'In the United Kingdom,' said Peev, 'journalists believe that on or off the record is a principle that's decided ahead of the interview'. Carlson was incredulous. 'People don't talk to you when you go out of your way to hurt them as you did in this piece,' he fumed. His attitude, widely shared by the mainstream press, is that the role of journalists is not to offend the powerful. It was the kind of journalistic slavishness that led me to grow increasingly impatient with media that viewed reporting in a fundamentally compliant way.

Aside from the compelling posts by the *Guardian*-published Baghdad blogger Salam Pax[10], Western readers before the war would have caught only an occasional glimpse of Iraq without a Western journalist's filter. Our understanding of the world was therefore greatly reduced. But the internet was a different story, filled with wonderfully anarchic discussions with citizens of varying opinions: pro-war, anti-war, undecided, vehemently anti-American and religiously pro-Bush. It left the mainstream media for dead. Blogs, websites and online forums, mostly uncontaminated by the Western media obsession with 'balance', could opine on the gravest decision of our time. It was refreshing to read the opinions of people in the Arab world who would be directly affected by the policies designed in Washington, London and Canberra.

It was a time that shaped my understanding of the role of journalism and I discovered how few friends I had in the mainstream. As John Pilger has argued, 'it is not enough for journalists to see themselves as mere messengers without understanding the hidden agendas of the message and the myths that surround it'. The profound failures of the mainstream media in the lead-up to the 2003 Iraq War—not least its blind acceptance of Saddam Hussein's non-existent weapons of mass destruction stockpiles—led to a huge upsurge in Western citizens sourcing alternative information on the internet. A study by the Tyndall Report in 2006 found that the coverage of Iraq on America's major television networks had fallen nearly 60 per cent since 2003[11] and they were failing at persuading their audiences: only half of Americans polled in 2006 believed that Saddam had WMD in 2003. Such results almost forced readers online to discover the real picture of the war-torn country. Charles Duelfer, the head US inspector who discovered the lack of WMD in Iraq, said cryptically: 'It would be a shame if one effect of the power of the internet was to undermine any commonly agreed set of facts.'[12]

An Iraqi writer and blogger, Faiza al-Arji, visited America after the 2003 invasion and was shocked to discover that the mainstream media was not 'neutral' as she had imagined. 'I started asking people in my interviews, in the past three years, do you remember seeing one Iraqi opposing the war in the mainstream media? They shook their heads and said no.'[13] Her incredulity towards the mainstream's ignorance of the Arab world highlighted the desperate requirement for new voices to be heard, especially those hostile to elite, pro-government thinking. How could it be, I was constantly asked in various non-Western countries, that in a supposedly free country such as America virtually every major commentator and news outlet marched in sync with the government?

The *New York Times,* the *Washington Post,* PBS and a host of 'liberal' and 'conservative' figures alike. This was only supposed to happen in repressive regimes. 'We had more debate here than in the countries going to war,' one blogger told me in Egypt.

We were treated to 'experts' such as columnist Thomas Friedman from the *New York Times.* A strong advocate of military action, his inclusion in the debate was deemed serious simply because of his vaunted position. The fact that he spent years after the invasion continually stating that the next 'decisive' six months would determine the outcome of the war seemed to be ignored by Western editors who continued publishing his discredited predictions.[14] The moment that perfectly defined my disillusionment with even the 'liberal' media[15] was when Friedman made the following comments in May 2003 to talk show host Charlie Rose:

> What they [the Iraqis] needed to see was American boys and girls going house to house, from Basra to Baghdad, um and basically saying, 'Which part of this sentence don't you understand?' You don't think, you know, we care about our open society, you think this bubble fantasy, we're just gonna to let it grow? Well, Suck. On. This. That Charlie is what this war is about. We could of hit Saudi Arabia, it was part of that bubble. Could of hit Pakistan. We hit Iraq because we could.[16]

Friedman's arrogance was startling. It revealed an insularity that defined so much of mainstream media thinking. Rather than relying on media whose resources would always dwarf a lone blogger, countless people all over the world simply went to the source of the story themselves. The traditional top-down relationship between writer and viewer/reader began to fracture.

The *New York Times* stated a few months before the 2004 US election that, 'a year ago, no one other than campaign staff and chronic insomniacs read political blogs'.[17] In fact, the shift to the internet had become a matter of faith long before. The media elite was in denial.

The Western media has spent the last few years resisting the internet onslaught until it became impossible to do so any more. Every major newspaper website around the world now has blogs and online forums to attract a younger readership.[18] But problems persist, not least declining circulation and media ownership concentration. Less than one-fifth of America's 1500 daily newspapers are independently owned.

The number of companies owning TV stations has dropped 40 per cent since 1995.[19] Six major corporations own the vast majority of American entertainment outlets and this figure is shrinking every year.[20]

These facts are rarely discussed in the corporate media but citizens are becoming increasingly sceptical. A Zogby International study in 2008 found that two-thirds of Americans now believe that traditional journalism is 'out of touch'.[21] A Harvard study in late 2007 found that nearly two-thirds of Americans did not trust coverage of the 2008 presidential campaign and a vast majority thought that the coverage focused too heavily on the trivial.[22] *Washington Post* journalist Dan Froomkin warns that mainstream political journalism is in danger of 'becoming increasingly irrelevant' if it doesn't 'call bullshit' and cease publishing spin as news.[23] *Post* veteran Walter Pincus takes this argument even further, challenging the mainstream media to refuse carrying any official comment that is 'designed solely as a public relations tool, offering no new or valuable information to the public'.[24]

The situation in Australia is equally dire. Successive governments across the political divide have, over the last decades, granted the media moguls, including Rupert Murdoch, Kerry Packer and the Fairfax Media group, unprecedented ability to own media assets. The Murdoch empire currently owns close to 70 per cent of the country's newspapers, one of the most tightly controlled markets in the Western world. Governments are also in the spotlight. A 2008 study of free speech in Australia reported that there was a desperate need for a 'more open and accountable approach to information gathering, dissemination and communication'.[25]

A 2005 Roy Morgan poll in Australia found that 71 per cent of respondents believed that media organisations were more interested in making money than informing society.[26] Two years later the poll found that, unlike the rest of the media, only a minority thought the information on the internet was biased.[27]

American media commentator EJ Dionne believes that the mainstream media and the internet can co-exist happily. 'What we need is to welcome the newly partisan and participatory outlets,' he said in Melbourne in 2006, 'while finding ways to preserve what is best in independent journalism.'[28] Investigative journalism—something most bloggers are simply incapable of, due to lack of time and resources—

is still vital in a democracy and is what quality media outlets do best. However, the internet has given non-professionals access to the political and media process. The most successful websites are those that embrace an online community and listen to what the users want. This is equally relevant in Sydney, New York, Riyadh and Tehran.

Many in the mainstream continue to ignore the changes. *New York Times* columnist David Brooks personifies this disconnect. Take his comment on American television from 2006: 'One of the things I've found in life is that politicians are a lot more sincere than us journalists and we are more sincere than the people that read and watch us.'[29]

The blogosphere became for me a respite from the grandstanding of supposedly respectable commentators and 'insider' journalism. I don't trust everything on blogs but September 11, and the reactions of many journalists to it, led me to the world's bloggers. The world was far more complex than an embedded mindset would allow.

Freelance journalist Christopher Allbritton raised money on his blog and travelled to Iraq and the Middle East to 'create a connection between the readers and me, and they trusted me to bring them an unfettered view of what I was seeing and hearing'. Allbritton's work was often picked up by mainstream news sources, but a borrowed laptop and rented satellite phone allowed him to maintain a personal tone throughout his work and an attempt to restore a sense of trust between a reporter and an audience that has steadily decreased in the last decades. Alaskan mountain guide Dahr Jamail flew to the Middle East in late 2003 with US$2000. With no journalistic experience, he soon started reporting the reality on the ground in Iraq and he has since become one of the finest chroniclers of the country's carnage.[30]

Journalists who straddle various media forms are redefining the association between the mainstream media and blogging, often finding the stories and angles ignored by a larger news organisation. It was 'stand-alone journalism', almost completely self-sufficient and able to reach readers directly without any unnecessary filters.[31]

The world's leading media companies have reduced their global footprint,[32] with reduced advertising revenue meaning fewer resources and a mainstream perception that audiences care less about the world. The editor of the *Sydney Morning Herald* told me in 2006 that studies proved his audience wanted more 'local' stories. Networked journalism[33] has therefore risen in importance. The horrific images and eyewitness accounts of the late 2007 Burmese uprising would never have happened without a handful of bloggers risking their lives to transmit them to the outside world.[34] A citizen in Gaza and the Israeli border town of Sderot launched a joint blog to better understand each other's plight, to overcome prejudices and misunderstandings.[35] *Alive in Baghdad* is an award-winning Baghdad-based blog that features weekly video reports by Iraqi journalists on life for average Iraqis under occupation. To stay afloat it requires readers' donations.[36] Riverbend, a female Iraqi blogger—now living in Syria—has published numerous scathing posts about the Americans in her country. She has achieved such success that two books of her blog writing have been published in America.[37] Women have been one of the major beneficiaries of the new technology, forcing out into the open issues that patriarchal societies would rather keep hidden.

During the 2006 war between Israel and Hizbollah, the Lebanese blogosphere exploded with opinions about the conflict and despite the government's ban on contacting Israelis many Jews and Arabs corresponded about, discussed and fought over the war. An Israeli mother and soldier's wife said: 'It's such a shame we had to have a war to get to know each other.'[38] Blogging has arrived in the region, although one Arab blogger highlights the relatively small community: 'We're not big enough to preach to the choir yet. There is no choir.'[39]

The most defining moment for me occurred in the 2005 election of Iranian president Mahmoud Ahmadinejad, which unleashed a wave of vicious rhetoric from Iran and the United States that appeared to be fuelling the case for a Western-led military strike against the country. Reading Iranian bloggers both in Iran and in the diaspora clearly indicated that there was robust debate about the renewed aggressiveness of the Iranian state, although this was largely absent from our media. Moderate, middle-class Iranian voices were sidelined in the rush to demonise the 'new Hitler'. The relentless political and media campaign against Iran was a key reason behind this book. I was furious and bewildered that Iran was being similarly lined up for action after all the egregious crimes in Iraq. What was the real Iran away from the headlines about Ahmadinejad's rants? I soon discovered that the internet and blogs offered an invaluable insight into the often contradictory but always passionate nature of the modern Persian state.

Iran wasn't simply a nation that threatened 'us'. Throughout my visit to the Islamic republic I was constantly asked why the Western media seemed obsessed with Ahmadinejad, when real power lay with Supreme Leader Ali Khamenei.

I had contacted countless bloggers, journalists and dissidents before I arrived in the countries I visited in 2007, and most of them were willing to meet me (though many feared for their safety and requested anonymity in print). I connected with others while on the ground and usually met with them in cafes, their homes or parks, hopefully away from prying eyes and ears. As a Jew travelling through the Middle East, I was curious how I would be received, especially in Saudi Arabia and Iran. It wasn't fear I felt though, perhaps slight apprehension. How Jewish would I want to be?

I chose the countries I visited for a variety of reasons. Iran held endless fascination for me. After the Islamic Republic, it was almost inevitable that the search had to be widened to include other nations that were too easily labelled 'repressive'. The internet was giving a predominantly young, middle-class population their first chance to express opinions and aspirations that could previously only be whispered among friends. Some were liberal and others were fundamentalist. I was keen to investigate the idea that the internet was an automatically democratising force. Blogs and online forums have created a space in places such as Saudi Arabia, Syria, Egypt and Iran for advocates of a more militant Islam to argue forcefully against those who wish for a more inclusive, compassionate Islam.[40] In Cuba, web access is far less common than in any other country I visited—partly as a result of the US embargo and the paranoia of the Castro regime—but dedicated communists openly call for greater transparency and efficiency in the current system while others argue for a tilt towards capitalism. The uncontrolled chaos of the net allows various opinions simultaneously to thrive and percolate. Some may be friendly to Western ears and many are critical of our way of life.

In every country I visited, except Cuba, the internet had become massively popular and was starting to challenge established rules of conversation and dissent. Were students agitating against Syria's President Bashar al-Assad? Or the Saudi Kingdom? Did the Chinese Communist Party maintain its tight grip, despite the country having the highest number of web users in the world? How was a close US ally such as Egypt coping with a growing insurgency from the Muslim Brotherhood and was blogging allowing President Hosni Mubarak to be mocked in a mass medium unheard of only a few years ago? Simply put: was the internet a subversive medium, intrumental in articulating an alternative vision in these nations or was it simply a new technology through which the regime could control its citizens?

I wanted to hear the sounds and smell the fears of new generations wary of a Western world keen to align itself with friendly dictators. More importantly, I was determined to reclaim words such as 'democracy', 'human rights' and 'freedom', beliefs that have been utilised to justify years of violent policies designed to subjugate nations to US foreign policy interests and Western markets.

I also wanted a chance to understand what these bloggers craved for themselves and their countries. Spending time with Iranian blogger Bozorgmehr Sharafedin, at twenty-five the then editor of the country's biggest youth publication, provided me with an insight into the daily struggles of simply telling the truth to readers about issues the authorities would rather see ignored. His life after hours was an inspiring example of a young guy desperately wishing fundamentalism would not survive another generation. Sharafedin loved his nation and its people but railed against its hijacking by mullahs and extremists in Washington.

Another blogger and journalist I met in Egypt, Wael Abbas, was a quietly spoken man who still lived at home with his parents while campaigning publicly against police-led torture. Unlike in the West, where condemning human rights abuses was generally risk-free, Abbas faced harassment and imprisonment. I couldn't help but wonder whether I would take the same risks if I lived in Egypt.

This book is a story of twenty-first century censorship and the struggle to overcome it. I've spoken to dissidents, writers, journalists, students, academics, citizens, bloggers, web obsessives and officials to gather a fuller picture of how modern states attempt to control the flow of information. Many regimes filter websites and excise 'subversive' content—China leads the world in this pernicious practice with the collusion and complicity of Western corporations. Some governments throw troublemakers in prison; China remains the world's largest jailer of journalists. Others condemn human rights activists as enemies of the state. A special report of the New York–based Committee to Protect Journalists stated in late 2007 that web-based reporters now constituted nearly 40 per cent of journalists imprisoned worldwide.[41] A June 2008 University of Washington annual report found that, since 2003, sixty-four people have been arrested globally for publishing their opionions on a blog. 2007 saw three times as many people arrested for political blogging than in 2006. The seeming futility of censoring websites, when users can always find a way around a roadblock, contradicted the utopian vision of the internet's founders. Was censorship an effective silencer or was self-censorship a greater problem in the countries I visited than state-imposed filtering?[42]

The role of Western internet multinationals in censorship has attracted headlines ever since Google, Yahoo and Microsoft began colluding with the Chinese regime and other non-democratic nations.[43] The power of these corporations was a cause for concern.[44] Although a company such as Google was consistently associated with innovation and the facilitating of freedom of information across the world[45], how far would it go to maximise profits, just like any other corporate entity?[46] I sensed in much of the Western media coverage that these issues were principally classed as 'their' problem but wouldn't affect 'us'. Yet when a professor at Britain's Royal Academy of Engineering announced in late 2006 that within five years anybody would be able to use Google to ask 'what was a particular individual doing at 2.30 yesterday and would get an answer'[47], it became clear that we have little understanding about what happens to our own online footprint. How much power do we allow Google—the fastest growing company in the history of the world—to accrue?[48] Do we care?

But if you thought censorship only happens elsewhere, you would be wrong. Across the Western world, authorities are starting to argue for web restrictions, often in the name of 'national security'.[49] In early 2008 a California judge blocked a leading website, wikileaks.org, that published sensitive leaked documents from around the world (though this was reversed on appeal).[50] A growing number of judges and legislators in the West are increasingly seeing the internet as a threat to elite power. 'If George Orwell had lived in the internet age,' writes the *New York Times*'s Adam Cohen, 'he could have painted a grim picture of how web monitoring could be used to promote authoritarianism [in the West.] There is no need for neighbourhood informants and paper dossiers if the government can see its citizens' every website, email and text message.'[51]

Many colleagues regularly asked whether it was more important to examine the steady erosion of internet rights in Western nations, including the Bush administration's collusion with telecommunication companies in spying on citizens' internet traffic and battles over net neutrality—the attempt by some of the same firms to restrict the speed with which information is accessed online.[52] These issues interested me and I've written about them elsewhere, but debunking the deliberate media distortions about countries with which the West regularly traded insults seemed more essential. I expected citizens in these nations to be suspicious of my questioning and wary of my probing. In every country they told me that many Westerners had made them feel they were living inferior lives because of their governments' authoritarianism. 'We love some things about the West,' a blogger told me in Tehran, 'but we love our countries, too.'

Surprisingly, the digital revolution in satellite television and the internet has had little effect on making Americans more knowledgeable about national and global events. A nationwide survey in 2007 found little difference between 1989 and 2007 in terms of public knowledge.[53] Doris Lessing, winner of the Nobel Prize for Literature in 2007, said at the time that the internet had 'seduced a whole generation into its inanities' and created a world where citizens know little.[54] Neuroscientist Susan Greenfield has argued that internet culture changes our neural configurations, shortens attention spans and reduces our imaginations.[55] I wondered if users in non-democratic nations, whose lives are defined by dodging social taboos, would regard a tool that allows access to a world of entertainment and political activism from around the world in the same way.

Ironically, while many citizens in non-democratic nations turn to bloggers and the internet to source critical material, writer Tom Wolfe dismissed the blogging phenomenon on its tenth anniversary as 'a universe of rumours, and the tribe likes it that way'.[56] Andrew Keen, in his book *The Cult of the Amateur*, expressed similar snobbery. He wrote that, 'millions and millions of exuberant monkeys ... are creating an endless digital forest of mediocrity'.[57] He longed for a golden age when only 'experts' would tell the uneducated masses what was right, moral and appropriate. His world-view starts to look shaky outside the Western world. This book hopes to challenge Keen's thesis by arguing that because the internet allows unfiltered, albeit partial opinions, to be expressed, citizens feel more empowered, involved and interested.[58]

This book doesn't intend to argue that the internet is a perfect, constantly evolving beast that allows every citizen to engage with the world. Nor do I claim that it should in any way replace papers of 'record' whose strength is long, considered and well-researched journalism. Rather, I argue that the internet challenges and expands what 'the record' is considered to be. A reader should be as sceptical and judicious towards blogs and networked media as towards the mainstream media.

Few journalist colleagues I know enjoy an eroding of their authority, but I welcome it, knowing that years of interaction with readers and critics of blogs have broadened my knowledge and information sources. Politicians who believe in the transparency of the democratic process embrace blogging to demystify the process's inner workings.[59] Political debate in the West and developing world should be far more compelling and provocative than the 'objective' journalism that demands a 'he said, she said' format.

I had always presumed that the internet was principally utilised by the middle classes and elites throughout the world—and most democracy activists I met were undoubtedly a minority—but the picture in a country such as China was vastly different. Rural users were rapidly taking up the web in record numbers, with 40 per cent of new users living in these areas. The result of state repression is often the opposite of what the authorities intended.

Across the world, however, web users are trying to bring the less privileged in from the cold. At internet cafes across Bolivia, the tools and techniques of networked journalism have been shared with members of unrepresented groups in society.[60] A small town in Chile was given free wi-fi access and President Michelle Bachelet said it was the first for the continent and would reduce the 'gap between rich and poor'.[61] Kosovo Albanian journalists and their Serbian colleagues launched a website to overcome the ethnic tensions between the two peoples.[62]

The One Laptop per Child association was formed to construct US$100 internet-connected laptops and empower children across the globe. Access to the web across Africa is severely limited and attempts are being made to widen it to even the poorest of countries.[63] Less than 4 per cent of Africans are online.[64] A Swahili blogger from Tanzania told a conference in South Africa in 2007 that one of the challenges of the medium in his continent was publishing rural stories and 'villagising' the internet, ensuring that anybody has the ability to tell their stories to the world.[65] Virtually none of these stories ever appeared in depth in the Western media.

Perhaps I had approached journalism in a different way. Many journalism colleagues were keen to be promoted in a news organisation and report on the daily political meanderings in Australia or overseas. Dining, talking and networking with the political and business elite were essential in these roles. None of this particularly fascinated me. I wasn't uninterested in what was happening within this elaborate dance, but I've long believed that the most insightful stories can be found elsewhere, by talking to people whose lives are affected by the decisions made by our leaders. Blogging was therefore the perfect medium for finding these voices.[66]

This book is about localisms that are challenged by the technologies of globalisation and vice versa. A reader in Sydney can now campaign for an activist in Tehran, and a journalist in Shanghai can read on overseas websites what his government is doing in Tibet. Many bloggers see themselves as 'bridge bloggers'—essential in filling the global information holes about a particular country, national disaster, coup or incident. The founders of Global Voices Online, a leading aggregate of blogs from across the world, have said that they see 'in the global blogosphere the emergence of a new kind of media ecosystem, in which journalists, bloggers and creators of citizen media increasingly coexist in beneficial and complementary ways'.[67]

Like blogs themselves, this book is designed to be a conversation, an attempt to challenge the presumptions about 'repressive' regimes and the West's relationship to them by tapping into national conversations that are happening on the ground. The internet is playing an increasingly central role in these debates, but blogging is only one piece of the puzzle. The 'Dictator's Dilemma' over a networked world—whether an authoritarian government chooses open communications and economic development or closed communications and banning of 'dangerous' ideas[68]—is one of the key issues of our time. Would the twenty-first century end up being a period of unparalleled democratic expansion or a time defined by exploitation and the tightening of control over dwindling natural resources? The only way to find out was to visit countries where, for those I met, these debates were often a matter of life and death.

Iran
Welcome to the Axis of Evil

I keep a weblog so that I can breathe in this suffocating air … In a society where one is taken to history's abattoir for the mere crime of thinking, I write so as not to be lost in my despair … so that I feel I am somewhere where my calls for justice can be uttered … I write a weblog so that I can shout, cry and laugh, and do the things that they have taken away from me in Iran today …

– Iranian blogger Lolivashaneh[1]

THE CLOGGED CITY OF Tehran sits at the foot of the snow-capped Elburz Mountains, the peaks usually visible through thick smog. The streets are polluted and chaotic, the motorcycles, vans and dilapidated cars all jostling for control of unmarked lanes. As my taxi roared at 140 kilometres an hour from Imam Khomeini International Airport into the heart of the city, I was struck by the sleekness of the buildings and the large billboards that dotted the sides of the road promoting Sony televisions and Kabooky Fried Chicken outlets. Brightly lit images of the first Supreme Leader of Iran, Ayatollah Khomeini, were everywhere, reminding first-time travellers that although the country had not established anything like the personality cult surrounding North Korea's Kim Jong-Il, public subservience to Khomeini and his successor Ali Khamenei was demanded.[2] Within minutes of landing, my Australian mobile phone sprang to life, despite my local provider having told me before I left that it would be 'impossible' for me to access global roaming there ('We have no connection with any Iranian phone companies, sir,' I was wrongly informed.)

This was not at all what I had been expecting—this brash modernity in which people used iPods and SMS with the same feverish attention as those in any international city. Tehran is a 'city without memory', wrote

Iranian author Amir Hassan Cheheltan. 'It hardly has any old buildings [and] infects its inhabitants with the virus of nostalgia.'[3]

A telling example is the former US embassy, the site of the infamous 444-day hostage crisis that started in 1979, which I discovered is now little more than a curiosity. A handful of murals feature crude anti-American images—such as the Grim Reaper inhabiting the face of the Statue of Liberty—and as I wandered around the sealed gates I recalled the faded colour images of hundreds of Iranians scaling the embassy walls, holding pictures of Ayatollah Khomeini and demanding nothing less than defeat of 'The Great Satan'.

It later emerged that the Iranian revolutionaries had entered the embassy and discovered a large cache of classified US government documents on a variety of sensitive subjects such as Israel, Iraq and the Soviet Union. Despite the American staff shredding much of the material before they arrived, the Iranians painstakingly re-assembled the information and published it in 1982 in fifty-four volumes under the title 'Documents From the U.S. Espionage Den'.[4] I saw copies of some of these in various markets in Tehran but such raw anger was largely absent from people that I subsequently met, the radical zeal reserved for the religious leadership (and even then, it often seemed deliberately created to generate fanatical support for the ruling mullahs).

To understand modern Iran it is important to return to 1953 and the CIA- and British-backed overthrow of the democratically elected government of Dr Mohammad Mossadegh. It emerged that the BBC assisted in the coup by using a code word in a broadcast that Winston Churchill had arranged for the Shah to hear. The overthrow of Iran's democracy by the West is conveniently overlooked in the proselytising today about bringing freedom to the Middle East. The coup installed the puppet dictatorship under the Shah of Iran that lead to his inevitable rejection in 1979 when an 80-year-old religious scholar from the holy Iranian city of Qom, the Ayatollah Khomeini, arrived in Tehran from France to a rapturous welcome by millions of Iranians. The Shah's rule was brutal, opponents were murdered and dissent was crushed. Darius Rejali, Iranian-born professor of political science at Reed College and author of *Torture and Democracy*,[5] has said that 'torture [by the Shah] was the inspiration for the Iranian Revolution. It pulled all the radicals to their [Khomeinei's] side. It was a revolution about human rights, not about religion.'[6]

Revealingly, many of the individuals who took over the American embassy in 1979 now despair over the theocracy that emerged and have become some of the country's leading independent voices. One of the former revolutionaries, Abbas Abdi, was an editor of the reform daily *Salam* and fell out with the regime. He told the *New York Times* in 1999:

> To understand us, you have to think of us as mammals who never lived out of water before 1979, and who are only now learning to walk on dry land. For Americans, freedom is an everyday commodity, but for us, under the Shah's dictatorship, it was something unknown. So when we took the embassy, we acted on the basis of what we knew, and that was despotism. Today we have chosen a different course, based on what we learned from the past 20 years.[7]

Many of these individuals have called for the normalisation of relations between Iran and America and paid a high personal price for doing so. Yesterday's religious fundamentalists, believers who helped strengthen a regime that brought decades of repression, are today arguing that the theocracy is beyond reform. A post-Islamic government is their aim.[8] As Nobel Laureate and human rights activist Shirin Ebadi has argued, the twenty-first century in Iran is not 'the century of revolutions. It's the century of reforms.'[9]

Iran enjoyed a brief relaxation of control and greater openness under the relatively moderate President Muhammad Khatami elected in 1997. However, his failure to deliver real reforms handed the election in 2005 to Mahmoud Ahmadinejad. The *New York Times* welcomed the new leader and 'wished him luck'.[10]

In just three years Ahmadinejad's presidency has seen crackdowns on various segments of society, from unionists to journalists and students to women.[11] 'Some factions in the government view all dissidents and critics as part of America's secret plan for a non-violent "velvet revolution",' wrote leading Iranian dissident Ahmad Zeidabadi.[12] 'Unfortunately, a significant part of the security and intelligence apparatus shares this view.'[13]

The rise of Ahmadinejad surprised many in the West, but the roots of his success lay not with the middle classes or the youth vote but in making promises to the disenfranchised.[14] An unauthorised biographer of the president, Kasra Naji, recalls an anecdote that perfectly captures his appeal and mystery. 'When Ahmadinejad was elected President in June 2005, anxiety replaced fever amongst many Iranians,' he writes. 'To let off steam they told jokes. Why did the new President part his hair so straight? To segregate the male and female lice. But while the laughter died down, the anxiety never went away.'[15]

One villager told *New Internationalist* that he had voted for Ahmadinejad in 2005 but by early 2007 felt disillusioned. Poverty has actually increased during his rule and, despite claiming to use oil revenues to aid the poor, his government's results have been lacklustre. 'He looked like a decent person, one of us,' said a 57-year-old man who worked part-time washing dishes in a restaurant in southern Tehran. 'I voted for him, but I wouldn't again.'[16] 'Who can believe this country exports $100 barrels of oil?' said one disgruntled blogger.[17] Washington-led sanctions were hurting average Iranians and small businesses far more than the ruling mullahs.[18] Foreign investment has also been minimal, not least due to Ahmadinejad's inflammatory rhetoric.[19]

Ahmadinejad, wrote Iranian academics Anoushiravan Ehteshami and Mahjoob Zweiri, is comparable to the American neo-conservatives, a group who finally came in from the cold after years of isolation. For many voters, at least initially, he represented the traditional lower and middle classes who felt that they had been betrayed by the reformers, too 'focused on political change and forgetting the role of social groups in establishing the Islamic Republic and protecting its ruling regime'.[20] The *Guardian*'s former Tehran correspondent, Robert Tait—thrown out of the country after three years in early 2008 after being found guilty of 'negative coverage'—explained that Ahmadinejad represents a great bulk of Iranians who came from the remote villages to the cities and rejected many elements of the modern world that the West takes for granted.[21] Despite these attitudes, however, a poll by WorldPublicOpinion.org in early 2008 found that, although the majority of Iranians viewed America negatively, they strongly supported 'direct talks on issues of mutual concern' and 'providing more access for each other's journalists'.[22]

The March 2008 parliamentary election delivered a setback for Ahmadinejad—who didn't run any of his own candidates with his political group, the Sweet Smell of Service—with the elevation of former nuclear negotiator Ali Larijani. One Western diplomat, describing him as a 'pragmatic conservative', said that Larijani 'sends a subliminal message that he has the backing of the religious mullahs'.[23]

Although conservatives won an easy majority in the election, principally because most reformist candidates were disqualified for 'lacking Islamic authenticity', discontent with Ahmadinejad was visibly growing. Rising disillusionment among the reformist base—one candidate even raffled off toasters and food processors to generate interest—meant that many supporters doubted their ability to gain power.[24] A former close ally of Ahmadinejad, Mohammad Khoshchehreh, publicly criticised the president for his populist policies. 'The failure of the government would make the system pay the price,' he said. 'Society will move towards secularism.'[25]

Explaining the dynamic of the democracy in the Iranian Republic, conservative journalist Bahman Hedaiati wrote:

> 'Populist-fundamentalist' is probably the best term for describing Ahmadinejad and his group. This group has a theoretic wing and also a populist one. Recent defeat of their supporters in the elections may result in weakening the populist side and strengthening the theoretic one. This means the 'carriers of God's message' may start to forget 'to save people's soul' and less strive at 'winning the nation's heart'.[26]

When I arrived in Tehran[27] many Western pundits and members of the Pentagon's inner sanctum were openly calling for military strikes against President Ahmadinejad's Islamic regime for allegedly possessing nuclear weapons.[28] Although the Supreme Leader Khameini issued a fatwa in 2005 that argued the production, stockpiling and use of nuclear weapons was forbidden under Islam, Ahmadinejad has undoubtedly argued the country's right to nuclear enrichment.[29] The disastrous Iraq War had emboldened the same commentators who actively supported the 2003 invasion to urge the US to hit Iran.[30] The Islamic Republic had started to challenge America's and Israel's regional hegemony.[31]

Aside from North Korea, there is perhaps no other country on the planet that is more fundamentally misunderstood than Iran. Impressions are inevitably clouded by Western media coverage. We are used to images of fundamentalist clerics shouting 'Death to America' and 'Death to Israel' and a nation buoyed by Washington's failings in Iraq.

I was in Tehran to speak to a host of bloggers, writers, dissidents and politicians. I had been reading Iranian blogs for a couple of years before I arrived and although many were written in Farsi, others were in English or I used Harvard's Global Voices Online, an invaluable source that translates blog posts from across the globe. I was transfixed by critical comments about the regime, religion, sex, drugs and attitudes towards the West that suggested Iranian youth were far from content to simply follow their parents' principles. In the privacy of people's homes, Iran's thriving internet culture was finally airing a divergent set of values for the first time since the 1979 Islamic Revolution. I was interested in discovering how important the internet had become to converse, challenge, provoke and flirt.

'So far the Iranian youth have used the internet with massive amounts of creativity,' said Hamid Tehrani (a pseudonym), the Persian editor of Global Voices, 'and in due time it will prove to become a dynamic instrument for the democratisation of a society'.[32] Tehrani told me that there was a perception in the West that all Iranian politicians supported nuclear enrichment but, he said, blogs were just one way to discover that this wasn't so.[33] Perhaps Tehrani was right, but could the internet on its own bring real revolutionary change to a country that actively embraces modern technology yet publicly dismisses non-Islamic influences? I was sceptical. Surreally, a blogger and journalist was detained in late 2007 for daring to reveal that Ahmadinejad's security staff had bought dogs from Germany for roughly $150 000 each.[34]

Iran has nearly one million bloggers—roughly 10 per cent of blogs are regularly updated—and the blog search engine Technorati lists Farsi among the top five languages used on the internet.[35] With a population of around seventy million, and 60 per cent of its population under thirty years old[36], Iran's burgeoning online community has fundamentally changed the national conversation and forced the ruling mullahs to at least recognise the necessity of reaching the massive youth population. In 2003 an Iranian dissident beautifully articulated the power that lies behind the new technology: 'At night, every light that is on in Tehran shows that somebody is sitting behind [*sic*] a computer, driving through [*sic*] information road; and that is in fact a storehouse of gunpowder that, if ignited, will start a great firework in the capital of the revolutionary Islam.'[37]

The high rate of internet penetration among Iranian youth has resulted in an explosion of views, but little original research has been done to determine the breadth of the movement. An exception is a study by Jordan Halevi (an online alias), a Canadian post-graduate student and author of the Iranian Weblog Research Project.[38] He collected over 300 surveys from various Iranian bloggers over four months in 2005 and 2006 and noted that although 'the results of the survey cannot be credibly projected onto the entire Iranian blogosphere ... there are observable trends'.

The majority of the respondents were men (though over 30 per cent were women) and the most cited year of birth was 1982. The vast majority were born in Iran in one of the largest cities (Tehran, Esfahan, Shiraz, Tabriz and Mashhad), though some now lived overseas. Most had completed at least some post-secondary education and called themselves either 'middle' or 'upper' class. The vast majority were Shiite Muslims (though interestingly, close to 30 per cent claimed they were 'totally secular'). Close to half of the respondents visited Iranian blogs more than once a day and said they had started reading Iranian blogs somewhere between 2001 and 2003. But a majority also said that 'only a few' or 'none' of their friends read Iranian blogs. Many respondents expressed dismay at the regime's censorship of many websites.[39]

I had simply emailed many of Iran's bloggers before I arrived, requesting a meeting—and was pleasantly surprised how many were willing to hang out. Nima Akbarpour is a 32-year-old journalist and blogger with slicked-back black hair and a trimmed goatee, almost a uniform for many male bloggers around the world.[40] We met in my hotel lobby in the southern, poorer part of the city (the north was far showier and oozed wealth), but I quickly noticed that Nima spoke softly, clearly not wanting to be heard by anyone milling around. This justified paranoia was widely shared. Only a handful of Westerners stayed at the hotel during my visit. The vast majority of guests were Iranian and Iraqi men on business, seemingly spending their days drinking tea and smoking cigarettes. An astounding number of them told me they had family living in Australia.

Nima said that although the last years had made covering sensitive issues far more difficult, it was still possible to provoke controversy. The latest edition of the magazine to which he contributes, *Chelcheragh*, that week featured a cover story about trans-gender sexuality. Nima said that his popular blog, Oysan.net, was routinely filtered by the authorities for days at a time, then mysteriously unblocked a short time later. He has never been given any reasons, but he soon realised that his government's fear of anybody who didn't subscribe to the conservative agenda resulted in irrational behaviour. For this reason, as I later discovered, it is futile trying to impose logic on a system of censorship that is essentially illogical and arbitrary.

I regularly visited internet cafes and discovered the randomness of the regime.[41] Using an internet search engine inevitably resulted in a screen saying: 'Dear customer, access to this site is forbidden.' Oddly, all the Australian newspaper sites were blocked but the English-language Israeli ones were available. On some days, certain political websites in the US were censored, then the next day I could view them clearly. The government blocks untold numbers of keywords, including any phrases deemed to be sexual or political in nature. But nowhere are these banned terms listed and they're constantly being changed and updated.

Some ISPs have blocked thousands of keywords. For example, if a user wants to search for the American songwriter Bruce Springsteen, they'll be unable to access his information because the word 'teen' has been filtered. 'Teen' is supposedly a potentially pornographic word. When I was told this, I thought it was a joke, but numerous other examples were presented. The word 'Asian' is often blocked, and so is 'dick'—searching for US Vice President Dick Cheney is not possible, but Richard Cheney is fine—and 'oral' and 'cock' are problematic. The lack of sophisticated filtering means that if a user wants to search for filmmaker Alfred Hitchcock or their favourite choral music, they won't have any luck. Gay and trans-gender sites are mostly blocked, but the words 'queer' or 'wanker' are viewable. The Google search engine and Gmail email service were briefly blocked in September 2007 and it's usually impossible to access Facebook or YouTube.[42] One major ISP even blocks searches for the word 'fashion'. There are untold numbers of other filters in place.[43]

Anything Western is suspect. 'The Iranian regime is well aware of the dangers of the work of imagination and thought,' writes Azar Nafisi, author of the best-selling *Reading Lolita in Tehran*.[44] 'After ... years of revolution, the Islamic government has failed to convince its citizens, and in fact many within the religious hierarchy, of its victory in the cultural domain.' When even works like Dan Brown's *The Da Vinci Code* are banned to prevent publishers from 'serving the poisoned dish to the young generation', it becomes clear that robustly censoring the internet is a way to challenge the curiosity and imagination of Iranians who want to fully engage with the global community. 'We are trained under the Islamic Republic to breathe with two different kinds of oxygen in private and public life', says US-based Iranian journalist Omid Memarian.[45] The internet has clearly allowed these once distinctly separate spaces to co-exist in an environment that makes the regime very uncomfortable.

There are numerous examples online of people challenging clerical rule and pushing for change, a fact rarely covered by Western media. Since September 11, one of the key messages from the Supreme Leader has been that the attacks in New York and Washington were the work of Israel and the United States to justify the subsequent invasions of Afghanistan and Iraq. Many anonymous bloggers challenged this interpretation. Soon after the September 11 attacks, one blogger wrote: 'So many dead ... Although the world only became aware of Islamic fascists on 9/11, as a society we have been forced to coexist with them for nearly a quarter of a century.'[46]

The Western media initially ignored these voices—arguably because blogs were not seen as official and verifiable or simply due to the tendency of Western media outlets not to publish material that isn't written by Westerners themselves. While our media preferred to maintain the 1979-style stereotype of a society in the thrall of charismatic, small-minded clerics, Iranian society has been shifting dramatically. The ban on alcohol, pop music and dancing remains in place, but the vast majority of Iranians were born after the revolution, therefore making the job of mullahs increasingly difficult. How could they maintain 'Islamic' values in the country's youth? With a literacy rate of more than 90 per cent across the country and more than half of university graduates being women, a spirited curiosity for the world outside Iran has strengthened. One female blogger, former parliamentary member Dr Jamileh Kadivar, unflatteringly compared the Iranian election system with the American one in early 2008. 'Suppose that this [2008 presidential election] was being held in Iran,' she wrote.

'First of all, Hillary Clinton couldn't be elected, because according to the Constitution, only male clergymen and politicians can be elected.'[47] Blogger Omid Memarian writes that many Iranians he knows are obsessed with Democratic presidential contender Barack Obama and seduced by his message of hope. 'Iranian people truly want to change their situation, get rid of decades of marginalisation and restore their reputation in the world.'[48]

This taste for Western culture has only increased with the arrival of satellite television. Tehran's streets are in fact filled with shops selling all manner of illegal, imported goods, from books to CDs and DVDs to pork products. I remember walking into a shop on one of the city's main boulevards and looking for a gift to take a friend I was visiting. I obviously couldn't easily buy a bottle of wine (and didn't know where to find one), but the store sold everything from cigarettes to cigars, canned food to Lindt chocolate. The more expensive items were in glass-covered cabinets—anything over around US$5 was in this category—and the staff seemed genuinely intrigued that I had even entered the store. It wasn't unlike the nearby massive bazaar, famous for centuries as the hub of commercial and political power. My presence, though welcomed, was seen as a curiosity, a number of men asking me in broken English if I was British or American. When I said I was an Australian, they said that they knew that we had troops in Iraq and wanted to know why.

Chelcheragh, one of the country's largest youth publications (selling around 30 000 copies weekly), provides a unique window into the ways in which journalists have to negotiate the red lines—the ever-changing, regime-imposed boundaries of public debate on political and social issues—set out by the regime. Its 25-year-old former editor, Bozorgmehr Sharafedin, told me that university students are the primary target audience, although parents also read the weekly edition when it enters the family home.[49]

The publication gained notoriety in 2005 after it hosted a ceremony titled 'A Night with: The Man with the Chocolate Robe' a few months after the collapse of Khatami's presidency. It was one of the first events of its sort in Iran's history, specifically designed to attract teenagers and young people in the celebration of a 'liberal' leader. It caused controversy with the hard-liners because it demonstrated that support for former president Khatami's reform program, though it was ultimately unsuccessful, still remained potent.

Bozorg told me that editing a publication in Iran is a daily high-wire act. The situation was challenging during Khatami's government, and now the magazine receives a weekly fax from the Ministry of Culture. Bozorg explained:

> We cannot write about women's protests. If you write any word about the women who are arrested for demonstrating in the streets we will be attacked. We cannot write about the teachers' protests last month. If you write even a single word about these kinds of protests, you will be banned. It was so sudden that we had to remove two pages of our magazine when it was publishing. We cannot write about the nuclear policy [unless we support the regime's stance].
>
> The Minister of Culture warned the magazine that if you write even a word against this plan or the police beating women in the street, we will treat this very severely. This kind of warning from the Minister of Culture was unbelievable, because we expect the Minister of Culture to support magazines, not be against them. [It] can be quite normal from police or the parliament, but not from the minister.

One day I was at the *Chelcheragh* office and Bozorg received a call from the ministry of culture. His demeanour suddenly changed and he stiffened. He was asked why over the last months the newspaper had been published without covers, 'making it look cheap'. He was confused, as glossy covers had been published but for some inexplicable reason the ministry had received their weekly batch without them. Bozorg said he would immediately send over copies with the covers intact.

I asked Bozorg how readers, predominantly reformist-minded, could respect a magazine that was seemingly unable to cover the main issues of the day in a frank manner.

> If I want to give you a message, I encode it and you decode it. Sometimes when I send a message I try to encode it in a safe appearance, and you understand, since you're a wise reader, and can decode it. So readers understand that by covering the cultural revolution it means we are against it, even if we have some interviews inside this part of the magazine in favour of the revolution. This process of encoding and decoding is kind of unique

in Iran because writers are wise and readers are wiser, and have become wiser in recent years. They know the restrictions, they know the red lines are so much and they try to read between the lines.

The newspaper's office in northern Tehran was in a nondescript white-washed building. I had been invited to a public meeting after the paper's sixth birthday to hear readers discuss their likes and dislikes and suggest ways to make the publication more relevant to their lives. The event was held in a large hall with a low ceiling and roman columns, a large screen showing a number of short films by the newspaper's contributors. Before commencing, mournful renditions of the Koran were played on a DVD while the crowd remained relatively silent.

The paper's publisher, editor and senior journalists all attended and spoke one by one, afterwards allowing the audience to ask questions. I had never seen anything like it in a major Western magazine or newspaper. Rather than simply presuming that an editor should make all the decisions, this meeting suggested that regular interaction with readers— rather than focus group–driven results—was the only certain way to ensure long-term survival and relevance.

Around 200 people were in attendance, from those in their late teens to those in their thirties. Both men and women spoke forcefully. Most enjoyed the newspaper's combination of politics, cinema, comedy, cartoons and sport. One girl said it had kept her sane during university. Some wanted harder political content, but the chairman explained that crossing 'red lines' would guarantee the paper's closure. It's notable that former president Khatami had recently met with the paper's heads and expressed support for its stance.

Another girl, 'a reformer', said Nima my translator, wanted the paper to embrace the reform movement's direction and not be so afraid to stand up to the creeping conservatism of the regime. However, slamming the president, even during a 'moderate' period, was a red line that no editor could cross. As I discovered throughout my visit, many Iranians were forced to have multiple identities, depending on the audience. Maintaining mystery wasn't obfuscation; it was pure pragmatism. This reinforced the impression that day-to-day living was a delicate balancing act. The inability to know the rules, both written and unspoken, even after decades of living in the country, must be frustrating.

Here, participants felt free to speak openly and push publicly for greater openness. No topic seemed off-limits in the forum. Nima reminded me that many young Iranians did support Ahmadinejad and I shouldn't presume that reformist policies enjoyed mass appeal. In fact, the meeting merely proved that more liberal-minded youth felt increasingly isolated in their own country. This explains why there are a growing number of citizens leaving for better opportunities in the West. Many head to Europe, Australia, Canada and America, with an estimated two to four million Iranians in the diaspora.[50]

One woman stood up and talked about surfing the internet and the absurdity of having so many websites blocked that seemed apolitical. Why couldn't the magazine talk about some of these blocked sites without mentioning them by name, she asked? She surely knew the answer to the question. It was deemed better to remain open and stimulate debate than be closed down on a matter of principle.

It was easy to dismiss these views as a minority in Iran. Bozorg, however, gave me a much-needed reality check. He told me that many Iranian bloggers 'write so boldly it's unbelievable. I don't know how they dare to write those kind of things'. He said that he often read blog posts about sexual relationships and drugs, saw pictures from parties of drinking and alcohol. Bozorg argued that reading blogs was the best way to 'understand the mentality of this generation'.

The online Islamic revolution

The Iranian blogosphere has become expert at speaking in code. When Iran-based, reformist journalist Hossein Derakhshan (known online as Hoder) posted a 'how to blog' article in Farsi in September 2001—at the same time that the government was cracking down on newspapers—an information explosion occurred. Numerous blogs started appearing on a multitude of subjects and although Derakhshan had fled to Canada after fearing for his personal safety, the 'godfather' of the movement remains a popular voice of criticism. His blog, Editor: Myself, operating in both Farsi and English (though blocked in Iran), is widely read in the country and in the diaspora. Derakhshan isn't without his critics. He is accused of remaining too close to the Ahmadinejad regime, abusing his high-profile status for personal gain and placing the life of opposition leaders in danger.[51] The Western media, however, consistently use him as the unofficial voice of Iranian 'Blogistan'.[52]

Derakhshan was invited to speak at a media conference in Israel in early 2007 and he told the Israeli daily *Haaretz* that although Ahmadinejad has undoubtedly cracked down on many segments of society,

> except for criticism of the spiritual leader Khamenei, you can write criticism of anyone. The press is so rough on Ahmadinejad that not long ago, he went to Khamenei and complained to him about the criticism. Khamenei told him that it was true that he was getting some harsh criticism, but that there was nothing to be done about it, that that's how the game works.[53]

Derakhshan wanted to insist that a sizeable degree of independence still existed between the media and Ahmadinejad.

Throughout the *Haaretz* interview, he expressed the contradictions that I heard myself while in Iran. It was not unusual for individuals to express support for the concept of an Islamic state but believe in the full emancipation of women. It was equally common to hear people despair at the path the country had taken since 1979, while still supporting its original purpose—a longing for the 'purity' of the revolution. While harshly critical of aspects of the regime, Derakhshan said that blogging had been instrumental in opening up public discussion on a range of issues. He claimed that Iran was the freest country in the Middle East, aside from Israel, and he believed in the Islamic Revolution and Khomeini. 'If Western journalists left the northern part of Tehran more often,' he wrote in February 2008 on the twenty-ninth anniversary of the 1979 revolution, 'they would be able to observe how much Ahmadinejad represents a passionate revival of the core values of the [1979] uprising.'[54]

Even as a self-declared atheist, Derakhshan wanted an Iran that embraced religion. 'Religion is an organic part of our society,' he said. 'It needs to be given a new interpretation. That is what Iran is offering the Muslim world.' *A new interpretation.* It is interesting to speculate on what that might be. A few months later, he wrote that, 'if the US waged a war against Iran, I would absolutely go back and defend Iran'.[55] Like every Iranian I met, Derakhshan's dissatisfaction with the current status quo didn't equate with embracing foreign intervention in any form.

Since the early years of the decade, bloggers have become an unofficial opposition and, although hardly unified, they are a disparate group of citizens finally able to challenge the dominance of the state-run media. On a raft of prominent issues, bloggers have challenged and supported the regime, condoned and feared the acquisition of nuclear technology and condemned the violent crackdown on dissent. Of course, daily life for journalists still remains tough. Take this moving explanation expressed by blogger Khabarnagar No ('New Reporter' in Persian) in August 2007:

> I want to write, but I fear whatever I write can be considered as an offence in the eyes of a Ministry. I say I am not writing about politics and I do not write about Orange or Velvet revolutions, I just write about technology and science. If I want to publish a photo, then I should cover the neck of foreign women in the photo, and create trousers or a skirt to cover her legs ... When we interview somebody, we should ask about the interviewee's personal life to ascertain that she/he has not gone to disco or drunk champagne ... You should be careful not to go to conferences abroad because you can be accused of spying.[56]

This frustration can only be expressed honestly online. Many writers, either professional or amateur, were simply not heard before the rise of the internet. The BBC Persian website remains one of the most popular linked sites in the Iranian blogosphere.[57] Whether it be criticism of the crackdown on women's dress (anyone displaying 'bad hijab' is routinely harassed by the authorities) or receiving an SMS to mark Journalist's Day in 2007 ('Why do you send an SMS to congratulate us?' a reformist blogger reporter asked the government rhetorically. 'Maybe because most of independent journalists of this country are jobless?'[58]) Another blogger wondered how Ahmadinejad could cry publicly in April 2007 when he announced nuclear enrichment and yet '45 teachers are presently imprisoned ... because they asked for better working conditions and women activists are in jail'.[59] 'I imagined it would be easy to create the ideal society I always dreamt of,' said jailed dissident Babak Zamanian. 'But I realised over time in Iran, democracy is a dream.'[60]

During the times that I left Tehran and travelled to other cities—the former Persian capital of Esfahan and the former centre of Zoroastrian culture in Yazd—I was constantly struck by the religiosity and propaganda on state-run television. Channel surfing one night, on one station I noticed a Persian-dubbed version of the Australian medical drama series *All Saints*—a rare program of decidedly light entertainment—and on another an hour-long program featuring a haunting Islamic prayer sung by a cleric. Hundreds of men, mostly bearded, were sitting and praying in a mosque, with a few young boys in the crowd, and their arms sometimes outstretched to the heavens. Some were weeping uncontrollably, the intensity of the chanting in unison or placing hands on their heads clearly overwhelming. I obviously couldn't understand a word but I was mesmerised and virtually in tears myself. Perhaps I envied something about their deep belief and intensity of feeling. It was something I had never felt in my Judaism.

US filmmaker Michael Moore popped up on TV one night, at the time when he was facing legal threats from the Bush administration for allegedly breaking the law by taking sick September 11 victims to Cuba for medical treatment for his documentary *Sicko*. Clips from the film were approvingly screened along with a few words from Moore himself. Interestingly, Iran was the only country I've ever visited where the words of the American intellectual Noam Chomsky have made headline TV news; they did so after he wrote that Iran had the right to a peaceful nuclear program.[61]

A constant theme on the 24-hour news channel was a montage featuring Muslims from around the world, including Palestine, China, Indonesia and Iran, all edited to rousing music. Muslims were seen holding signs protesting the US occupation of Iraq and Israeli brutality in Palestine, all clearly designed to signify a global, pan-Islamic struggle against the US and Israel. The regime wanted viewers to believe that, united, Muslims could achieve anything. The launch of Press TV in 2007, an Iranian attempt to rival the satellite dominance of al-Jazeera, is just the latest attempt by the Ahmadinejad regime to counter what it sees as a heavily biased Western press and Iran's intellectual class. Due to the staid and predictable nature of state-run radio, TV and print, the healthiest sign of debate is often between reformers and hard-line elements on each other's blogs. In mid-June 2007, conservative forces called for a second Cultural Revolution to 'purge universities of secular and reformist thought'. This resulted in a furious online slanging match between various factions and accurately reflected the tussles occurring in public between the reformists (generally lacking in political power) and the conservatives (currently in the ascendency.) One reformist deputy in parliament wrote on his blog that 'people who encourage a second Cultural Revolution should remember what happened from the first Cultural Revolution in the early years of the Islamic Revolution ... Many Iranian students and academics were fired and asked to follow strict rules, but after a few years the authorities turned back on their decisions when they realised that the Cultural Revolution didn't work.'[62]

Chelcheragh editor Bozorgmehr says that 'most of the people [I know are] in favour of reform, not revolution, because people are too tired to experience another revolution'. As a person who used to be a devout Muslim, he is happy to express dissent against the government but wonders what would replace it. 'I think Tehran is a modern city, but deep inside it is an Islamic city,' he argues.

> Deep inside me there is an Islamic core that is against insulting the Koran—not me, but I mean any typical person in Iran. They love Imams and they love Islamic values, so maybe they are afraid of another government that is against Islamic values. These complicated situations make it difficult to answer a question like 'Are people satisfied with this government or not?

After the election of Khatami, Bozorg and his friends believed they were the majority and that the intellectuals and reformists were widely supported. But, with the elevation of Ahmadinejad, they realised that their views had been marginalised. 'Iranian people are unpredictable,' Bozorg says.

> Even if the US attacked Iran tomorrow, maybe all the people would go into the streets and welcome them, but it is just as possible that people would go out into the streets and fight them, house by house. We cannot predict it. Will they fight against the foreigners or will they welcome supporters for the changing of the government? We have an unpredictable nation that makes answering such questions so difficult.

Hard-liners want online friends

Aware of the internet's influence, Ahmadinejad has embraced blogging and occasionally posts on his own site, Ahmadinejad.ir, in Farsi, English, French and Arabic.[63] Predictably, he only allows comments that praise his leadership, but it's a sign that his government has undoubt-edly recognised and embraced the importance of the new technology. An Ahmadinejad post from late December 2006 explained his feelings when publicly challenged at a university. 'In this country,' he wrote, 'a small group of people, sure about everything, assert their will on the government which is elected by the majority.'[64] He conveniently forgot to acknowledge that millions of Iranians had boycotted the 2005 elec-tion due to a lack of credible candidates. His principle aim was to portray the protesting students as dangerous, destabilising anarchists, in con-trast to the religious figures who could be trusted.[65]

The government is now helping every religious student to open a blog. The Muslim Bloggers Association (MBA), formed in January 2005, hosts numerous bloggers from a variety of backgrounds, including a Hizbollah list, and membership requires being a Shia Muslim and believ-ing in the Islamic Republic. MBA 'fights enemies and causes such as secularism, feminism and atheism', negates the Holocaust and is vehe-mently anti-Zionist. The group praised the slain Hizbollah leader Imad Mughiyeh in early 2008 and said that thousands 'like him will be ready to fight against oppressors and become martyrs'.[66] There are around 100 bloggers involved and one of MBA's key allies is Mohamed Ali Ramin, adviser to Ahmadinejad and key organiser of the 2006 Holocaust con-ference in Tehran.

Iran's Islamist blogs are popular and unwisely ignored in the Western media, where only liberal bloggers tend to be read because they write in English. According to a report written by Global Voices' Persian editor Hamid Tehrani on Iran's Islamist blogs, these sites 'provide one of the best places to learn information about news and state-related issues in the Islamic Republic, because some of their writers have close ties with Iranian leaders and some of them are even leading figures in the regime'.[67] A report on Iran's anti-Semitic blogs, released by Tehrani in June 2008, found that some Islamist sites discuss conspiracy theories associated with Ahmadinejad, including Holocaust denial and allegations that September 11 was a Jewish plot. Despite the relative unpopularity of the blogs, Tehrani stressed that many Iranian politicians are anti-Israel but not anti-Semitic.[68]

In the holy city of Qom, the home of Iran's Shiite clergy, the coun-try's clerics have also been quick to recognise that the internet is the perfect tool with which to spread the message of the revolution. Years ago, a prominent cleric had stated a position that was widely shared within the regime: 'Blogging, due to its very nature, has the capacity to nurture the spirit of vulgarity … [and is] a destructive plague.'[69] These days, according to the cleric who heads the Aalulbayt Global Information Centre in Qom, 'it was decided to have access to the internet in order to spread this Islamic knowledge all over the world'. Four global websites in thirty languages spread the political, personal and spiritual word to believers everywhere. The Centre's director, Hojatoleslam Lajarvardi, claims that Qom hosts more websites per head of population than anywhere else in Iran.[70]

Countless men and women are trained by clerics in Qom to blog about their religious beliefs and enter into discussions about issues as diverse as moon crescent sightings to life in an Islamic seminary. Although these courses existed before Ahmadinejad's regime, they have grown exponentially since 2005. One blogger told Iranian youth magazine *Chelcheragh* about the Office for Religious Blogs Development (ORBD), which specifically aims to harness the internet for solely religious purposes. To demystify the process, one popular blog was called 'Mullahs are not Martians'. 'A hawzeh [Islamic seminary] student is the same person who used to be a high school student like you, sitting next to you,' Najmi told *Chelcheragh*, 'and now as you have become a university student, he has become a student and studies, too.'[71] Other bloggers talked about using podcasting, posting photographs, YouTube and Google Video to pursue Islamic values in Iran and beyond.[72] An entrepreneurial web user even launched FarsiTube in late 2006. Co-founder Sherwin Noorian told Global Voices that the site was 'targeted towards Iranians, and has all kinds of videos about Iran and Iranian culture'.[73]

The 'children of the revolution' are logged on

The first Iranian email message was sent in 1993 by Dr Larijani, director of the Institute for Studies in Theoretical Physics and Mathematics, and received by administrators at the University of Vienna.[74] Developed within the university system, the internet was initially promoted by the regime as a way to prove the country's technological prowess in the years that followed the Iran–Iraq War. The authorities were initially happy to allow educational and commercial interests to access the net without censorship. The explosion in the youth population virtually guaranteed a healthy enthusiasm and a strong desire to engage with the outside world, something hard to achieve only a few years before. The subsequent rise in universities brought internet access to untold numbers of students from across the social classes.

The 2003 Iraq invasion was a catalyst for the regime to rapidly increase the banning of numerous political websites under the guise of eliminating 'pornography'. The crackdown even led to the head of the national association of ISPs resigning in protest at the growing censorship.[75]

A draft law was released in 2005 'on the punishment of crimes linked to the internet'. It proposed jailing citizens who wrote 'nauseating' material on homosexuality and sex acts and 'false information' on the Supreme Leader and pressured ISPs to comply with strict intrusion into their customers' records.[76]

During my visit to Iran, I could obtain little more than anecdotal evidence about the prevalence of filtering—government officials simply refused to discuss it—and instead discovered the absurdities of the system from Iranian bloggers and web users. In the months before my visit, there had been talk by authorities in the state-run media about implementing a national internet and email, the idea being to set up a completely separate online presence with only approved foreign sites available. It seemed like a practical impossibility but was clearly being considered by Ahmadinejad's regime.

A report issued by global advocacy group OpenNet Initiative (ONI) in mid 2005 claimed that 'Iran's filtering system is one of the most substantial censorship regimes'.[77] ONI alleged that the regime relied upon 'commercial software developed by for-profit United States companies to carry out its filtering regime'. It targeted SmartFilter, a filtering package made by the US-based company Secure Computing and claimed that it was 'configured as part of the Iranian filtering system to block both internationally-hosted sites in English and locally hosted sites in local languages'. ONI tested many sites and found 34 per cent were blocked, including pornographic sites, much gay and lesbian content, some politically sensitive material, women's rights sites and many blogs. Sites in Farsi were far more likely to be blocked than comparable content in English. ONI said in its report that by providing filtering to a non-democratic regime, Secure Computing was 'complicit in Iranian breaches of the UN Declaration of Human Rights'. ONI tests in 2007 found the situation had only worsened.

Days after this report was released, SmartFilter issued a response denying that its software had been bought by the Iranians. It claimed that 'any use of Secure's software by an ISP in Iran has been without Secure Computing's consent and is in violation of Secure Computing's end user licence agreement'. The company's chief executive in the US, John McNulty, said: 'We have been made aware of ISPs in Iran making illegal and unauthorised attempts to use our software. Secure Computing is actively taking steps to stop this illegal use of our products.'[78]

I contacted Secure Computing in the US to further enquire about its role in selling software to various countries for the purpose of filtering websites. Sarah Tolle, the company's Director of Global Public Relations, told me that its web filtering software SmartFilter 'allows organizations to customise the internet based on specific needs. We classify internet content into over ninety-one categories so that customers can chose, by category, what types of web content they want made available to their organization.' When pushed about selling the product to foreign governments, she said that these clients:

> can use any of these categories to tailor the internet to their cultural needs ... Secure Computing has no control over, or visibility into, how an organization implements its own filtering policy, but the company does not provide any categories that would allow someone to discriminate on the basis of race, religion, political persuasion, gender, sexual orientation, or any other personal characteristic.[79]

An examination of the categories of SmartFilter on the Secure Computing website suggests, however, that the company could allow users to filter political material. For example, the entry under 'Blogs/wikis' reads:

> This category is intended to cover the risks associated with content that may change frequently according to user interactivity and therefore may range from harmless to offensive. Because many Web logs and wikis focus on a particular theme or subject, this category is often used in conjunction

with others such as Education, Sports, Politics/Opinion, or Nudity depending upon the focus or theme of the site.[80]

The clear impression is that a non-democratic regime, like Iran, could set its SmartFilter to 'cover the risks' of politically sensitive material and block access to it. This is the kind of Western complicity that led leading Iranian dissident Akbar Ganji to argue that international pressure must be placed on companies that 'keep Iranians from using the web'. Western profits, he said, should not be at the expense of Iranian access to the internet.[81]

Caroline Nelleman is a Danish researcher who has completed a master's thesis on Iranian blogs.[82] She tells me that even if Secure Computing didn't directly sell its software to Iran, there would be no problem with the regime obtaining it, even with the current sanctions in place. (SmartFilter, she said, is clearly being used by the Iranians and the software has the ability to be used in a highly aggressive manner.) The government could simply order the filtering system online from the US or Europe, and then have it sent to Iran.

Western internet multinationals have started to implement their own restrictions on Iranian web users. In 2007 Yahoo and Microsoft removed Iran from the list of countries on their email services. Both companies claimed the move was to abide by US government restrictions (though Yahoo still included North Korea and Syria).[83] It was a seemingly futile move, as Iranian users could simply register under a different country. Neither Microsoft nor Yahoo provided satisfactory answers to me when challenged on this behaviour, only citing US government rules. Google has also restricted access to Google Desktop and Google Earth and other projects, offering the same reasons, though the company claimed sanctions did not preclude it from including Iran in its Gmail country list. A Google spokesperson told me the company was acting 'in accordance with US export controls and economic sanctions regulations'. Furthermore, the spokesman said, due to concerns in a country such as Iran over protecting customer privacy, 'we have no plans to host Gmail, Blogger and a range of other such services'.[84] Legal opinion is divided over whether the firms are obliged to restrict access or are simply pre-empting demands from the Bush administration.

Many Iranians I met used proxies to view filtered websites. Iran Proxy, formed by young Iranians and claimed to be the first anti-filtering group inside Iran, has developed articles and proxy websites to allow users to access restricted pages. The group claims that over ten million sites are blocked in Iran. One blogger told the *Boston Globe* that many Iranian web users use fast-changing online addresses and proxies to avoid detection. 'They block us and we evade the blocks,' she said. 'It goes on every day. They code, we decode.'[85]

Iranian authorities routinely defend the actions against free expression on the internet by claiming that parents demand the blocking of pornographic material. This rationale was shown to be disingenuous when later versions of Microsoft Windows provided an option for users to specify some of their own restrictions, therefore ruling out the need for external filtering.[86] The manager of a major ISP in Tehran told the *Boston Globe* that filtering was appropriate because 'all governments have ways to control their societies. It's natural that when we see someone wants to destroy us, we limit them.'[87]

Living away from meddlers

One evening Nima took me to a private party in the heart of northern Tehran. A friend of his regularly hosted these events in his small apartment, a relatively modern place with a squat toilet. The lounge-room was completely cleared, with seats positioned against the walls. A table of bread, dips, sausage and olives sat in the corner. A computer with Danish speakers pumped out songs by Bryan Adams, Celine Dion and Dire Straits.[88] Women, who arrived covered, took off their coats to reveal tight, low-cut tops, short skirts, heavy make-up and styled hair. As soon as they came through the front door, their demeanour changed and they became relaxed, flirty, normal. The men, dressed in pressed shirts and jeans, shared cigarettes with the women.

'Would you like whisky or vodka?' Initially stunned at the question, knowing that alcohol is officially restricted, I was slightly embarrassed by my naivety. Within an hour, the party was filling up and the music getting louder. One man, whose girlfriend kept on telling me that he hadn't proposed, was an architect and said that the rise of Ahmadinejad had made it more difficult for private businesses because the regime preferred publicly funded works or favoured companies. He later whispered that it was very important for Iranian women to get married. Another woman, an engineer, asked me if parties were similar in Australia and I had to admit that they were. Aside from the unhealthy obsession with Mark Knopfler of Dire Straits ('He's a hero to us here,' one man told me), the atmosphere was reminiscent of any party in Sydney, London or New York.

Suddenly, the music shifted from Western songs to Persian techno. Couples started dancing, the men looking awkward while the women moved confidently around them. After initial hesitations, I was persuaded by one of the few single women, Zhila, to follow her lead and move my arms and legs in ways that I had never done before. She told me later, and the cheering crowd around us seemed to confirm it, that my efforts to master an Iranian dance style were appreciated, if nothing else. Both Nima and Zhila said that they attended these kinds of parties at least once a week, the only option to socialise and 'be free' in a nation that didn't have bars, nightclubs, pubs or an unpatrolled public sphere. It was the only time during my visit that I saw people truly unwind. 'This is who we are,' Zhila said. The separation between private and public spaces was never starker.

What struck me so powerfully at the party was that most guests didn't really want to talk about politics, despite my incessant questions. It was time to escape the daily need to assume a public role, to be what society, and especially families, expected. Farouz Farzami, the pseudonym of an Iranian journalist who is banned from publishing, wrote in the *Wall Street Journal* that increased government repression on all sectors of society had not affected the wealthy, too busy, she said, to care about lessening freedoms. Alcohol and satellite dishes were a way to insulate against troubled times. A friend told her: 'Why should I bother to organise a protest against seizing our satellite dishes? We may be forfeiting our freedoms, as you say, but when the price of avoiding the authorities is so affordable, why would we risk everything to take on the regime? We have to wait until society itself is disillusioned, and the masses open their eyes.'[89] At least the bravest bloggers I was reading were not waiting for change to be organised by somebody else.

The following day Zhila, a petite girl with pale features and brown hair, drove me into the nearby mountains for lunch. She told me that she is an atheist Muslim—a secularist who identified culturally as

Muslim—but that acknowledging such things in public was impossible. She was born in Kurdistan, works as an architect and had lived in Tehran for fifteen years. She said that nobody liked the government but she preferred to stay out of politics. During her university years she had consumed the political scene, but these days she didn't like to read the newspapers or watch TV. I sensed that she was disengaged more out of frustration than apathy. Despite the social restrictions in the country, Zhila said she wouldn't want to live anywhere else.

It was cooler in the mountains, a welcome respite from the searing heat and pollution in the city. We sat on cushions and carpets in an outdoor restaurant alongside a river, large overhanging trees protecting us from the sun. It almost felt like a date, and maybe it was, but it was Iran, and gender relations were hard to fathom. Around us young couples sat holding hands and families tried to shepherd their unruly children. Zhila, in her early thirties, said that she wanted to find a husband but it was hard to convince a man to settle down. It was impossible to have children on your own, she said, or risk being completely ostracised.

The contradictory relations between men and women are hard to understand for an outsider. Tehran's underground metro system—far cleaner and more efficient than, say, those in New York or London—was technically supposed to be segregated according to gender, though whenever I rode in the carriages both sexes travelled together, giggling, flirting and smiling at each other. Women all wear the hijab, their bodies covered in either the heavy chador or body-hugging mantou. Many wear heavy make-up and red lipstick with hair that is held up with excessive amounts of hairspray. Young men wear tight jeans and shirts and Elvis-style coiffures. They could be straight off the set of *Grease*.

Most men and women dismiss the regime's strict dictates and date and sleep together like anywhere in the West, though much more covertly. The country's policy of free education and national literacy programs has allowed many women to enter universities and become active bloggers, but they undoubtedly still suffer discrimination by not having equal legal and social rights. Few women took seriously the pronouncement of Supreme Leader Khamenei in mid-2007 that he was willing to liberalise women's rights though not along Western lines. In some remote towns, stoning of allegedly adulterous women still takes place.

During an international film festival held in Tehran in February 2008, the official state news service, FARS, blurred out the faces of female guests, rendering them virtually unrecognisable. Feminist Farnaz Seifi said it was the first time that such an extreme action had occurred. 'The current government is simply against women in every way,' she lamented.[90] The closure of Iran's most important women's magazine, *Zanan*, in early 2008, for 'offering a dark picture of the Islamic Republic', only confirmed these fears.[91] One female blogger wrote with irony, '*Zanan* just reflected women's voices in the magazine, and they are women who threatened the so-called psychological security of society'.[92] Protests against 'gender apartheid' still existed, however. Hundreds of students protested at Shiraz University in early 2008 against a policy that separated men and women in the classroom.[93] Positively, however, a growing number of female bloggers are openly writing about their bodies and sexual desire.

A famous website dedicated to 'temporary marriage' ('muta' in Persian)—a process sanctioned by the Islamic Republic to allow young couples the freedom to have sexual relations either for a few minutes or as long as ninety-nine years—was an intriguing example of Islamic values being co-opted by modernity (not unlike one of Bozorg's friends, who worked in a silicone company, telling me that a growing number of Iranian women are getting breast enlargements and a great many recipients of these procedures are mullahs' wives). The Iranian interior ministry announced that 2008 would herald a massive campaign to encourage the nation's sexually frustrated youth the opportunity to embrace 'muta'.[94] Hamid Tavakoli, the twenty-year-old founder of the website, described as shy and religiously faithful, said that the greatest number of visitors came from the holy cities of Qom and Mashhad.[95] 'Our website intends to revive the Holy Prophet's tradition,' he argued, though my friends said that sexually explicit material was commonplace on the site.

Iranian nudity exposed

When I saw artist Golnar Tabibzadeh, a striking twenty-three year old with long black hair and piercing blue eyes, she quickly struck me as somebody whose strong opinions would not be welcomed in mainstream society.[96] We met at a posh restaurant in northern Tehran with other citizens of the upper classes, the mood lighting reminiscent of trendy bars in the West, except alcohol was obviously not served. Golnar told the *Toronto Star* in 2006 that her art, often depicting naked and tortured figures and therefore hidden in Iran, 'is one of the few places where I can express myself without self-censorship—not like in the outside world, in the Islamic Republic, where a lot of people filter their words'.[97]

She was preparing for her first international exhibition in Germany and being critical of the government meant she was seriously considering moving overseas 'for a better quality education'. She was tired of being constantly harassed by Iranian men. For simply wearing a little make-up, she said, a woman would get hassled in the street after 8 pm. Years ago at university, a lecturer became fixated on her exposed, sandal-encased feet.

Despite being part of the post-revolution generation, Golnar believed that life for Iranian women was deteriorating. She recalled seeing her mother being bashed a few years ago by baton-wielding female policewomen for simply demanding women's rights. She asked them why they were beating women who were fighting for their rights.[98]

A friend of Golnar's, who had lived in Canada and China, asked whether being a Jew made my journalistic success more likely. It wasn't an accusing question, merely curiosity. Although I didn't advertise my Judaism to most people I met, I wasn't averse to mentioning my religion with people I trusted. It was a curious question for somebody who, having lived abroad for so long, was not solely exposed to the highly prejudicial Iranian state-run media that broadcast *The Protocols of the Elders of Zion*. I was very aware that the notion of Jewish power and influence is ubiquitous in the Middle East, but I answered that my religion was irrelevant. I did note, however, that being a Muslim in the West post–September 11 could perhaps adversely affect your career.

Golnar had barely left Iran, but she spoke English virtually fluently and appeared comfortable with my Western ways (she said she rarely read blogs but tried to engage foreign media websites.) The day I met her she was wearing black jeans, a beige tank-top and open-toed sandals. She was in Greece a few years ago and wore a bikini on the beach. She said it felt strange at first, the freedom and normality of this simple act, and although she openly wore bikinis at private parties in Tehran, she hated having to become a different person on the street, trying to avoid eye contact with men.

The following day I was invited to Golnar's family home in western Tehran. She lives with her parents and brother in a modest house filled with her evocative paintings, her father's sculptures and many books in Persian and a handful in English. She told me that most Iranian families wouldn't allow a Western man to visit their house and spend time with their daughter/sister.

Behind drawn curtains, Golnar showed me many of her large canvases, figurative in style, with dark social commentary on a society that is largely forced to hide private thoughts. Large, often Picassoesque nude bodies lay disfigured or covered in various shadows. None of them can be displayed publicly because the depiction of any nudity is strictly prohibited. There were some nude self-portraits, virtually unrecognisable in their abstraction.

Much of her work was moody and she said this reflected her view of the world and those of her friends (one had tried unsuccessfully many times to commit suicide and another had an abortion after she fell pregnant to her boyfriend and was forced to visit Tehran's only semi-official abortion doctor, a man who charges US$2000 for a procedure). During our time together in her studio/bedroom, we listened to a host of Western rock, from Belle and Sebastian to Arcade Fire and Joan Baez to Dire Straits.('Mark Knopfler is very popular here, we love him.')

That evening Golnar took me to a gallery and cafe run by a woman, the only place of its kind in Tehran. The owner, a plump woman in her fifties, had lived in San Francisco for nineteen years, running a florist's and working in public relations. She travels regularly and writes film criticism for *Film International* magazine. She spoke with an American accent and had decided to return to Iran to see her ailing father, then stayed to 'give something back to my birth country'.

She explained the constant struggle of running a cafe as a woman in Tehran. The endless bureaucracy, hassles by police, unannounced raids—to condemn patrons smoking or women whose hijab was too far down their heads. The cafe had been closed by the authorities months before my visit because a particular permit hadn't been obtained (one

which was notoriously difficult to get). Previously, authorities had criticised the cafe for allowing smoking, so signs were put up asking women
not to smoke inside and light up on the street. This was also problematic, but took the issue away from the cafe itself.

The owner said that she accepted that her liberal views represented
the minority position in Iran and that Ahmadinejad was widely popular.
If the laws requiring women to wear hijab were removed, she said, only
a minority in Tehran—and even fewer in other cities—would do so. 'We
have a long way to go here,' she said. But she didn't idealise women's
lives in the West, rightly pointing to societal pressure in our countries to
convince girls 'that they must always be thin and beautiful'.

I sensed that Golnar wanted to show me a side of Tehran that
wasn't limited to regime propaganda, proving that a liberal intelli-
gentsia existed to counter the mullahs. Before we left her home she
changed clothes and covered herself completely, leaving virtually no
flesh exposed, and on the way to the cafe she cursed the green-clad
religious police speeding past on a motorcycle, their jackets removed
and shirts untucked.

Whispering truths

Journalist and blogger Azadeh Akbari had worked for many foreign
news companies, including Associated Press, ABC News America and
Frankfurter Allgemeine, but was now translating for UNICEF. She had
a warm smile and wore a black hijab. She wasn't upset that work for
Western media companies had dried up, except for the money, because
'these agencies only want to know about nuclear problems and al-Qaeda.
They don't give a shit about what happens in the country'. When she
worked as a staff reporter for Associated Press, the regime called her
a 'spy'. 'Anywhere we'd go, they told us that the American spies are
coming, the servants of the US are coming.'

Azadeh (meaning 'free woman' in Persian) writes a blog in Persian
and English and focuses on Iran's often hidden social problems, such as
drug addiction, prostitution and street children. Azadeh, who is thirty,
told me that, when she worked for Iranian newspapers, editors would
tell her that she had to write articles about prostitution without mentioning the word 'prostitution' or 'condom'. When she wrote about a 'sexual

calendar' on her Persian blog—the calendar explained that it is forbidden to have sex on special days and revealed the characteristics of a desirable woman and her ideal size and shape—she received a great deal of flak from her male colleagues. 'Their faces are modernised, but their thinking is not,' she said. 'Some of my male colleagues started to write, "Look at these intellectual girls, they've studied for four years and they want to lead the world." It was humiliating.'

On her English blog, Azadeh explained the challenges facing an independent journalist in Iran:

> The other problem is that in Iran an average person reads less than 5 minutes a year. There are only 6 TV channels that are all led by the government. Reformist newspapers are under censorship. If we write a word against the government they close down the newspaper. Self-censorship is very common between journalists.[99]

Azadeh was the only person I met in Iran who was willing to talk openly about endemic drug problems among the country's population (and although very few newspapers were willing to publish these stories any longer, her blog remained a vital outlet and surprisingly unfiltered). She told me that heroin remained a massive problem, but the rise of crack and crystal meth posed an even greater threat. A gram of heroin cost around US$9 and crack US$2. Afghanistan is the primary source of the drugs and the US-led war has led to the market being flooded.[100] There are an estimated three million drug users in Iran and the last few years have seen a more pragmatic approach to the problem, with fewer addicts being thrown in jail.[101] Azadeh talked about her investigations of male prostitutes and how many of them told her that the internet had finally allowed them to find like-minded souls in Iran and internationally. She said that there are around two million gay people in Iran.

During Ahmadinejad's speech at Columbia University in September 2007, he claimed that 'we do not have homosexuals in Iran like you do in your country'. The *Guardian*'s Brian Whitaker, author of a book about gay life in the Middle East, wrote that he discovered similar views across the Middle East. 'Some concede that a few gay people do exist, but claim they are victims of Western influence, since homosexuality is a "foreign" phenomenon.'[102] 'He [Ahmadinejad] must know gay men and women exist,' wrote David Shariatmadari in the *Guardian*, 'because he supports the laws used to persecute them.'[103] Considered an illness waiting for a cure, transsexuality and sex changes are, ironically, tolerated and encouraged by Iran's ruling elite. Iran carries out more gender change procedures than any other country in the world besides Thailand (unofficial figures suggest up to 150 000 Iranians are transsexuals).[104] Ahmadinejad has even increased public funding for hormone therapy.[105]

As a supporter of former president Khatami, Azadeh believed that the reason Ahmadinejad won power in 2005 was that people preferred justice to freedom (something confirmed, she said, in a study conducted by the Ministry of Culture). Freedom was important for the intellectuals, but Iran's poor were more worried about bread on their table. The new reality hit her when she was trying to research a story about a mosque in America that allowed women to pray without covering their heads. But when she typed 'women' and 'mosque' into Google, the words were blocked. For some mullahs, she said, being a woman is a 'sin'.

Azadeh displayed contempt for the Iranian regime but felt similarly offended by the destabilising role played by America. 'Iranians have never forgiven them for the 1953 coup,' she said. 'People don't accept it when Americans talk about democracy for Iraq or Afghanistan. We were really trying democracy [in the early 1950s].'

The Iranian Jewish question

While I was in Iran I met blogger Mohammed, a twenty-five year old with a neatly trimmed goatee.[106] He asked that I didn't reveal his name in print or record our conversation. When we had started communicating via email months before I arrived, he asked that we not discuss politics at all. I was unsure about his request, but I naturally agreed. When we met, I started to learn the reasons for his concern.

As we sat in a bohemian-style cafe in Tehran, the walls adorned with photos of Al Pacino and Marlon Brando in their Godfather roles, Mohammed told me he had seen the word *Israel* on my website and feared that the authorities might discover we had met and block his chances of studying in the United Kingdom later that year. Although he said he had read about me online, he had deleted any evidence of this from his Google history. His paranoia was understandable because Israel was demonised on a daily basis in the state media. Any possible association with somebody writing about Israel could be held against him.

After Israel, Iran has the largest Jewish population in the Middle East, around 25 000—a little known fact. Before I arrived I had tried unsuccessfully to contact the Tehran Jewish community (their English-language website, http://www.iranjewish.com/English.htm, is a rich source of information but contains no contact email or phone number) and had read that Iranian Jews were able to practise their religion without persecution. Through some contacts, Bozorg—who said he had never been to a synagogue before nor knowingly spoken to Jews—arranged a meeting with a Jewish family on the Friday Sabbath.

We were invited to Tehran's main synagogue, situated near the centre of the city behind a high fence and guarded by two police officers from the government. Hebrew lettering was proudly displayed on the outside wall facing the street. Children played on the footpath wearing the kippah (skull-cap), clearly not afraid to show their Jewishness to the passing traffic. Our host, David, a heavy-set 26-year-old computer engineer, led us both inside. The hall was sparkling and brightly lit. As in Orthodox synagogues around the world, men were sitting downstairs and women upstairs (although I noticed some women sitting downstairs near the back). Most men wore a suit and tie and the prayer books were only in Hebrew, though most visitors dispensed with reading them. The congregation talked incessantly, with some of the old men trying to 'shhh' the restless crowd. We could have been in Sydney, New York or London, such was the universality of the service. I felt distinctly proud to be Jewish at that moment, able to dispense with my usual discomfort around observance, and simply enjoy the moment of a connection with Jews on the other side of the world.

My own ambivalence towards Israel, even sometimes hostility towards its foreign policy, made me wonder how I would feel spending time with these devout Jews. For many Jews in the West, Judaism and Zionism have become intimately intertwined. Despite the increase in my ambivalence about Judaism over the years, I always try to venture to a synagogue and Jewish community centre in whichever city I'm visiting. It isn't about regular worship; it's merely a desire to experience, and admire, the tenacity of fellow Jews in a host of challenging situations under often repressive regimes. This is the kind of Judaism of which I am proud—not the unthinking, Zionist flag waving that has infected many diaspora communities.

David, speaking in Persian while Bozorg translated, told us that the weekly Friday evening service was a chance for friends and family to catch up. 'The community here is very tight,' he said, with men and women generally marrying within the faith. I had to ask David about his views on Israel, despite the sensitivity of the subject and the regime and media's almost daily attacks against the Jewish state. 'Israel is political and I really can't talk about that,' he initially said. But then he opened up a little. 'We don't agree with everything Israel does, but we feel solidarity with Jews around the world.' David's answer was revealing in its sparseness.

The service started at seven o'clock and finished around nine. The Rabbi tried valiantly to discuss the week's Torah portion but the congregation rarely quietened down. I remember hearing at Orthodox synagogues in Australia that the men spent the entire service talking about football while the women discussed shopping and men. I wondered if similar stereotypes existed in Iran. At various times during the proceedings, people rose to recite prayers, in unison or in silence, genuflecting towards the Ark (behind which sits the Torah).

At the end of the service, a number of men approached me to ask who I was. When David told them that I was also Jewish, they immediately commented that I clearly wasn't very religious because I had not been closely following the prayers. The outsider had been discovered. Bozorg and I walked back towards the street and noticed men and women mingling and laughing together—many women allowed their hijab to slip from their heads.

David invited me to a Sabbath meal at his parents' home, an apartment near the city centre. We went with his wife, who had nearly finished an engineering degree, and her plump, moustachioed father. Outside the door was a sign in both Persian and Hebrew and a mezuzah (affixed to the doorposts of many Jewish homes and containing Hebrew verses from the Torah). David said in his broken English that both signs stated that all visitors were welcome to enter and should have good health when they leave.

The apartment was alive. David's parents, the smiling, partly toothless father and kind-looking mother, were chatting to his sister and her grey pony-tailed husband while her children ran around. The grainy TV screen beamed incessantly in the background, playing what looked like a Chinese soap opera. It was what we'd think of as a kitsch apartment, every corner seemingly packed with old treasures, fans and vases, which reminded me of the kind of house a grandparent in the West would inhabit.

We sat down at the dinner table. Nobody spoke English with any proficiency, so there were many curious glances. David was being bombarded with questions about me from his family. Everybody was inquisitive about Australia—David's sister wore a Billabong-brand T-shirt with indigenous dot-painting emblazoned across her chest—and wanted to know how many Jews lived there, what I did, why I wore an earring, where my family came from, how I looked no older than twenty-eight years old and whether I had had a Bar-Mitzvah. When I said that most of my family had been killed in the Holocaust, David said, 'Our president doesn't believe it happened.' 'That's because he's ignorant,' I responded. There were audible gasps around the table. They may have shared my view but were clearly taken aback with my brazenness, especially in front of strangers. Later in the evening, David said that he was aware that his country was viewed fairly negatively in the West but implied that Ahmadinejad was only one president and a passing fad.

Following the generous entrée came the main course, which consisted of duck stuffing, mountains of rice, mixed salads, duck stock soup, fish and a host of other meat dishes. Throughout the meal, glasses of whisky and home-brewed kosher wine were passed around. David's family were clearly proud to be Jewish. Although cagey about Ahmadinejad's views on Israel and the Holocaust, they said they wanted to stay in Iran as they were able to freely practise their religion, despite suffering some discrimination like other minorities—such as not being able to publicly express opinions on contentious issues like Israel and the Palestinians. A number of Iranian bloggers have even started engaging with Israeli bloggers in an attempt to better understand the other's culture.[107]

David told me that he often disliked the anti-Israel programs on television but refused to explain exactly why. I think I understood his hesitation. David and his family lived relatively comfortable lives in Iran, could practise their religion and work freely. The community was allowed to celebrate the religion's Persian roots.[108] Expressing any comments that may be construed as critical of the government or overtly political, especially to a relative stranger, was simply seen as naive and counterproductive. David struck me as not fearing the current president but hopeful he would soon lose office.

During Ahmadinejad's controversial speech at Columbia University in September 2007, he argued that 'we are friends with the Jewish people. There are many Jews in Iran living peacefully with security'.[109] Then he asked, provocatively but not without merit, 'why is it the Palestinians are paying the price for an event [the Holocaust] they have nothing to do with?'[110]

After Ahmadinejad's appearance at Columbia University, where he was introduced by university president Lee Bollinger as a 'petty and cruel dictator', the Jewish community in Iran published a statement condemning Bollinger's speech.[111] 'The constant disrespect and disturbance ... prove once more that those claiming to be peace loving people have no real grasp of the concept,' it read.[112] I sensed that the Jewish community establishment had to be seen to support the government, though not always uncritically. Iranian Jewish parliamentarian Dr Siamak Morsadegh said on the occasion of Israel's sixtieth anniversary in May 2008 that his community would not be celebrating and that they protested the 'murder of totally innocent Palestinian civilians'.[113] Ahmadinejad would have been pleased, given that in his view Israel was a 'stinking corpse ... on its way to annihilation'.[114]

The situation for Jews in Iran, while not perfect, is hardly equivalent to that of Nazi Germany. Indeed, the comparison is obscene in its dishonesty. After the Columbia appearance, the Jewish weekly *Forward* editorialised that the American Jewish community was doing itself no favours by comparing Iran to Nazi Germany, over-demonising Ahmadinejad or alleging that Jews in Israel were about to be exterminated by Iran:

> Sixty years ago, Jews were alone and friendless, mistrusted by most Americans and hated nearly everywhere else. When Hitler came to kill us, nobody cared. Today our position is vastly different. We are full citizens of most countries we call home. We have gifts our ancestors could scarcely dream of. We dare not squander them.

For years Jewish American and Israeli groups have been using cash incentives to try to lure Iranian Jews to their respective countries, with little success. Despite being generally allowed to travel to Israel and emigrate abroad, only 152 out of 20 000 Jews left Iran between October 2005 and September 2006, a fall from the previous years.[115] The chairman of Tehran's Jewish community, Dr Siamak Morsadegh, and Jewish MP Maurice Motamed released a statement in July 2007 that 'Iranian Jewish citizens will never exchange their identity with money … [and] the Iranian Jewish people do not show any interest in immigration to the occupied territories of Palestine for the reason of enjoying full religious freedom in Iran'.[116] A group of forty new emigrants left Iran for Israel in late 2007, the largest exodus since 1979.[117]

For David's family, emigrating just wasn't an option because they did not feel that they were being unduly persecuted. While there is no doubt that many Iranians believe the conspiratorial and at times pathological rantings of Ahmadinejad[118] on the right of Israel to exist, most Iranian Jews have no desire to leave.

The problem with the 'Iran as Nazi Germany' line, wrote commentator Jonathan Cook, is that Iranian Jews simply don't fear genocide will be committed against them.[119] As David and his family told me, there are kosher butchers in Tehran, synagogues and even a Jewish hospital that Ahmadinejad has partly funded. It was announced in August 2007 that the regime was building a new cultural and sports centre for Jews in Tehran.

Ahmadinejad has undoubtedly unleashed inflammatory anti-Semitic rhetoric against the Jewish state—though his desire to see Zionism obliterated is little different to the position of every Iranian leader since Ayatollah Khomeini.[120] Ahmadinejad's pronouncements have undoubtedly played into the hands of the 'crazies' in Washington keen to portray the Iranian president as the logical successor to Hitler.

Before I arrived in Tehran, I was keen to engage with Jews in the country. I had read in the Jewish press in both America and Australia that the country's Jewish community was forced to adhere to an anti-Zionist agenda to curry favour with the regime and survive. This is not what I discovered; in fact, I found quite the opposite. There were undoubtedly areas that David and his family didn't want to discuss, but they barely knew me. They seemed genuinely happy to allow me into their lives—David even offered to show me around the city's hidden Jewish treasures—and not afraid to proudly display a quiet Zionism.

Introducing the former vice-president

One of the central figures in the reformist and blogging movement has been Mohammad Ali Abtahi.[121] During Khatami's reign, he was the president's Chief of Staff, Vice President for Legal and Parliamentary Affairs and Personal Advisor. He remains close to Khatami and although his power base has shrunk during the Ahmadinejad years, he is of the view that a reformist revival is possible in the 2009 presidential election. He was the first Iranian cabinet member to start a blog and currently heads the Institute for Inter-Religious Dialogue in northern Tehran.[122] His office is a well-appointed multi-storey building, with a large library filled with books about the world's religions.

Although he is a reformer, Abtahi is an Islamist and belongs to an association of Islamist bloggers called Yaran Baran (Fellows of Rain).[123] On the YB website, the bloggers, despite impressions in the West, are neither liberal nor pro-democracy. They believe in pluralism but reject Western liberalism and Western freedoms. Their aim is to achieve democracy through Islamic frameworks. Former Tehran-based *Financial Times* journalist Gareth Smyth has written that the vast majority of Western commentators have little idea about Iranian political life or the diversity of attitudes among reformers. 'When I arrived in Iran in December 2003,' he explains, 'before the polarisation between Iran and the West escalated over Tehran's nuclear programme, there was a strong western view that the reformists (popular, goodies) were confronting the conservatives (unpopular, baddies) over social freedom and women's clothes.' Less than two years later, Ahmadinejad came to power.[124]

I had been reading Abtahi's blog for at least a year before I travelled to Iran (he writes both a Persian and an English one) and enjoyed his insights into official thinking and criticisms of the ruling elite. Abtahi said his websites had never been filtered but were hacked twice by officials. He believed that his prominent public profile lessened the chances of his online presence being shelved. In a post written in the aftermath of Saddam Hussein's execution, Abtahi wrote:

There is no doubt that the greatest crime done by Saddam was the war with Iran when the entire world especially America accompanied him. Although the main guilty person does not exist now anymore ... the crime should not be forgotten. It is now the time that Iran holds an international seminar about Saddam's crimes to Iranians and damages which were made. The occupiers of Iraq who were the ex-friends of Saddam should be accountable now.[125]

Rather than directing extreme rhetoric against Washington, Abtahi's well-reasoned call was to hold the Western powers to account for their years of funding and arming Saddam. This was an Iranian reformer whose suggestion was barely heard in the West.

Abtahi's think-tank inevitably receives financial assistance from overseas, said Bozorg, my translator, but even saying such things in Iran was difficult. Any foreign involvement could be portrayed as attempting to undermine the Islamic Republic.

Abtahi is a short, round mullah with a permanent cheeky grin. He seemed determined during our two-hour interview to challenge my Western prejudices about his country and its government. As we spoke in a small room with plush couches adjacent to his office, cups of hot tea were brought in. He regularly warned me against adopting some Western ideal of what Iran should be. Many Iranians were deeply conservative and not necessarily keen to follow Western notions of gender equality and freedom of speech. He also reminded me of something regularly forgotten in the West: that the country's president is not the head of state and, although he holds considerable power, he is always subordinate to the Supreme Leader.

Abtahi was eloquent about chastising what he saw as the counter-productive rhetoric of Ahmadinejad and the need for an alternative vision of the country. But his definition of democracy is not related to our own. Abtahi both praised the importance of the 1979 revolution and talked longingly about the 'democracy' that existed before (although he didn't specify, I presumed he meant the period before the 1953 coup). I challenged Abtahi on a system that clearly dictated strict boundaries of public debate. He responded:

[Debate] belonged to the time [before the 1979 revolution] when democracy was the basis, fundamental to society. We're so far from that time. The most important achievement of the reformist government was injecting such literature to the body of society. People recognised their rights, that is so important. Those who sanctioned the election, those [*sic*] intellectual generation, their demands from the president, Mr Khatami, were not democratic demands. They asked, 'Why don't you confront civil liberty protestors?' and that's different from what you call democracy in the West.

When I challenged him on the inability to criticise the Supreme Leader in public, he chastised my equivalency. 'One of the misunderstandings is that you try and compare the institutions of countries which are not similar to each other. It should be compared with countries that are just like us.' He suggested Egypt, 'which has the same population and the same civilisation background'. He confusingly said that discussing women's rights was a more appropriate issue for comparison. It was a typical contradiction within many reformers, at once wanting to embrace greater liberties but also seemingly incapable of imagining a nation without strict public controls.

One of the most revealing sections of our interview revolved around the Iraq War. Although Abtahi was vehemently opposed to the invasion and occupation, and believed that whatever role Iran had developed in Iraq was 'natural', he supported the regime aligning itself with Shia groups inside Iraq. Surprisingly, however, he didn't advocate a rapid withdrawal of American troops, fearing the consequences for Iraqi civilians (this view was shared by many Iranians). Like most Iranians I met, Abtahi complained that Washington simply didn't understand the Middle East and that its boorish actions were convincing Muslims that there was a battle against everyone in the region. He opposed a worsening relationship between the West and Iran and believed that the disastrous Iraq War made a US attack on his country highly unlikely.

It was sobering to hear Abtahi, as a reformer, state that the regime should never talk to Israel. 'I consider the behaviour of the Israeli government to be primitive and ancient … [Iran] doesn't have any reason to have a relationship.' When he said that no Arab countries maintained diplomatic relations with the Jewish state, I reminded him of Egypt and Jordan. 'They are not proud of this relationship,' he shot back.

After the interview was over, I was fascinated to see a different side of Abtahi emerge. Bozorg, Abtahi and I were talking over cups of cold tea, and the former vice-president acknowledged that he did in fact advocate the banning of websites that supported assassination or violence, pornography (but not sexual education sites) and a host of other unspecified sites. As Bozorg later told me, many reformers had split personalities: they were both modernisers and highly conservative, unsure of the true role of democrats in a repressive regime. They loved power but were also aware of the revolution's shortcomings.

Abtahi was at the centre of power during Khatami's leadership and, unlike everybody else I met, he spoke the language of regaining political influence. He wasn't liberal in the Western sense, spoke lovingly of political Islam and dismissed the rights of the Jewish state (although a reformist spokesman, and colleague of Khatami, denounced Ahmadinejad's Holocaust denial in late 2007 as 'unnecessary political adventurism ... which harmed the country').[126] Abtahi, and reformers like him, are framed in the West as the moderates in Iran—and compared with Ahmadinejad, they probably deserve this tag—but they are certainly not likely to embrace Washington's idea of co-dependence. I liked him, though, this witty, funny and very personable man. I was deeply sceptical of his ability to institute the changes of which he spoke, but on many key issues I was forced to face the reality of a moderate Islamist, an almost invisible term in the West, open to ridicule and scorn. But throughout the Middle East, such men and women are without a doubt growing in stature and political power.

The Iranian paradox

I had discovered an Iran suffocating on a lack of oxygen for dissenting views of any kind. But another Iran exists, especially online, and largely out of the Western consciousness. Iran's blogging community is probably the healthiest in the Middle East, despite a political leadership intent on stifling these outlets.

Iran's online community is providing the strongest indication yet of how a predominantly young population under thirty wants to articulate an alternative Iranian identity. A growing number are expressing the desire for a 'post-Islamic' country, values that are being fiercely fought by the ruling elite. I heard this term 'a post-Islamic state' regularly during my visit, although it was not clearly articulated what that might be among the people I met. Some writers wished for an Iran that embraced secularism, but they recognised that many Iranians would not want Western-style democracy. The shift in the political mindset and institutions would be enormous. A democracy with Iranian characteristics would require an undoing of nearly thirty years of religious and political rule.

Hasan Yousefi Eshkevari, a reformist cleric, was released from jail in 2005 after serving five years of a seven-year sentence. His supposed crime was speaking out against the Islamic Republic, and one of the conditions of his release was that he would no longer be allowed to wear his cleric's robes.[127] He has told Pulitzer Prize–winning writer Anthony Shadid that one of the threats facing Iran is that citizens are becoming critical of Islam itself, not just the government.

> We say under the banner of religion that there will be equality, under the banner of religion, there will be development, under the banner of religion, there will be a successful economy. But what if there is not, this failure of the religious state will be a failure of religion. The failure of the government, therefore, becomes a failure of the faith.[128]

It is notable that not one Iranian I met during my visit talked lovingly about the country's recent history. 'What is to be done with our own Islamic fascists?' wrote blogger Godfather in 2003. 'Our electoral system does not give us the opportunity to vote against them. Have we put up a fight? Yes, for 25 years our prisons have seen the best packed to the rafters, we have seen the best kind sent to the gallows and buried in mass graves. Are these fascists in the minority? Yes ... but they are armed and willing to kill for their beliefs and we are only willing to die for ours.'[129]

Conservative forces pushing for stricter Islamic laws may well lose the long battle against the largely young population, but it is unequivocal that there has been a seismic political shift towards political Islam across the Middle East—from Palestine to Lebanon and Afghanistan to Iraq—that suggests that Iran's influence is only now starting to be felt.

If we want to truly understand the nuances of the Islamic Republic, Ahmadinejad is just one small piece of the complex puzzle. While the conservative forces will tighten their grip in challenges to their authority, liberal and conservative bloggers are far from united. The vision of these bloggers—whether of a post-Islamic society or a nation where Islam remains the central pillar—is often contradictory but they should be acknowledged as the voice of Iranian youth and, indeed, the future for Iran.

I found an Iran that was as vibrant and challenging as any country that I have ever visited, principally because it confounded my expectations of a repressed society and instead embraced private revolt by many citizens unable to express themselves in public. I was relieved to discover that the accepted Western narrative of oppressed Iranians was only partly true. The myriad restrictions placed on daily life have inevitably led to a vibrant online, art and written culture, but the end point of the 1979 revolution is still to be decided. I felt welcomed by Iranians who wanted to show me that they lived 'normal' lives like any other young people in the world. Like any proud people, most innately distrusted Washington and its aim for the country.

The thriving internet community showed that political engagement was probably far higher in Iran than in many comparable Western nations. Yet the internet cannot, on its own, bring about the required dismantling of decades of repression. It can simply be a tool with which writers, journalists, women, unionists, teachers and other citizens engage with the political process and advocate for change.

Technology never brings true reform; only people do.

Egypt
Challenging a 'Moderate' American Dictatorship

'Search for Egypt on YouTube, and all you'll find is tourism and torture.'
Egyptian blogger Alaa Seif, 2007[1]

'If you see how bloggers and students used the internet ... this is the happiest thing that happened in Egypt in the past ten years.'
Human rights lawyer Gamal Eid, 2007[2]

US SECRETARY OF STATE Condoleezza Rice arrived at Cairo's American University in June 2005 and delivered a speech of startling clarity. 'For sixty years,' she argued, 'my country, the United States, pursued stability at the expense of democracy in this region here in the Middle East—and we achieved neither. Now, we are taking a different course. We are supporting the democratic aspirations of all people.' She demanded that Egypt's dictator, Hosni Mubarak—one of America's closest Middle East allies—allow free elections and release imprisoned opposition figures. The regime, she insisted, 'must put faith in its own people'.

Without context or history, Rice's words were inspiring, but ultimately they remained empty and even hypocritical. Egypt is the second-highest recipient of US foreign aid annually (only Israel receives more and Jordan is third). The money has been a reward for good behaviour towards Israel after the country reached a peace deal with the Jewish state in 1978.[3] Military aid over the last twenty-five years has equalled US$33 billion, yet consistent opinion polls find anti-Americanism far higher than in any other Middle Eastern country.[4] 'The Americans now prefer stability over democracy,' said an opposition leader in early 2007. 'I will never trust them again.'[5] There are at least 80 000 political prisoners in Egypt and the annual budget for internal security is higher than the entire budget for health care.[6]

After the initial democracy-laden rhetoric, the Bush administration unsurprisingly realised that 'stability', not 'democracy', was more important.[7] Indeed, the Iraq War caused massive anti-American demonstrations across Egypt and hampered any opposition attempts to unseat Mubarak. The first opportunity in the country's long history for people to choose their leader by democratic means came as late as 2005. Since that election, which saw the Muslim Brotherhood gain eighty-eight seats in the 454-seat parliament and the rise, before imprisonment, of liberal presidential candidate Ayman Nour, the regime has steadily increased the pressure on alternative voices.[8] Washington hasn't complained and even actively encourages the silencing of local dissent.[9] In fact, the US ambassador to Egypt praised Mubarak in 2007 for his government's 'commitment to the opinion of the common Egyptian citizen'.[10]

The Bush administration has also colluded with Egypt in its 'extraordinary rendition' program—including the kidnapping and torture of Australian Mamdouh Habib—housing and torturing terror suspects in the same jails as dissident Egyptians. The day after President Bush visited Egypt in early 2008 and praised its 'vibrant civil society', the regime prevented demonstrators from protesting in central Cairo.[11] Where Egypt is concerned the moral high ground adopted by the US is severely compromised. One of the Arab world's most respected NGOs, the Cairo Institute for Human Rights Studies, released a report in early 2008 that found that at least fourteen of the region's worst human rights abusers were close allies of Washington, including Egypt.[12]

It is impossible to spend any time in Egypt and not discuss the Muslim Brotherhood. Formed in 1928, the party is banned and many of its members are imprisoned, with up to 10 000 Islamists behind bars.[13] (The regime occasionally allows its members to run in elections, though 90 per cent of Islamist hopefuls were disqualified in April 2008 local elections.) The regime sentenced some of the most senior members for up to ten years in prison in April 2008. The Brotherhood has tens of thousands of members, though exact figures are impossible to determine due to the decentralised nature of the organisation and its understandable refusal to keep written records of personnel in case state security obtains them.[14] The regime clearly fears its power—and its actions in Egypt, Syria and Palestine have often been brutal against civilians—as does Washington, knowing that open and free elections would likely deliver victory to an Islamist, anti-Western party, as elections have in Palestine with Hamas.

Everybody I met in the country had strong feelings about the growing influence of the group. I was told that its public visibility, from protests and graffiti to street signs and women wearing hijab, had rapidly increased in the last decade. Many women, predominantly Muslim, were suspicious of, if not hostile, towards them. Men, often secular, seemed far more willing to acknowledge the greater tolerance within the Brotherhood over the last years.[15] Members of the Brotherhood claim that the group is a safety valve for moderate Islam. 'Without us,' says a leader, Essam al Eriyan, 'most of the youth of this age would have chosen the path of violence.'[16] The rise of the movement in the Palestinian territories (including the 2007 Hamas takeover of Gaza) and its close ties to Hizbollah have further forced the Mubarak regime on the offensive, though its beliefs and use of political violence in other nations warrant careful scrutiny.

The regime has portrayed the group as incubating terrorists, offering assurances that only its toughness can suppress the Hamas and Hizbollah tendencies of its members and maintain the country's peace deal with Israel.[17] Mubarak has launched dozens of secret military tribunals for Brotherhood members over the last years, despite civilian courts acquitting them of all charges.[18] Although the Brotherhood officially ditched the use of terrorism in the 1970s, the Egyptian prime minister, Ahmed Nazief, stated in 2005 that the group 'will never be a political party'.[19]

Its embrace of Islamic law unsettles many Egyptians, but Mahdi Akef, the group's supreme guide, has said he believed in an 'Islamic democratic model, to show it works in practice'. With the slogan, 'Islam is the solution', the regime's attempted strangulation of the movement has merely strengthened it. Not unlike the political effect of the US invasions of Afghanistan and Iraq, the electoral success of political Islam has surged at the ballot box, despite the best wishes of the neo-conservatives. Across the Middle East in the years since September 11, 2001, a growing number of young people are observant Muslims.[20] I was in an Egypt that wasn't afraid to increasingly display a devout face to the world.

Mubarak, president since 1981 after the assassination of Anwar al Sadat, rules over a nation that is the Arab world's most populous but whose influence has declined in the last decades. A state of emergency has remained in place for over two decades, granting legitimacy to repressive measures against opposition figures. Religious freedom is non-existent if an Egyptian citizen isn't Muslim, Christian or Jewish.[21] Despite the brutal suppression of the leading opposition group, the Muslim Brotherhood, dissent against one-party rule continues to grow. The internet has played a key role in this facilitation and Egypt was the country in which I found bloggers the most willing to meet and publicly oppose their leader's rule. I visited the country at a time when there was a renewed crackdown on journalists, the Muslim Brotherhood and bloggers,[22] I was sometimes taken aback by their brashness in the face of possible imprisonment, torture and concomitant Western silence.

Cairo, one of the dirtiest major cities in the world, looked like it was trapped in a bygone era, its architecture weighed down by blackened buildings and oppressive humidity. The level of noise, according to scientists with the National Research Centre, equates to having a lawnmower running next to your head.[23] Hitler's manifesto *Mein Kampf* was available at popular bookstores and could be bought from street vendors. The sight of a decrepit but functioning Iraqi Airways Co office in central Cairo was a sad reminder of that country's parlous state. A shop with the sign 'Power Rangers for Transport' promised speedy deliveries, but this was probably wishful thinking. And yet, not unlike Syria, Egypt was deceptively liberal; some women were dressed in Western clothing and alcohol was relatively freely available.

In a city of approximately 16 million people, it was impossible to miss the desperate poverty and the sight of men, women and children with severe deformities.[24] Outside my hotel, families spent countless minutes standing in front of shoe shop windows pointing to shoes among hundreds of brightly lit pairs crammed into the tiny spaces. I enjoyed catching beaten-up taxis to crisscross the city, the fumes often circulating through the interior. It was a city that had seen better days.

'Yes, we practise censorship,' said a Ministry of Interior spokesman in 2005. 'So that he who is afraid will not talk.'[25] The regime ordered the seizure of the German news magazine *Der Spiegel* in early 2008, claiming it was insulting to Islam and the Prophet Mohammed.[26] Despite the rhetoric, Egypt's internet is rarely filtered and the regime has preferred to imprison and intimidate bloggers and opposition figures in the vain hope that dissent will be crushed. And this repression of opposition has occurred under the watchful and supportive eye of Washington. Dissatisfaction with the Mubarak regime threatens to explode at any time. In no other country I have visited did bloggers and opposition figures from across the political spectrum so brazenly flout regime regulations to challenge one-party rule in both cyberspace and on the streets.

The vast majority of the media is state owned and projects a pro-Mubarak line. A number of outspoken newspaper editors were imprisoned in 2007 for allegedly defaming the president and his son Gamal, the likely successor.[27] During my visit I read an article in the English-language paper *Al-Ahram Weekly* about the torture of Sudanese refugees in 'preventative detention'.[28] Such reporting now routinely appears on blogs and online forums, forcing the government on the defensive.

Walking along the Nile at the end of a long day, as the sun swept across the water, young men and women sat, talked, walked and held hands. A polluted haze hung over the city to the horizon. Two teenage boys with guitars sang romantic Arabic songs to two adoring girls. It was a fairly normal scene with a notable difference. When Egypt was appointed a seat on the United Nations Human Rights Council in 2007, the regime insisted that it wasn't about to conform to 'Western' standards of rights. 'Egypt cannot allow homosexuality or sexual liberties for teenagers under the pretext of promoting human rights,' an official said, 'because even if there are some groups that advocate these rights, the vast majority of society is simply and strictly opposed to these Western values.'[29]

Human rights limited

Elijah Zarwan, thirty-two, is a former Egyptian researcher for Human Rights Watch (HRW).[30] An American–Canadian Jew who lived in New York for many years, Zarwan invited me to a spacious office in a high-rise building in a wealthy part of Cairo. Most of the rooms were fairly bare, and a handful of staff sat at their desks with laptops perched on telephone books. Zarwan said that all the staff often suffered harassment from the state. He told me he knew his mobile phone was tapped and sometimes heard the telltale clicking sound and even state security voices during conversations.

Zarwan said that the government had a 'schizophrenic' relationship with the internet. It wanted to embrace the economic benefits of the new technology but was also wary of internal dissent. A number of journalists joked to Zarwan that they would find it impossible to write a story with the headline 'No Brotherhood members arrested today'.[31] Over 1000 members were arrested in 2006 and 2007.

He expected greater internet crackdowns in the coming years, but not necessarily an Iran-style filtering process. (The only known site blocked in Egypt, and other Middle East countries, is the Jewish dating website JDate, though it's quite possibly the company itself that is refusing connections from Egypt.)

Talking with Zarwan reinforced for me the need for the universality of human rights. He told me with disdain that many Western human rights activists refused to protest when members of the Brotherhood were imprisoned or tortured, preferring to campaign only for individuals whose views they thought were moderate or Western-friendly. Islamists were treated with suspicion, their views and actions deemed dangerous. It was universal human rights—for some. This explained, he said, why so many Western-based activists remained silent when HRW attended sham court trials or visited activists in jail. They didn't want to be seen to be sympathetic to perceived anti-Western forces.

A few months after I left, Zarwan issued a stern challenge to the regime about the refusal of authorities to allow human rights groups to monitor 'the military trial of 33 leading members of the Egyptian Muslim Brotherhood, undercutting the government's claims that civilians will have a fair trial before military courts'.[32] In a blog post in early 2008, Zarwan strongly stated that he was 'fundamentally opposed' to the Brotherhood's platform and 'distrust[ed] their new discourse of freedom and democracy'. But he notably argued that he campaigned against the government's treatment of them 'on moral and practical grounds'. It was an admirable position for a secular Jew to take.[33]

Islamism is a way of life for many in the Arab world. Leading Egyptian democracy activist Saad Eddin Ibrahim lamented the fact that Washington ignored these developments, but 'the Western world must come to grips with the new reality, even if the US President and his Secretary of State continue to reject the new offspring of their own policies'.[34] Ibrahim, who was convicted in 2001 of preparing slanderous reports about Egypt and spent years in prison before being acquitted in 2003, now faces fresh charges but chooses to remain in the US. He told *Democracy Now!* in October 2007 that Mubarak was using death squads to eliminate opponents and that he wished the West would cease supporting the 'autocrats' in his country. He stated that the opposition remained small 'because we don't have access to the state media, nor do we have access to the mosques'. He said that 77 per cent of the country stayed home during the last parliamentary elections. 'We believe the majority [spiritually] is with us.'[35]

When Zarwan first arrived in Cairo in 2000, he had to walk forty-five minutes to find an internet cafe, and then the connection was mediocre. Today, much of the capital has free wi-fi access and even the poorest sections of the city have web cafes. Zarwan praised the regime for a program that allowed anyone with a computer, modem and phone line to get online for the price of a local phone call. 'It's really had a huge effect [on internet penetration],' he said, 'and provided a model for other developing countries in the world.'[36] Zarwan said Mubarak realised that the country was failing economically and needed to better engage with the world. The internet came along at just the right time.

Zarwan's personal story was intriguing: a Jew who ended up falling in love with Egypt and Arabic and wanted to immerse himself in a culture utterly removed from his own. He was my sort of Jew—the questioning kind.

The last years have also seen profound changes in the ways in which the opposition, bloggers and activists have used the internet. Zarwan recalled talking to journalist Wael Abbas in 2005 and hearing his frustration that the press syndicate didn't take bloggers seriously. Online reporters weren't given respect. State repression in 2006, and the arrest of many bloggers for peacefully advocating judicial independence and free elections, helped raise the profile of blogging and led to a renowned al-Jazeera documentary.[37] By the end of 2007, a group called Arab Bloggers Union had formed and campaigned across the Arab world for the release of an imprisoned Brotherhood blogger. 'Him today ... it could be you tomorrow' was the headline of the campaign. It was the sign of the times that such a group could exist and campaign publicly in the case of an anti-torture blogger.[38]

One Egyptian blogger, Amr Gharbeia, led an online discussion about whether exposing the identities of torture victims harmed his or her ability to cope with the inevitable shame:

> I believe that a lot has been achieved in the previous year and a lot of it is due to the efforts of activists and the bloggers. It is a source of pride as the Egyptian public opinion is now aware that torture takes place a lot in this country. It would be worthwhile now to look into the future and avoid repeating the mistakes of the past. Something of this sort may be happening now. Lately, [blogger] Wael Abbas tried to think of the victim. The latest film he published shows a man forcing a woman to take off her clothes in front of a camera and in the presence of others. He only published a still picture and an audio recording. I would like to know whether Wael's motive in protecting the woman was because she was a female or whether his motive would have been different had it been a man forced to undress.[39]

Discussions about societal shame in a deeply conservative country was something only online writers were willing to tackle. 'We are a society which doesn't wash off its dishonour,' Gharbeia blogged, 'except with blood.'

Zarwan and I left the office and headed for an outdoor cafe. His English friend followed some time later. A charming and almost Hugh Grant type, Robin had lived in Cairo for more than six years as a translator and spoke fluent Arabic but said that 'there's never really assimilation, no matter how long you've been here'. Zarwan agreed. The cafe, a regular hang-out, was dirty, the blue chairs looking like they'd seen cleaner days. There was no food, only very strong tea and coffee. A few men were smoking shisha pipes in the corner. Stray cats ran around us. I saw dozens of similar places across the country, a place for mainly Egyptian men to congregate and shoot the breeze. Both Zarwan and Robin said they had fallen in love with the freedom they had as 'outsiders' in the city compared with what they considered the constrained worlds from which they had come. And unlike so many expatriates I met in other countries, they regularly mixed with the local population.

Despite a population of 72 million people, 6 million internet users[40] and an estimated 4000 blogs (up from a mere 30–40 in 2005)[41], Egypt still has an illiteracy rate around 40 per cent. The web therefore remains an elite pursuit, but one case, recalled Zarwan, catapulted the medium into the public consciousness. Imad al-Kabir, a micro-bus driver who refused to pay a small bribe to the police during an altercation between the officers and his cousin, was taken into a local police station in January 2006, horribly beaten and sodomised with a stick. The officers filmed the incident on a mobile phone camera and distributed the film, via Bluetooth, to other bus drivers to intimidate them and 'break his spirit'.

Kabir initially stayed silent but finally came forward to report the assault when his brother was arrested and placed in the same police station. The video, soon circulating on various Egyptian blogs, showed Kabir sprawled on the floor, naked from the waist down, hands bound behind his back and legs held in the air. Kabir was begging and screaming for mercy. The officers' faces were not visible on the footage.

Lawyer Nasser Amin of the Centre for the Independence of the Judiciary persuaded Kabir to bring the case to the public prosecutor, but in early 2007 a court charged the twenty-one year old with resisting arrest and assaulting an officer and sent him back to the same police station in which he was assaulted. Unlike most torture cases, however, bloggers were integral in creating a wave of outrage at the regime for condoning abuses. The opposition press forced the issue into the mainstream arena. Zarwan said that bloggers had succeeded in forcing the state to detain a police captain and put him on trial. 'This is extremely unusual for Egypt, a country where torture is widespread and officers are rarely, if ever, tried for it.'

Unlike the vast majority of previous cases involving abuse of power by police officers, Zarwan argued that the last few years have seen blogs feed into the traditional media, newspapers and satellite television. After the Kabir case, 'the government realised that it can no longer afford not to take this seriously. The bloggers have succeeded in doing something that years of standing on the street corner and shouting no to torture or no to the interior ministry had never managed to accomplish.'[42] The two officers who abused Kabir were found guilty in late 2007 and sentenced to three years in prison. 'I've regained my rights,' shouted Kabir after the verdict was announced. 'I don't want anything more than that.'[43] It was the first time in living memory that an Egyptian police officer had been found guilty of torturing a suspect.

Opposition activist and blogger Mohammed al-Sharqawi knows what it's like to be imprisoned and raped in a police station. He was detained in Cairo in May 2006 after a protest commemorating the anniversary of police violence against journalists and protesters the previous year. He was forcefully dragged by a group of plain-clothes policemen and beaten, before being sexually assaulted. He remained in jail for three months for no discernable crime and was never charged.[44] Fellow bloggers suggested that al-Sharqawi and others had been arrested for their 'citizen journalism' and reporting on information ignored by the mainstream media, such as torture.

I met al-Sharqawi in central Cairo after his initial hesitation in talking to a Western journalist.[45] It helped that I had befriended some of his opposition friends and HRW's Zarwan, all of whom had vouched for me (though I suspect being an American or Israeli journalist would have been a problem). He wore an Adidas football jersey and had a nervous but constant laugh. He looked about twenty-five. We caught up near Tahrir Square, the chaotic space that required precision running to avoid being hit by rampaging drivers. Al-Sharqawi lived in a small apartment above an outdoor restaurant which regularly sent its smells and smoke into his rooms, he said. Like many eating establishments across Egypt, the smell of rotting food seemed to linger in this restaurant. I asked al-Sharqawi about this and he joked that it was healthier to eat at a street stall because you could see the food being prepared. The waiters all knew him and he joked with them throughout the night.

Al-Sharqawi's contempt for Western media was quickly revealed after he told me that a Western reporter had wanted to visit him soon after his release from prison. He was about to enter hospital for an operation and the journalist asked if she could speak to him right after he came out of surgery. He was incredulous. '"Go to hell," I wanted to say, but she came and we spoke.' He couldn't believe that Western journalists would care so little about the people they were writing about.

Al-Sharqawi was keen to tell me his story, though he constantly looked around the restaurant as he talked. He was justifiably paranoid: state security agents watched his every move. This is what he told me anyway and, as he picked at the limp lettuce salad in front of him, I sensed that his imprisonment and rape had made him realise that he wouldn't be able to live a normal life again for a very long time, if ever.

He said that his girlfriend didn't always cope well with his newfound status; it had caused constant problems.

Like most Egyptians I met, al-Sharqawi was vehemently opposed to Washington and its consistent support for Egypt's dictator. He was unrepentant in his views against the regime. He said that when he was arrested he had no idea where he was going and was refused medical treatment for health problems. 'I suffered a lot then and felt pain, but they didn't care.' Friends and family were able to bring him food every few days. He remained sceptical towards the Muslim Brotherhood and opposition group Kifaya[46], the relatively small but vocal Egyptian Movement for Change, saying they spent too much time talking and not enough doing, though both supported him during his imprisonment. I was surprised that he was happy for his sexual assault to be raised in such a public way, considering the shame of male rape in Arab societies. Another opposition figure later told me that the incident had made al-Sharqawi more arrogant, as if his experience had given him a greater authority to act impulsively, even recklessly.

The night we met he said he intended to write a long post describing his experiences over the last years. He told me he wanted to explain to Arabic readers that the incident had only made him stronger and more determined against the regime. 'I want people to know that they can't hurt me any more,' he said. During our time together I wondered if his bravado was a way to manage his ordeal. I asked him directly about the likely future of Egypt and the effect of blogging on it. He wasn't overly optimistic. 'Mubarak's son will probably take over, but we'll keep throwing stones in his direction.'

Al-Sharqawi continues to campaign against torture and writes about these issues on his Arabic blog; he was re-arrested in April 2008 after distributing material to promote a general strike against the regime (though he was released a few weeks later). He remains unafraid of returning to jail though feared having his laptop stolen, which explained why he carried it with him everywhere, including to our dinner. He had joked to me that he had numerous photos, audio and video files and documents that were 'worth sleeping with'. Human Rights Watch reported in early 2007 that the Egyptian authorities continued to refuse to investigate his case or the men behind it. He told HRW that one of the officers present during his abuse 'always seems to be waiting downstairs from my apartment' and in March 2007 he arrived home to find his laptop, containing an unreleased video of police abuse, had been stolen.[47] This explained his paranoia when we met a few months later.

It was difficult to warm to al-Sharqawi, his tough exterior seemingly impenetrable. As the large bottles of beer flowed, he certainly opened up, but he bristled at the sound of the Muslim call to prayer. He wanted a secular future for the country and planned to open a publishing house to ensure that alternative voices were heard. He told me he wanted to publish a collection of the country's best bloggers. He launched the Malameh publishing house soon after we met but faced ongoing harassment. The police force broke into its Cairo office in April 2008 and confiscated a novel they alleged to have political connotations.[48]

Bloggers such as al-Sharqawi represent only a tiny proportion of Egyptian society, but the State Security Investigations department of the Interior Ministry issued a report to prosecutors in March 2007 that accused him and sixteen other bloggers, including Wael Abbas, of 'spreading false news' likely to negatively affect Egypt's international image.[49] Organising protests were also deemed illegal, though Zarwan said many bloggers now filmed public events and quickly uploaded them to their websites, partly to be able to identify officers engaged in violence. It was also a way to communicate with foreign journalists and even foreign embassies.

Anonymous blogging has become more common in the face of a regime crackdown but, Zarwan said, 'there is a sense amongst bloggers that the government is waiting for an excuse to go after them', so open discussion about the Mubarak succession or torture has been tempered, 'but in the end committed opposition bloggers haven't toned down their criticisms at all'. Coptic Christian human rights bloggers are also threatened—but the real reasons for the harassment are rarely revealed.[50]

Moroccan–American journalist and blogger Issandr El-Amrani[51], a Cairo resident for seven years, has been published in the *Economist* and the *Boston Globe*. He stressed that people like himself and Zarwan had far more freedom than the average Egyptian because of a foreign passport. We ate at a pricey restaurant in the French embassy, surrounded by tables of the city's elite. The tight security revealed that such targets were popular with the extremist minority.

El-Amrani was personable and cynical, his thick-rimmed, black glasses perfectly framing his face. He constantly reminded me, like Zarwan, that the regime should at least be 'given credit … for granting internet access to a lot of people, even poorer people', adding: 'The current prime minister was formerly the minister of communications. He basically put together all this and essentially created a situation initially where the state was subsidising the internet. The telephone company was making an initial loss so that the ISPs could prosper.' Mubarak's regime, like many dictatorships, he argued, was more complicated than initial impressions allowed. El-Amrani was keen to dispel what he said were my unfortunate prejudices about the government. 'Freedom of the press isn't irrelevant, but it's not the only barometer,' he said.

The site that El-Amrani started in late 2003, The Arabist (http://arabist.net/), quickly became an essential stop for journalists, diplomats and foreign observers keen to understand the attitudes of the Arab world in the wake of the Iraq invasion. He told me that the website aimed to investigate internal Arab politics, something virtually ignored in the Western press. According to the site, it 'seeks the very opposite of romanticizing the Arab world or trying to explain it through essentialist cultural theories. Debunking ill-informed, culturalist or alarmist works about the region is one of the main preoccupations of this site.'

El-Amrani explained in the *Guardian* in 2007 how the Egyptian blogosphere (including his site) 'harms no one and escapes the limitations of accepted discourse in the real world'.[52] He wrote that the Western media were missing the increasing solidarity between secularists and Islamists online in their opposition to the regime and The Arabist was unafraid to document these societal shifts. He hoped the site would be just one space where bloggers could express solidarity:

> While journalists in the Arab world still have, in theory at least, unions and laws to protect them, bloggers enjoy no such protection … The fact is that young political bloggers in undemocratic countries have little awareness of the legal resources potentially available to them, of how to avoid detection, or of libel and other laws their writings might be attacked for. Now that the well-honed repressive skills of Arab security services are catching up with them, who will stand up for bloggers?

El-Amrani saw himself as a commentator and not an activist, though the simple act of posting information about government abuse such as torture and detention made his protestations questionable. He said that the regime had a greater problem with activists than bloggers, though often the two groups' aims collided. He was encouraged by state-controlled media starting to get news tips from bloggers, rather than the other way around. Despite this, however, the regime's seemingly random repression of the internet proved that it had no 'coherent policy towards bloggers'.

After a long and heavy lunch of lamb, meatballs, sautéed fish, beef and mushy vegetables, cooked in a supposedly French style in the middle of Cairo, I wanted to escape the searing heat. I found the Mosque of Ibn Tulun, an Iraqi-style space with relatively non-pushy attendants. There were many ceiling fans roaring inside and a number of sleeping men sprawled on the green carpet. Although the mosque wasn't overly opulent it was peaceful and a welcome respite from the constant hassling outside. It was calming to see some men intently reading the Koran from intricately inscribed editions.

It is patently clear that the regime won't be toppled by the power of bloggers alone; however, through the internet, the opposition has cleverly exploited the government's insecurities. Disparate groups, from the Brotherhood to liberal secularists, have sometimes united to oppose Mubarak's authoritarianism. Hossam El-Hamalawy has been at the forefront of this struggle.[53] A 30-year-old activist, journalist and blogger, he studied economics at the American University of Cairo (AUC) and started working in journalism in 2002, freelancing for the *Los Angeles Times*, Bloomberg, Human Rights Watch and the BBC. He was intense, with short, greying black hair, a committed Marxist, and openly advocated for a socialist state.[54] His student activist days left him with a security file and therefore inadmissible to teach at most universities in the country (except AUC, who apparently don't require regime approval before hiring staff).

We met near the AUC at a cafe filled with students drinking coffee and eating focaccias. It was a stifling day outside, and although I had spent hours walking through the backstreets of the city past crumbling buildings and posters of Mubarak looking into the future through old-fashioned sunglasses, I still found Hamalawy's message both fascinating and confronting. He spoke in revolutionary language, though was implacably opposed to violence. He told me that he had worked as a researcher on journalist Stephen Grey's book on 'extraordinary rendition', *Ghost Plane*, and discovered that the Australian prisoner Mamdouh Habib had once been a prisoner at a notorious jail near his home on the outskirts of the city. 'We don't believe in democracy here, believe me. And the Americans know it, too.' Hamalawy's message, spoken in exceptional English, was perhaps the most critical voice I heard in Egypt. Uncompromising and angry, his conversation was more of a barrage. I liked this man who was unafraid to speak his mind.

Hamalawy told me about life as a blogger–activist and the atmosphere in the country in 2006. 'Cairo was a city under occupation then,' he said, telling me it felt like the streets were filled with foreign troops. He faced police brutality, along with his friends, simply for the act of demonstrating for democracy. 'It's similar to the kinds of pictures you would see in the Indonesian revolution in 1998 where initially the students mobilised but then the security services mobilised that urban pool of thugs, armed them and unleashed them on the students.' In both countries, America had provided military and political support for the actions. State violence spurred Hamalawy into action. He set up an email mailing list for journalists and human rights workers and dispatched information daily. He said he felt proud to be part of a blogging movement united by its anti-torture and anti-authoritarian stance.

Not all Egyptian bloggers were critical of Washington, however. One of the most popular Egyptian bloggers is the neo-conservative Sand Monkey. Sand Monkey, whose blog has a large American audience, temporarily stopped blogging in 2007 because 'there has been too much heat around me lately. I no longer believe that my anonymity is kept, especially with State Security agents lurking around my street.' Condemning state-sanctioned torture, even for somebody who praised Washington, was a precarious business for this blogger, no matter the political persuasion. He later explained that he felt frustrated at the inability of Egyptian bloggers to better organise themselves into a force to challenge authoritarian rule. 'That we now have the media attention, the people's admiration or at least interest, and the "zeitgeist" is ours if you will,' he wrote in 2007, 'so it's time we use it wisely.'[55]

The biography on his blog reads: 'Be forewarned: The writer of this blog is an extremely cynical, snarky, pro-US, secular, libertarian, disgruntled Sand Monkey. If this is your cup of tea, please enjoy your stay here. If not, please sod off.' Sand Monkey supported the Iraq War because, as he explained in early 2008 about US President George W Bush's visit to Egypt, 'hate him or love him, the man shook up the region with his push for democracy in Arab countries, especially Egypt'.[56]

The vast majority of Egyptians I met didn't share this view. Hamalawy said he supported Hamas and Hizbollah, and a one-state solution for Palestine, 'not because I'm an Islamist—I'm an atheist—but because they are anti-imperialist movements'. He argued that the largest protest in Egypt for years was in 2000, to express solidarity with the Palestinian intifada. This mobilisation, he said, led to a stronger opposition in 2003 and beyond, and the rise of political blogging emerged from that scene. There was a direct line through it all, he told me. The main organisers behind the 2000 protests became the leaders of the Kifaya movement. Unsurprisingly, during the 2006 Lebanon war, the group demanded an end to the country's peace treaty with Israel. The movement launched a petition to collect one million signatures towards its goal.[57]

Autocratic regimes—and Mubarak's was just the latest—were worried about their reputations abroad. Hamalawy said that the leaking of torture videos seriously embarrassed the government, but the authorities didn't seem to understand the ways in which the internet had democratised information. For example, if you tried to photograph public buildings you were likely to be stopped by over-zealous officials. 'These guys don't know that we can get photos of everything on Google Earth,' he laughed, 'and I can see the president's house on Google Earth. The ruling elite in Egypt is very phobic towards information. The blogosphere is the antithesis of everything they believe.'

Blogging the female experience

The Egyptian blogging community, not unlike Iran's, is filled with women who struggle against both government repression and outdated presumptions about their societal role. I met Shahinaz Abdel Salam in central Cairo near my hotel in Sharia Talaat Harb, a bustling boulevard that fell asleep for a few hours from four in the morning and awoke five hours later, at nine. A 29-year-old architect from Alexandria, Abdel Salam had startling red hair and wore a wide smile. I had been told by a number of opposition figures that she was the perfect example of a brave female activist who skilfully dodged official sanction. After introducing myself—something I was advised against doing in detail over the mobile phone network, due to probable tapping—I jumped into a taxi with her and we went to a Western-style shopping mall across town.[58]

Abdel Salam was intrigued about Australia, she told me; she had never met anybody from there before. Then she asked the question that followed me around the Middle East: she wanted to know why our government had troops in Iraq. She was also curious about my views on Mubarak. 'Does he get much media coverage in Australia?' she asked.

We were at the mall because she said we were likely to be watched by the regime in any cafe downtown. The security services were ubiquitous and the sight of a Western man and an Egyptian woman automatically generated curiosity and suspicion. She later told me that Egyptian society didn't really allow her to have male friends, so she labelled her fellow male bloggers as colleagues or activists.

Abdel Salam was forthright, passionate and focused. She had started blogging in 2005 as a way to express previously private thoughts. But she was at pains to highlight that she was blogging 'as an Egyptian first, and a woman second'. She told me:

> For a long time I wanted to have a space for my ideas and be able to comment on what's been happening around me, on the street, my country, my family, about women, about politics. I was taking the train from Alexandra to Cairo to attend demonstrations, taking pictures and putting it on my blog. Sometimes it was like commenting, why women couldn't get into the mosque through the principal gates, why we have small gates in the back. I didn't like that. I was talking about that, about what I feel, what I see, how I was reacting, and people were reacting with me sometimes.

Abdel Salam recalled attending protests with the Islamists during her university days and being the only woman not wearing a veil. They were usually protesting Israeli violence against the Palestinians. The demonstrations would automatically place the men at the front and the women behind, but Abdel Salam resisted these calls and told her male colleagues that it was absurd to place the women at the back during a public protest. These colleagues even tried to convince other women to force Abdel Salam to comply with their arcane rules.[59]

I asked her whether she maintained friendships with Islamists, either men or women. She said it was often an uneasy relationship but they sometimes came together to oppose the Mubarak regime. I sensed that she feared the growing Islamisation of Egypt but felt powerless to do anything about it. In a society where gender relations weren't as codified as in Iran or Saudi Arabia, there were still clear boundaries. Abdel Salam told me that family pressures were also problematic. Her mother wanted her to settle down and find a 'nice' Muslim man but she said she wasn't ready for commitment.

She remains friends with imprisoned blogger Abdel Kareem Nabil Suleiman, sentenced to four years in prison in 2007 for 'vilifying religions', 'inciting hatred of Islam' and defaming Mubarak. Shortly before his detention in November 2006, Suleiman wrote defiantly on his blog: 'I am not scared at all ... I will not back away one inch from what I wrote and handcuffs will not prevent me from dreaming of my freedom.'[60] Suleiman, twenty-three, was disowned by his conservative family in the week of the sentence and remains a highly controversial figure. For some he is an attention seeker, and for others the test of a moderate and inclusive Islam. After his jailing, there was an international outcry: the Middle Eastern blogosphere exploded in anger and solidarity, and pressure was placed on Western governments to protest the first example of a blogger being jailed for personal remarks. In late 2007, Suleiman alleged torture against his captors, and supporters said he was looking haggard and in desperate need of release.[61] It was a clear case of governmental over-reach and a warning to other bloggers to watch what they wrote.

For Abdel Salam, as for virtually every blogger I met in Egypt, the Suleiman case was a lightning rod. He is a 'very shy man', she told me, 'and then you see how strongly he writes on his blog'. A senior fellow at the American libertarian think-tank the Cato Institute had met and corresponded with Suleiman in 2006 and found a quiet man who strongly believed in women's and minority rights. They had kept in touch by Gmail chat and as soon as Suleiman was informed that he would have to attend an interview with prosecutors, a network of Middle Eastern bloggers swung into action and quickly found him a lawyer.[62] Protests were held outside Egyptian embassies and global debate soon turned to the fact that a key American ally was imprisoning a young man to shut him up.

The case had proved two points about the strength and weakness of the Egyptian activist blogging scene. The government was clearly taking the medium seriously and hoping that an excessive jail term for a small-time blogger would intimidate others into silence. But it also showed that bloggers could no longer be ignored and were starting to be feared as a credible alternative voice. Abdel Salam admitted that she was far braver in conversation than on her blog and said she now feared retribution from the regime. She still posted information about protests and included photos and videos from demonstrations. Her mother had even been contacted by authorities and encouraged to convince her daughter to stop her blogging activities.

As our conversation progressed, Abdel Salam expressed deep concerns about the role of the Muslim Brotherhood and its attitude towards women. 'They may win a free election,' she said, 'but they are too extreme.' She told a story about a recent local election when a woman from the Brotherhood approached her and asked whether she was a Muslim. When she said yes, the woman responded, 'So, you're voting for us.' Abdel Salam's hesitation incurred the woman's wrath. There was simply a presumption that a Muslim would support the Brotherhood. Abdel Salam hoped that some of her friends, who closely associated with the main opposition party, would be able to influence what she saw as their narrow, intolerant ideology. When she talked about wanting to obtain freedom and democracy for Egypt, she wasn't willing to accept any group that claimed to be able to achieve it. As a woman, Abdel Salam wanted to know why women were not able to achieve positions of importance within the Brotherhood. For them, she sighed, to be a woman is to be a wife.

Although a critic of successive American administrations, particularly in relation to Iraq, Palestine and its support of Mubarak, she liked American people and had recently returned from a visit to New York. She loved the fact that she could shout obscenities against Mubarak in Central Park without risking imprisonment or worse. She supported the Iranian regime for standing up to Washington and being 'independent' but criticised its human rights record. The outlook of this highly educated Egyptian woman was far more nuanced than that represented by mainstream media in Western countries, often determined to classify attitudes towards foreign affairs as either 'pro-US' or 'anti-US'. Abdel Salam said she knew that most Egyptians would prefer to be at war with Israel and ditch the peace treaty. This suited Mubarak because he told the Americans that only his tough attitude could protect the Jewish state. As we were leaving, she questioned the number of Jews killed in the Holocaust—'I know that it happened'—and wondered if the Nazis targeted other groups. It was an incredible blind spot, though one I sensed was more out of ignorance than bigotry. It wasn't an uncommon question throughout the Arab world.

During my first visit to the Middle East many years ago I was stumped by this question. How could people not know the history of the Holocaust?, I wondered. But I soon discovered that my naivety was based on blindness. The issue was mainly avoided in the schooling of the region, state-run media regularly demonised Jews and Israel, and Palestinian suffering was paramount. Abdel Salam was not unlike many others in the Middle East (aside from the undoubted number of people who truly loathed Jews and were anti-Semites) who craved information and remained open to reason. She was anti-Zionist, I soon discovered, not anti-Semitic.

The relative openness of Egyptian society offered me the opportunity to meet more female activists and bloggers there than anywhere else in the Middle East. Many of these women were undoubtedly Westernised and anti-Mubarak, but they didn't hesitate in speaking to foreigners. I admired the stance they took despite a fear of imprisonment and torture. Many told me that to speak the truth wasn't brave, merely a necessity.

Salma Abu Taleb was a striking twenty-one year old with curly black hair whose family was communist.[63] We met near the AUC in a Starbucks-style cafe (many activists who vehemently opposed Washington spent a disproportionate amount of time hanging out in them). Abu Taleb spoke nearly fluent English with a distinctly British accent, the result of taking classes from the British Council.

For Abu Taleb, not unlike Abdel Salam, her gender was not the primary reason for her foray into blogging, but challenging presumptions about the rights of women in Egypt became increasingly important.

She told me that she had been sexually harassed since she was seven years old, like other female friends, and her blog was 'good therapy' and allowed women to share 'Muslim ideas about how to react, to beat the man and shout. Also to tell the men who say these things don't happen.' She was strongly against Mubarak's rule—'if you want to make things better you probably need to blow up half the country and rebuild it' but equally she feared a violent rejection of his rule in the coming years.

Walking the streets of Cairo and Alexandria I was struck by a disparity, one that I would again note in Lebanon and Syria. These were societies struggling to define their attitudes towards women and emancipation. It was not strange to see an abaya-clad woman walking alongside a young girl in a short skirt and tiny t-shirt. They appeared to co-exist without serious trouble, but Egyptian female bloggers challenged this superficial interpretation.

Dalia Ziada was a moderate, proud, female Muslim who criticised both Washington and Middle East dictators, including her own. She wore a pink hijab—because of her mother, she told me—and represented an Islam almost invisible in the Western media.[64] I liked her immediately, at once devout yet cheeky. She was a blogger, an activist and a translator who had started her own NGO to help money-poor NGOs translate documents free of charge. I had caught a rusty taxi across town to meet Ziada near the American University. It was a precarious experience as the driver asked if I was in a rush and when I unwisely said yes he sped through red lights to deliver me on time. It was customer service Egyptian-style.

Ziada had started blogging to promote human rights and to campaign against 'female circumcision' (female genital mutilation). Many young girls were subjected to the practice out of a deluded religious belief, she said, when it was in fact simply a way to oppress women. Many of her friends and family approved the behaviour—'all the girls in my family were subject to the operation'. I wasn't brave enough to ask about her own situation but she saw her role as educating 'the grass-roots and not the elite' about why it should stop. Ziada spoke eloquently about her struggle and it was impressive to hear this young, 25-year-old woman standing up to a centuries-old practice. She worried that no Egyptian man would accept a politicised and vocal woman to be his wife. She wanted to marry but was in no rush.

An Egyptian 2005 government health survey found that 96 per cent of the women interviewed had undergone genital mutilation.[65] It was no longer taboo to discuss the issue in public, thanks in part to a coalition of government and NGOs campaigning to stop the practice (outlawed in 1996, but the new law was rarely enforced). Even Mubarak's wife, Suzanne, joined the calls against it. Ziada told me it would take time to unwind hundreds of years of tradition instituted by both men and women but that various female bloggers had contributed to this important shift in Egyptian society.

Ziada's blog has made her distinctly unpopular with large segments of the Islamist population. She said that many Egyptian Muslim men resented her 'meddling in tradition'. She argued that Egyptian society, like many in the Muslim world, was resistant to change:

> Let me tell you something really strange; some men give their wives many rights, and the wives refuse to take these rights because they think they are not jealous and don't love them. For example, a man tells his wife, 'You go to work any time, and you can stay late any time and I trust you, you are a good woman.' She may say that he does not love her.

It was shocking to hear her discuss a recent incident in Cairo when somebody threw boiling water on the back of a woman who was wearing a tight T-shirt. The woman survived but was badly disfigured. Ziada said her brother Mohammed had been seemingly programmed to accept only strict Islamic doctrines. He was a 21-year-old engineering student and his friends from the Muslim Brotherhood told him that 'the girl he dreams to have as a wife should be wearing the hijab. He does not want anything else. He does not ask about her mind, how she thinks.' Not surprisingly, Ziada opposed the Brotherhood and even supported the regime's crackdown on its members. Ziada said they were radical and determined to implement a fundamentalist doctrine on all Egyptians, discriminating especially against non-Muslims. She acknowledged the group's opposition to Mubarak; although she criticised the president, she said she never insulted him because he 'deserves respect'—but perhaps naively thought that free elections would not elect the Brotherhood into power.

We walked around the university after meeting at the cafe. I noticed some men looked at both of us suspiciously, probably wondering why a Western man was with a devout Muslim woman.

Ziada seemed genuinely interested in hearing about my previous girlfriends. The fact that I had dated and not married was intriguing enough but she also wanted to know why I hadn't proposed to any of these women. A fair question.

The internet will not bring liberation

During a day at the Pyramids near Cairo in Giza my guide said he supported the regime's toughness against 'troublemakers'. 'Why do you think we have so little trouble here?' he asked. He said that opposition parties could publish anything they wanted and criticise Mubarak freely. When I said that such actions could land someone in jail, he didn't really respond. He put forward the equation given by many Middle East dictators (supported by Washington). If Mubarak lost power, he warned, the Islamists would take over and cause trouble. After the chaos in Iraq, this was understandable. The reality is that it is far too easy in the West to believe that every citizen is against a one-party state and repression. In fact, the majority in most autocracies are far more concerned about a decent job, health care and education than free speech and internet access.

The Pyramids beggared belief. Despite the tourist hordes, it was possible to admire the majesty of the structures in relative peace. Towers of windswept rock rose from the middle of the desert. I'd seen Angkor Wat, Cambodia's ancient former temple complex, but here I felt overwhelmed by the sheer scale of the Pyramids and the massive pieces of carved stone that seemed impervious to time.

Back in Cairo I met one of Egypt's most successful bloggers and independent journalists. At thirty-two, with a goatee and slightly buck front teeth, Wael Abbas had recently returned from a fellowship at online magazine Slate in Washington. He said that life in America was like working in a machine and the 'robots' couldn't step out of line. One hour for lunch, long work days and little time for relaxation made Abbas feel like it was a country that didn't know how to live properly.

We talked in a bustling alleyway near Midan Talaat Harb, packed with young people drinking tea and smoking shishas. During our conversation numerous friends approached Abbas to ask about his US visit. Bow-tied waiters raced from table to table trying to manage the demanding customers. The street was draped with fluorescent lighting. I liked the way cafes in Egypt were often little more than wobbly plastic seats placed in the middle of an alley.

Abbas had started his blog in 2004 as a way of distributing material about the growing anti-Mubarak sentiment on the streets. 'I decided to tell people in Egypt there is something going on in Egypt,' he said. He wrote about police brutality, torture, labour rights, election rigging, internet freedom, opposition parties and rallies. Unsurprisingly, he was soon targeted by the regime and received threatening, anonymous messages on his blog and his mobile phone. He was warned to cease his activities or end up in jail. At times he had to hide from the authorities after filming demonstrations and placing the footage on his website. But he continued, despite the threats, and claimed to now receive a million hits per month. Activists started giving him incendiary footage of torture in police stations and his site soon became an essential source of information about the hidden Egypt.[66] The material quickly moved into the mainstream press, opposition papers and satellite television.

Abbas, who lived at home with his parents, was risking his freedom. But blogging merely strengthened his resolve. If he received calls from the security services, he would publish a transcript of the conversation on his blog. The anonymous figures stopped calling. He was asked to spy on some opposition figures. He agreed, called a government phone number, told them some false information and then posted the conversation on his site. The next tactic was spreading false rumours about Abbas. He was accused on state and independent media of having a criminal record, converting to Christianity—'Egyptian people cannot be tolerant of changing religion,' he said—and being gay. It was all designed to damage his credibility and hopefully force his angry family to convince him to cease his activities. Although he expressed concern that he could be arrested at any time, his energy and determination were infectious. He was the first blogger in 2007 to be awarded the prestigious Knight International Award for Excellence in Journalism in recognition of his work.

Abbas was upset that the Western media still insisted on portraying Mubarak as a 'moderate' and frustrated by the disorganised nature of the Egyptian blogosphere. He told me, as we drank copious amounts of piping hot tea, that although he craved a more stable media environment than offered in Egypt, he couldn't imagine living anywhere else.

Like most bloggers I met, Abbas was insistent that the only way Egypt could move forward successfully was through democracy, freedom of expression and respect for human rights. He offered no particular solutions but feared a number of eventualities. Mubarak would hand over power to his son Gamal[67], the Islamists would take power, the military stage a coup or the people institute a revolution. He thought any of these was possible. He was adamantly against Washington's funding of the regime. 'They are afraid of the Muslim Brotherhood coming to power and I found in the latest USAID report that the American government is actually funding the regime to counter the opposition yet it claims to be funding democracy in the country.' Abbas wished he knew where all the billions of dollars of annual aid actually went. 'How much is enough to make Americans question why their money goes to support this government?' he asked in the *Washington Post* in 2007. 'We Egyptians want a fair struggle for our freedom. We'll never have it as long as Mubarak and his corrupt regime are propped up by USAID.'[68]

Bloggers should not be expected to provide a roadmap towards democracy for any country, let alone one in the heart of the Middle East closely aligned to America, but Abbas advocated Egyptian, not Arab, nationalism. He said that the concept of Arab nationalism had existed in the region for decades but had utterly failed in uniting the efforts of disparate groups towards shared goals.

During my time in Alexandria, the ancient coastal city a few hours north of Cairo on the Mediterranean, the languid pace of life almost seduced me into believing such shared goals were achievable. The relatively small town had a European feel, with a tram running through its centre, crumbling buildings and rambling outdoor cafes. My hotel room was sullen but it had a superb view across the sparkling harbour. Families walked along the beach, fishermen spent hours perched on the water's edge and the pollution was almost invisible compared with that in Cairo.

The Bibliotheca Alexandria, the ancient world's finest library, which re-opened in 2002, is situated on the Corniche and projects itself with a starkly modern design of glass and steel. Designed by Norwegian architects, with enough space for eight million books and an enormous granite wall inscribed with characters from all the world's written languages, the massive terraced reading room allows visitors space to reflect, web surf at no charge and admire this Babel of books. It was the cleanest building I saw in Egypt. For a few days in Alexandria, it seemed possible to believe that Egypt wasn't a police state controlled by a US-backed dictator. It was a tranquil and romantic place, only now rediscovering its 'mojo' after decades of neglect.

Who's afraid of the Muslim Brotherhood?

Ibrahim Houdaiby is a moderate face of the Brotherhood.[69] A fluent English speaker and blogger with short black hair and trimmed beard, the 23-year-old business consultant had been actively involved in the Brotherhood since 2003 and is a board member of the group's official English website (http://www.ikhwanweb.com/).[70] His family has occupied senior positions in the Brotherhood since the 1950s—both his grandfather and great-grandfather ran the organisation until their deaths.

We met near the American University in a small cafe that served pungent coffee and sticky pastries. Houdaiby radiated confidence, a worldly businessman who travelled around the Middle East on a regular basis. He was happy to meet me and I wasn't sure what to expect. My image of the Brotherhood before I arrived in Egypt was influenced by my attitude towards Hamas. I had supported its election win in Palestine in early 2006 and believed that the Western world's global boycott of the organisation was counter-productive and anti-democratic, but I had also read in the Western media about its perceived extremism.

Houdaiby was almost seductively compelling, but perhaps too dismissive of the more militant wings of the group. The West's attempted isolation of the Islamist movements since September 11, 2001, he argued, has only raised their viability in the eyes of many in the Arab world. The fact that there is a clear difference between 'Islamist' and 'radical Islamist' is deliberately ignored in Washington. Houdaiby struck me as somebody who was both willing and capable of engaging with anyone willing to discuss the Brotherhood. He wasn't afraid to disagree with certain decisions of the group's leadership but remained convinced that time was on the side of the Brotherhood and he would see it in power in Egypt in his lifetime.

The Brotherhood had become Egypt's most powerful opposition group because of its ability to infiltrate the body politic through Mubarak's initial willingness to engage with them, the president agreeing in principle to the implementation of Sharia law.[71] The Brotherhood engaged student bodies, business and unions and it reacted quickly after the 1992 Cairo earthquake. Its members were competent and disciplined. When it became increasingly clear that Mubarak's regime was unable to deliver on fundamental services, the Brotherhood started to fill the void.

Houdaiby portrayed the group as an open-minded force, utterly removed from its extremist international image. 'It's not an organisation,' he said. 'To me it's an idea. An idea for reform. An idea for development. A reform that fulfils my materialistic and spiritual needs and aspirations. And does not contradict my principles and beliefs.' The draft release of the Brotherhood's political manifesto in late 2007 was a sign of the movement's 'openness, tolerance and confidence', according to Houdaiby.[72] He disagreed, however, with the manifesto's position of refusing Brotherhood support for women and Coptic Christians running for the presidency.

Houdaiby was keen to persuade me that since September 11 the West had deliberately lumped all Islamists together. Al-Qaeda and the Brotherhood clearly had different ideologies. 'There is not a single person in the Muslim Brotherhood who adopts using violence the way al-Qaeda does,' he argued. Then he surprised me. 'I'd rather live in the United States than under the Taliban,' he said. 'I think the United States is more Islamic in a sense, not religiously, but in the sense that it represents the core values of Sharia. There is freedom, equality, justice and mercy. Although mercy is questionable there because of the high levels of individualism within the society, but at least the other core values are there.' The Brotherhood offers each legislator a free trip to anywhere in the world to educate themselves about other countries' political and social realities.[73] But Houdaiby has written that Mubarak's pro-American policies—despite his state-run portrayal as principled critic of Washington—was simply leading to growing hatred of Americans on the Egyptian streets.[74]

He said his ideal model was Turkey—though he seemed unaware of that country's repressive policies towards dissent, such as its botched 2005 prosecution of Nobel writer Orhan Pamuk—and dismissed concerns that the application of Sharia law would discriminate against non-Muslims. 'All these misconceptions come from the application of Islamic Sharia by authoritarian regimes.' I never expected to hear an Islamist, especially during the various excesses of the 'War on Terror' years, express admiration for America. This probably said more about my own ignorance than anything else. All of us have been undeniably affected by the 'War on Terror' rhetoric, despite the best efforts to resist. I asked him how he would manage living in America at a time when Muslims were feeling under siege and targeted as 'terrorists'. He replied in his typically calm way that he would advocate for their rights and live as a law-abiding citizen.

The definition of terrorism was always a deeply contested issue in the Middle East and Houdaiby didn't disappoint. He supported the resistance in Iraq against the foreign, occupying forces but said any attack on civilians was terrorism. Similarly, he backed the Palestinians against Israeli occupation, 'as long as they are trying to liberate occupied territories'. When I said that the occasional suicide bomber specifically targeted Israeli civilians, he argued that he 'could not really blame the people of Hamas for targeting civilians. Because they have no other choices ... I would not do that, but I could not blame the person in this position.' One person's terrorist is truly another person's freedom fighter, whether it's being discussed in Cairo, Sydney or New York.

The Brotherhood has cannily used the internet to generate coverage of its members residing in jail, often on spurious charges, and sends these messages across the Arab world. By spring 2007, there were an estimated 150 bloggers in the group, compared with virtually none a year earlier.[75] Liberal Arab voices had dominated the blogosphere for many years and Islamists soon recognised a need for their own positions to be advocated. Mubarak's ongoing crackdowns against the movement resulted in a sophisticated and coordinated campaign of web activism and linked young Brothers and general Egyptian youth. While many in the Brotherhood dismiss the moderates in the movement who discuss popular culture alongside politics, it has been estimated that such reformers comprise only around 15 per cent of the group[76] and the Brothers' blogs still offer an unprecedented insight into the Islamist movement.

Brotherhood families write blogs about how they are coping with their loved ones away in jail and revealing the dire prison conditions of their relatives. Houdaiby told me about men whose parents died while they were imprisoned and who had been refused permission to attend the funeral. I asked why he thought the authorities hadn't also arrested the families of the Brotherhood members to further intimidate them. 'I don't think they have the guts to arrest any of the family members,' he said, 'because that would be unjustifiable for anyone. It's really hard to ask anyone to cope when their father, uncle and husband are in prison.' Houdaiby celebrated his engagement with his fiancée's family in jail, because his future father-in-law was a Brotherhood member and awaiting trial. He shared his personal moment in a prison lounge in April 2008 with dozens of Brotherhood activists and family members.[77]

The voice of female Brotherhood members remains strong despite many of them having brothers, fathers or husbands in prison. They often discuss the military tribunal process, but one, Shaza, wrote in early 2008 that, 'my tongue fires Molotovs. Some of them are intentional and others are unintentional. I hope you be aware lest you get wounded.'[78] Asmaa, daughter of the Muslim Brotherhood leader Dr Essam El-Erian, issued a warning to Mubarak: 'We love Egypt. We won't stop. We won't travel abroad. We won't leave this.' I asked Houdaiby about these female bloggers and he didn't miss a beat. Looking around the cafe and pointing to a few women sitting in colourful hijabs and laughing into their mobile phones, he told me that they were most probably Brotherhood members who blogged. 'It's natural that they would,' he said.

One popular Brotherhood blogger, Abdel al-Monem Mahmoud, used his popular site to post messages from families of jailed members. Before being arrested in 2007 for allegedly inciting students to stage a military parade, he told the *Wall Street Journal* that new media was an essential aspect of the Brotherhood's armoury in updating its image. 'People don't know what a Muslim Brotherhood member is like as a person ... and some are wary of the Brothers. We want to tell them that we are ordinary Egyptians. We want our freedom, just like the seculars, leftists, socialists or poor Egyptians do. The only difference is that we have an Islamic identity.'[79]

After being released from prison, Monem wrote in late 2007 on al-Jazeera Talk—but not on the Brotherhood website or his blog—that the Brotherhood's blogging trend was threatened. He claimed that one of the major mistakes of the group's bloggers was becoming 'identified with a specific ideological and political trend—which made it too easy for them to be portrayed by internal and external critics as a "faction". Blogging was supposed to be a personal thing, not a political trend, and its growth into a movement doomed the experiment.' The airing of the Brotherhood's internal politics was playing into its enemy's hands, Monem argued, after senior leaders criticised the airing of internal deliberations. He strongly hinted that the leadership was moving towards 'discipline' over 'openness'.[80] On his personal blog (http://monem press. blogspot.com/), Monem continued to highlight the regime's ongoing crackdown on the Brotherhood.

New York–based commentator and Egyptian-educated Mona Eltahawy, after meeting the Brotherhood's Supreme Guide, Mohammed Mahdi Akef, in 2005, revealed the contradictory nature of the movement. She asked Akef whether Egyptian Islamists would treat women as badly as regimes across the Middle East. He responded: 'No. And my proof is that although you're naked [Eltahawy was not wearing a head-scarf], you were allowed to enter my office.' She was disappointed that, when challenged on his interpretation of the Koran, he claimed his comment was appropriate because 'there is only one interpretation' and 'according to God's law, you are naked'.[81] Yet despite her reservations about the Brotherhood, Eltahawy defended its presence on the political stage because 'if I don't, then I am just as guilty as the regime that has for decades sucked the oxygen out of the body politic'. She doubted whether the Brotherhood would secure a majority of votes in a free election. I wondered if this was wishful thinking. The Brotherhood enjoys broad popular support but is often endorsed by citizens who see it as a viable alternative to the corrupt regime. Like the Palestinians in the West Bank and Gaza who endorsed Hamas in early 2006, this was more a rejection of the incompetent status quo of Fatah rather than a wholesale belief in Islamic values.

Houdaiby countered that although he supported the Brotherhood's stance on the wearing of the hijab—'we believe it is an individual woman's choice to uphold it'—it was 'a choice that the state should not interfere in'.[82] He praised Eltahawy's 'uncompromising position on human rights and her defence of freedom for all', a rare commodity in Western commentary on the Brotherhood and a position I rarely heard expressed by supposed believers of democracy in Washington or London. Houdaiby offered an almost convincing entry point into a movement that was predominantly demonised in a post-September 11 world and urged Western policymakers to engage with the group.[83]

Essam El-Erian, chief of the Brotherhood's political bureau, warned in the Jewish weekly *Forward* in early 2008 that the regime's 'failure to provide for the people's basic needs' would have 'disastrous' consequences locally and internationally.[84] Unprecedented national protests in April 2008, not officially supported by the Brotherhood, highlighted this frustration. Citizens were killed lining up for bread. Food shortage and low wages were key concerns and tens of thousands of workers at the Middle East's biggest textile mill chanted, 'Down, down, Hosni Mubarak! Your rule is shit!'[85] Activists and bloggers were arrested, including Esraa Abdul Fattah, a woman who helped launch the Day of Anger Facebook group and spread the word about the protests.[86] Although Fattah was released a few weeks later after appeals to Mubarak from her mother, her use of Facebook scared the regime, with over 70 000 people joining the group.[87]

Mubarak's sledge-hammer approach to civil society was leading to a worrying increase in extremism, Houdaiby said. 'With the crackdown of moderates, and I'm not just speaking of Islamist groups, all moderates were making the radicals more relevant. You are sending a key signal that will increase radicalism. We as the Muslim Brotherhood do not do that [resort to violence] because our peaceful orientation is not a radical thing. It's an ideological, ethical stand.' Houdaiby was highly likeable, friendly, intellectual and moderate, but did he really represent the Brotherhood's core beliefs? I wasn't entirely convinced.[88] His constant refrain about not resorting to violence was also questionable, especially in countries other than Egypt. Despite these hesitations, I left with no doubts that the West had to engage the Islamists if they wanted to understand a growing portion of the Arab world.

Houdaiby told me about a protest that evening at the Syndicate of Journalists headquarters in downtown Cairo. I wanted to attend to show solidarity with the demonstrators, who were marking the two-year anniversary of a previous crackdown against activists.

As we arrived in a busy street during peak period, a cacophony of horns and drivers shouting obscenities filled the air. The Syndicate, with Arabic writing imprinted in its design and tall columns, gave the headquarters an imposing feel. I was slightly nervous as we approached the protest—although I was told that foreigners were never targeted by the authorities—but felt inspired by the passion of the screaming and shouting demonstrators. We found a group of around 200 noisy activists chanting anti-Mubarak slogans and holding colourful banners (I was later told that anti-US and anti-Israel comments were also made.) The protest was led by the opposition group Kifaya; Houdaiby told me that a number of Brotherhood members were also present and I recognised many activists and bloggers I'd met over the past weeks. They seemed genuinely surprised to see me and welcomed me warmly. Traffic crawled along the streets in front of us as hundreds of riot police surrounded us on all sides. Many empty trucks sat nearby, ready to detain arrested activists. Nonetheless, I knew that after last year's anniversary protest a number were beaten, arrested, kidnapped and (in Mohammed al-Sharqawi's case) raped. I stood still and just observed the proceedings.

I noticed a man in his sixties who was standing at the front of the protest, virtually breathing on the police, holding a placard with a caricature of Mubarak. Underneath the image read the words 'The Dictator'. It was a powerful and brave stance. He didn't say a word, merely stood there for what seemed like minutes, almost challenging the riot police to arrest him. They looked at him impassively but didn't react. He was endlessly photographed by the phalanx of media observing the protest. Some were probably government officials gathering information on opposition activists.

The protest started to dissipate after around forty-five minutes and a few of us, including Shahinaz Abdel Salam and al-Sharqawi, walked away. The two constantly looked over their shoulders, worried that, like the year before, police officers would surprise and arrest them. It was extremely brave for al-Sharqawi to return to the scene of his kidnapping. He showed us where he had been detained and beaten the previous year. As we wandered towards Tahrir Square in central

Cairo, we noticed a small group of activists ahead of us begin to shout slogans. 'I'm not that brave,' Abdel Salam said to me. We stopped and put some distance between them and us. We soon saw a truck emptying of riot police up the road, but it appeared to be only for show. For whatever reason, the authorities had decided not to intervene in the demonstration.

Later that night a group of us grabbed soft drinks in a poorly lit alley and discussed the recently released Amnesty International 2007 report. It was noted that the state media had endlessly covered the violations by America and Israel but had conveniently forgotten to include Egypt's transgressions. A number of Muslim women were amazed to meet a Jew who criticised Israel. They said they had only seen Zionists on television defending violence against Palestinians. One said that they wondered if Jews existed who publicly criticised the Jewish state.

The web genie is out of the bottle

Bloggers and dissidents continually told me that they resented the Western media's description of Mubarak as a 'Western-friendly' dictator. The clear implication was that Washington's dictates were far more important than the human rights of Egyptians. It was only since the rise of the internet that much of the Western media seemed to express any interest in an ally's abuses, though the torture videos, bravely disseminated by Wael Abbas among others, haven't created nearly as much international controversy as Iraq's Abu Ghraib. Why, some bloggers asked, shouldn't torture committed on Egyptians by officers financed by US aid not be as shocking as persecution of Iraqis by US defence contractors?

Washington cannot argue about democracy and human rights while supporting a regime that actively tortures its own citizens and assists the Bush administration's 'extraordinary rendition' program. I didn't meet one Egyptian who believed in the rhetoric emerging from the Western political elite. Some of these activists love aspects of American culture—and even want to live there for a time—but they have seen the disastrous effects of Mubarak's repression on friends, colleagues and family members. Optimism was in short supply. Muslim Brotherhood member Ibrahim Houdaiby wrote in early 2008 that he could not remember a period in which such a wide cross-section of society felt 'that the future of Egypt is rather gloomy and uncertain'.[89]

Egypt remains the Middle East nation with the most effective online dissent, and the authority's brutal reaction proves the potency of the threat to its security. The government has pushed the internet as a key driver of reform, and though a report on Arab web censorship noted: 'It is ironic for Egypt to see internet cafes and computer clubs affiliated to the Ministry of Telecommunication in the areas deprived of essential utilities and facilities such as drinking water and sanitary drainage'[90], it remains resistant to serious engagement with the issues important to both secular and Islamist bloggers.

Throwing bloggers in jail and refusing to recognise a legitimate opposition party in the Muslim Brotherhood merely gives oxygen to radicals who believe in the violent overthrow of the regime. However, supporting the Brotherhood's oppressed community remains a key test of human rights advocates. Far too often the concept of human rights is applied selectively by Western commentators in a rush to damn Islamism as an enemy of freedom. In a country with an aging dictator, fear and arrogance don't allow the West to fully engage with a group that speaks for millions across the Arab world.

Syria
Dissent behind the Assad Curtain

'The internet is really important, but it doesn't make any change in the end, because the hand of security is still so strong. People can get information now, but they can't do anything with the information. Maybe you have a window on the world, but you don't have a window on what's going on inside, and that makes you blind.'
Syrian pro-democracy activist Maan Abdul-Salam, 2007[1]

THE AIR IN DAMASCUS seemed far fresher, perhaps deceptively so, than in Egypt or Iran, but there was an unmistakable difference in the streets—a sense of openness that I hadn't felt in those other two countries. Perhaps this was because Syria is a secular state where religious fervour is less publicised and certainly the religious leadership is far less vocal. I had long been told of the relaxed pace of Syrian life and found it first hand in the capital.

Appearances are deceptive, however, and a police state can reveal itself in less than obvious ways. With a population of 19.3 million people, Syria, led by dictator President Bashar al-Assad, is repressive and undemocratic. When leading Syrian dissident Dr Kamal Labwani was sentenced in 2007 to twelve years in prison with hard labour for 'undermining national security', one blogger responded: 'When will the Syrian people reach their limit? What is it going to take to light a fire under our collective Syrian asses?'[2]

Advocacy group Reporters Without Borders claimed in its 2007 annual report that 'state control of the media and the ongoing state of emergency continue to be used as an excuse to arrest many media workers ... Three people are in jail for criticising the regime, making Syria the biggest prison for cyber-dissidents in the Middle East.'[3]

During my two weeks in the country[4] I noticed a willingness of writers, bloggers and dissidents to openly criticise the leadership and highlight its failings. They take a risk in doing so, but the internet has provided a forum for the dissemination of opinions that simply didn't exist in the public domain only a few years ago. The Syrian blogosphere remains small and opposition groups are fragmented, but growing alliances between Islamists, liberals and reformers are starting to take shape.

One of the most influential bloggers about Syria is Joshua Landis, Professor of Syrian History and Politics at Oklahoma University and founder of the leading English-language blog on Syria, SyriaComment. We agreed to meet for lunch in a casual restaurant in the wealthy part of the capital, distinguished by wide, tree-lined streets with perfect views of the nearby Anti-Lebanon Mountains. Landis explained how he fell in love with Syria and was attracted to the idea of a country that remained mired in mystery, even today. For him, the internet has become a space to dissect daily news about Syria and the Assad regime and debunk the myths that exist in the West over the regime's supposed terrorist status (even if the country has committed aggressive acts in Lebanon). Landis offers another perspective on Syria. 'Bashar al-Asad is the best president Syria has had in over 40 years,' he blogged in 2004, 'and could be a valuable ally to the US. Syria has been the most successful country in the region at accommodating the demands of its highly diverse population and in promoting tolerance among its people.'[5] Landis praised Assad for holding the various ethnic groups together—not unlike Saddam Hussein in Iraq—though he wasn't blind to the social and political cost of doing so.

Landis is a lanky, chain-smoking, bespectacled, pasty American with wavy blond hair and prominent front teeth. He's generous, is highly knowledgeable about Syria and the region, and, while often embraced by the foreign affairs establishment (he proudly told me that 'friends at the State Department say the first thing they do in the morning is open up SyriaComment ... because you get a summary of the country'), he remained highly sceptical of the Bush administration's self-described democratisation plans for the Middle East. 'I don't think Syria is ready for democracy,' he said. 'I think if you did have this regime crumble there would be chaos, like Iraq.'

Landis recounted a fascinating story, told to him by Imad Mustapha, the Syrian ambassador to America and fellow blogger, which reveals the challenges of introducing the internet into Syria at the turn of the century. In 1999, Mustapha headed the Syrian Research Centre at the University of Damascus and Hafez al-Assad was still president.

In 1999 the Prime Minister invited a little meeting of about thirty people to talk about whether Syria should legalise the internet. At the time there was no legal internet, but the University of Damascus and the dean had the internet in his office. You could telephone to Lebanon and Egypt and use the internet through a normal telephone line. It was very hard to stop this kind of thing, of course it was expensive, but people were beginning to do it. It was only text, no graphics. The question was should Syria legalise and set up an IT infrastructure.

The main guys at the head of the table were the Mukhabarat [state security] heads and one of them said 'this is a Zionist conspiracy and run by the Jews' and nobody else around the table felt at liberty to say anything different from this line: they all mumbled something similar. Imad Mustapha said nothing, but at the end of the meeting the Prime Minister said 'You've been very quiet. What do you think?' and he said, 'I don't agree with anything that's been said here.' He was not asked to elaborate, and the meeting adjourned.

Within a few weeks he got a call from Bashar Al-Assad's office—this is before he became president, but he was still the head of the Syrian Computer Society—and he was asked to give a lecture about the internet at the Assad Library, the major national library in Damascus. He said 'I was young and churlish so I decided to give a lecture on Israel, Syria and the internet.' He had good overhead computer projectors and knew how to use PowerPoint, so he downloaded a lot of Israeli websites (particularly on the Golan Heights) that interest Syria, and the foreign ministry website that presents Israeli history, and he showed the audience what Israel was doing to promote its version of history, its position on the Golan and its culture and excitement to the rest of the world. When he got to the last section on Syria he just put up a black picture on the wall, and said 'this is Syria's participation on the internet' and then he sat down.

There was a lively discussion and it turns out that Bashar had come and was sitting there. He didn't say a lot but after the lecture Mustafa was asked to come back and give that same lecture several more times at the Assad Library and each time there was another ministry that turned up—the foreign ministry and so forth, and one of them was the Mukhabarat and all the guys he had seen show up for the PM's original meeting came back and were there around the table, and clearly this was the real purpose of his lecture—to get this message across to the Mukhabarat who had put their foot against the door originally.

Mustapha then didn't hear much ... for another year until he got a call from Bashar's offices (once he became president) saying to him 'Well, enough words—now it's time to implement' and he was asked to join the Ministry of Foreign Affairs and introduce the internet and the web there, and [to] set up systems and get everything working so that the one ministry would have [its] face to the world, and it would run through the other ministries. After he had done this he was appointed to the embassy to Washington and shortly later became ambassador.

Landis told me that the Syrian security services viewed the internet before 2000 as a Zionist plot to infiltrate the state. Since then there has been a technological explosion but the relationship between the internet and the regime has been a contradictory one. The number of users has skyrocketed from 30 000 in 2000 to one million today and, according to a study by the Jordan-based Arab Advisor's Group, Syrian users are 'projected to exceed 1.7 million by 2009'.[6]

Online freedom has certainly improved since 2000, but according to OpenNet Initiative, a group that monitors filtering and web surveillance, censorship is 'pervasive'. The group reports that Syria's filtering takes place at the ISP level. Syria targets the websites of Syrian-specific and Arabic news sites, Kurdish organizations, and foreign-based Syrian opposition parties that are all critical of the government. Access to the country code top level domain of Israel, '.il', is also blocked. Facebook was filtered in late November 2007 (along with a local online forum for young people, Shabablek). Syrian authorities issued a new directive in early 2008 to force internet café users to reveal their identity. The Syrian Media Centre denounced the move and spokesman Mazen Darwich said that, 'open forums have been used by thousands of Syrians to launch a counteroffensive against the government's curb on public expression'.[7]

Amr Nazir Salem, Syria's former minister of telecommunications, was strident in an interview in *Reason*, when challenged on his country's online censorship: 'Syria is under attack, we have to admit that, by several powers, and if somebody writes, or publishes or whatever, something that supports the attack, they will be tried.'[8] In April 2008 Prime

Minister Mohammad al-Otari accused the electronic media of spreading false news and being 'nouveaux riches' figures trying to establish new media empires for profit.[9]

When Landis started SyriaComment at the beginning of the Iraq War, he quickly realised that there was little independent information about Syria in the mainstream media. 'There is no free press here and there is no place for Syrians to express their opinions,' he said. 'Syria is not covered outside of Syria, so lots of people began to comment [on my blog] and you saw these radically different, diverging opinions: you saw the sectarian splits, the Lebanese versus the Syrians and the Israelis versus the Syrians. Today there are around 9000 people who subscribe via email … and roughly 2500 readers every day.' Landis said that, while it was important for the West to better understand Syria, it was more essential for Syrians to understand what other Syrians thought about their own history and politics.

I read the local English press during my visit and found a motley collection of propaganda rants against Israel and Washington. They were predictable and badly written and I wondered if the Western popula-tion, the only obvious audience for the articles, could take them seriously (Landis said he knew the content of the pieces before he would read them, which he no longer did). Assad was praised on a daily basis and portrayed as a benevolent master constantly helping his needy servants. One front-page story featured a picture of Assad receiving a bunch of flowers from a young girl after the president had opened a new school in her area. It reminded me of the photos Iraq's Saddam Hussein would transmit to the world or Republican-aligned blogs in America after George W Bush announced 'Mission Accomplished' on an aircraft carrier in 2003.

Landis is married to an Alawite woman and spends many months in Syria every year. He told me that when he lived in Damascus in the 1980s there was virtually no intellectual class. Access to the outside world was severely limited and ideas about Israel, Jews and America were one-dimensional. Even today, he said, there was vast ignorance of Syria in the West, though this hadn't stopped the US Government-backed National Endowment for Democracy (NED) continually funding projects to undermine Assad's regime, including a 2006 grant to 'support democratic reformers through the use of Internet-based technology and political process training'.[10]

Landis imagined a debate in Syria between Noam Chomsky and President Bill Clinton's former Middle East advisor, Dennis Ross. This, he argued, was the real way to discuss matters of peace and war, not via pre-packaged discussions between two individuals who essentially agreed with each other. He disliked the growing tendency for Western elites to analyse the Middle East only in terms of 'democracy promotion' and 'civil society' and the role America could play in this transformation.

Landis argued that this book—without, it must be said, knowing my intentions in writing it—could be read in a similar vein, as an attempt to impose Washington-style democracy on the region. He told me that a number of conservative analysts from leading American think-tanks were currently researching the role of blogs in non-democratic regimes. I responded that although I certainly believed in free speech and an unfiltered internet, I was not calling for regime change or American meddling. Rather, I simply believed in the right of citizens to access and disseminate information without the control of the state, in all nations around the world.

Nevertheless, Landis forced me to seriously reassess the rationale for this book. I didn't question my interest in telling the stories of bloggers and dissidents usually ignored in the Western media, nor did I shy away from slamming despotic regimes that deserved sanction (despite a number of leftist friends wondering why I wasn't spending more time focusing on the crimes of Western nations).

When Landis first started his blog using Blogger, he ran into trouble with the authorities for publishing anonymous comments about Assad's wife being a prostitute, an attempt by Lebanese and Syrian opposition writers 'to get their frustrations out about the regime'. He even published gossip about regime figures and inevitably faced threats of closure and expulsion. He was eventually protected because an English blog wasn't regarded as a threat to Syrian security. Local bloggers and activists, Landis recalled, have faced far greater pressures.

Human Rights Watch reported in October 2007 yet another example of government inference, detailing two years' prison for an individual who had 'undertaken acts or writing or speeches unauthorised by the government ... that spoils its ties with a foreign state'. His crime was posting comments online that attacked Saudi Arabia.[11] 'This is an authoritarian state,' Landis said, 'and they don't they like opposition growing and organising. It's security's job to make sure it doesn't. They lost the battle to keep the internet out of the country and they don't really understand it very well.' Landis spoke approvingly of a leading young lawyer in Damascus who, in a website[12] to which she emails a monthly link, details who has been brought before Syria's security courts. It was a small sign of much-needed transparency. Despite arresting the occasional dissident or journalist, it was seen as far easier to simply block access to Blogger, however, forcing any opposition to find alternative strategies to spread their message.

Stories abound about the regime's ruthless repression of dissidents. Amnesty International found in its 2007 report that 'hundreds of political prisoners, including prisoners of conscience, remained in prison'.[13] The advocacy group highlighted numerous cases, including eight men detained incommunicado for initiating a political discussion group. The men were sentenced in June 2007 to between five and seven years in jail for 'exposing Syria to acts of aggression'.[14] Anwar al-Bunni, a prominent human rights activist, was imprisoned in April 2007. According to his lawyer, he was found guilty of spreading false information to weaken national morale and contacting a foreign country (he had used EU funding to establish a human rights training centre in Syria).[15] Blogger Tariq Baiasi was abducted for posting a comment on a website that criticised the state's security apparatus. He simply disappeared in July 2007.[16]

During my visit, there were ubiquitous posters of President Assad, who had just netted 97.6 per cent of the vote in a recent referendum securing his hold on power. 'We love Bashar,' read the posters plastered all over the city. *Syria Today*, the country's first independently produced English-language magazine, asked a number of citizens in Damascus what they thought of the president. Although none of the respondents criticised their leader, many expressed moderate support for his efforts to move the country into the twenty-first century.[17] One of its major contributors acknowledged to me that the magazine, if it wanted to survive and thrive, had little choice but to endorse Assad, or at least not criticise his leadership.

Like any repressive society, however, a small minority will inevitably rebel. Landis recalled an early meeting that he attended in May 2005 of the Association of Syrian Bloggers and wrote that it 'was one of those evenings that make you feel good to be alive'. It may have been small, but within a few years the scene had grown greatly. Landis blogged enthusiastically about the event:

> There were a mere 5 blogs or so in Syria at the beginning of 2005. Now there are some 34 or 35. 'A veritable blog explosion is going on,' Ayman [Haykal, founder of the group and Damascene blog] announced. All the same everyone was dismayed at the small number of Syrian blogs. 'It is because we are afraid of the written word,' one explained. 'We base our blogs around photos. They can say a lot.' We spoke about many subjects: Syrian identity, Arab nationalism, democracy, US policy, and, of course blogging as it related to each. Almost everyone said he was optimistic about Syria's future and believes the country is changing quickly and for the better.[18]

By the end of 2005, there were over 100 bloggers in Syria, writing in both English and Arabic. One of the most popular independent Syrian news websites, http://www.syria-news.com/, today ranks in the top 2000 popular sites in the world, according to web ranking tool Alexa.[19] The Arab Bloggers Union, whose president is Syrian but based in Sweden, is raising its profile, even calling on fellow bloggers to report 'offensive' blogs 'which exceed the limits of opinion and belief by trespassing God'.[20] Notions of free speech were still being digested by users of the internet, even those who praise the benefits of blogging. The Arab world has spent decades saddled with state-run media that offered only government propaganda. Satellite television and the internet are changing perceptions of what's possible, but the limits of speech are robustly debated. I found many bloggers in Syria, happy to call themselves liberal and Westernised, who felt that slamming Islam or the Prophet Mohammed in public was unacceptable. Some of them scoffed at the ability to slander Jesus and Christianity in the Western media without punishment.

While bloggers are much thinner on the ground in Syria than in Iran, their views are just as passionate. When Egyptian blogger Kareem Amer was sentenced to four years' jail in February 2007 for 'insulting Islam' and defaming Egyptian President Hosni Mubarak, the Syrian blogosphere exploded. The opinion of Abu Kareem at Levantine Dreamhouse (now based in New York) was typical:

The language of the charges is sickeningly familiar. It is the language that paranoid authoritarian governments use when they feel threatened, when someone tells the TRUTH. They ring hollow as if drawn up by a bored bureaucrat, the same set of charges paraded out thousands of times before; all they had to do was change the name of the accused. And for what? Abdel Kareem just expressed his thoughts, he did not incite or threaten violence, he did not undermine the security of the country. His only true crime is that of having and expressing critical thoughts, an inexcusable deviance for an autocratic and corrupt regime, much more difficult to deal with than a bomb tossing terrorist. Citizens of such countries are expected to be subservient automatons without critical thought. They are supposed to act like castrated sheep, bleating meekly and bowing to the almighty, infallible leader, Hosni Mubarak (or Bashar al-Assad, or ...).[21]

Within a few weeks, a number of leading Syrian bloggers issued a joint statement against the lengthy prison sentence. It was posted on a number of Syrian blogger sites:

We, as a community of Syrian bloggers, condemn the arrest and sentencing of Egyptian blogger Abdel Kareem Nabil Soliman for the peaceful expression of his dissenting views. We ask the Egyptian government to reconsider its decision to arrest and prosecute Abdel Kareem. The stated reasons for their action include the preservation of the public peace and state security, and the prevention of incitement against Islam. We contend that his arrest will achieve neither. Silencing such dissenting voices as Abdel Kareem's, serves only to strengthen the hands of extremists who will not shy away from violence to achieve their goals. Moreover, we remind the Egyptian government that his arrest and prosecution violates at least two articles of the 1948 United Nations universal declaration of human rights to which Egypt was a signatory.[22]

It was a heartening response for a fellow Arab suffering under repression in a neighbouring country. Such solidarity came only a few months before Syria's former communications and technology minister, Amr Salem, issued a decree that stated all website owners must display 'the name and email of the writer of any article or comment ... clearly and in detail, under threat of warning the owner of the website, then restricting access to the website temporarily and in case the violation is repeated, permanently banning the website'.[23] One popular news website, www.damaspost.com, was temporarily blocked soon after a commentator criticised the nepotism within the Journalists' Union.

Dodging online bullets

One night I ate dinner with an Australian journalist, John Dagge, living in Damascus's Old City. Walking along the winding, cobbled streets, we saw young boys playing football, old men smoking and watching the world go by, store owners sitting in cramped shops selling thousands of pirated DVDs and perfect photocopies of Edward Said's memoir. Away from the crowded and polluted parts of Damascus, the Old City— established as early as 8000 to 10 000 BC and one of the oldest continuously inhabited cities in the world—felt pleasantly atmospheric, one of the more beautiful examples of relatively untouched ancient history.

Dagge's three-storey house was a shambolic creation with paper-thin walls, roaming cats and a traditional Arab interior. He was working as a freelance journalist and lecturer in Damascus, while learning Arabic, and told me that life in Syria as a writer was constantly about grasping how to discuss sensitive political issues in code.[24] Dagge said that the government was undoubtedly starting to crack down on online dissent, closing internet cafes in the Old City and arresting users who accessed human rights websites. He told me about a friend who had designed a computer game where you played a Palestinian who had to kill Israeli soldiers. You lost points if you killed nurses. It was a response, Dagge said, to games where American soldiers killed Iraqis and was one of the few games that was copyrighted in the country. It cost US$10 instead of the usual pirated US$1. The regime was more than happy to use computer technology for what it considered legitimate purposes such as this.

Dagge told me about a bizarre trend among many young Syrians who had become obsessive about their mobile phones. It was discovered that three-second calls were free, so people would call each other in restaurants or other various public places and have a one-hour conversation, hanging up every three seconds and calling back. Dagge said he was often at cafes and noticed young men and women making numerous calls to the same person within rapid succession simply to save some money.

In 2005, when Assad gave a speech at the Baath Party congress, he completely ignored the war in Iraq, problems in Lebanon and relations with Israel. Instead, he warned delegates about the threat of technology. This new information, he said, had 'overwhelmed Arabs and threatened their existence and cultural identity, which has increased the doubts and scepticism in the minds of young Arabs ... The ultimate objective of all this is the destruction of Arab identity.'[25] Assad clearly recognised that even a relatively small number of dissidents can sow doubt in the minds of citizens.

'It is a mistake to conclude that the regime acts more harshly when it is under pressure,' wrote blogger Rime Allaf in early 2007. 'On the contrary, it is never so severe as when it has the time to "take care" of its citizens.'[26] The political elite, like Joshua Landis, is allowed to write freely and suffer no consequences. I suspect that permitting Landis unfiltered access in Syria was an attempt by the Assad regime to prove to the world that they really did believe in the free flow of ideas after all.

Political scientist Dr Sami Moubayed operates in a similar space.[27] An author and journalist, he writes regularly for the *Washington Post, Al-Ahram Weekly* and *Asia Times*. I met him in his office in central Damascus, a large room with scattered piles of *Newsweek* magazines. He had a receding hairline and an arrogant air about him, as he spoke proudly of being part of Syria's elite, only writing in English and therefore appealing to a small section of Syrian society (though a much larger international one). He advocated 'Syrianism', a rejection of the traditionally accepted notions of Arabism. 'I preach Syrian nationalism,' he wrote in early 2008.[28]

Moubayed said that members of the regime still didn't understand the internet but were not intelligent enough to institute an intensive filtering process as Iran had done. He told the amusing story of a webmaster coming to a Syrian minister and saying, 'Sir, the ministry site is ready. Would you like to come and see it?' The minister replied: 'Yes. Should I take my car, or is the site close to here?'

As an associate professor at a private university in Damascus, he had seen firsthand the effect of the internet on his students.

> I'm thirty, ten years older than my students. When I was twenty, I was never so outspoken or courageous in my rhetoric. These people are not

like that. Why? Because when they were eighteen there was the internet, there was satellite television, there was the democracy of information. When we used to read in the 1980s or early 90s when something critical of the government came in our hands we were to afraid to read it—frightened that someone was watching. It's not like that, and that's thanks to the internet. It's incredible what it's done for people.

Like virtually every conversation that is had in Syria, politics soon entered the equation. Moubayed said that the war in Iraq had bolstered the stature of dictators in the Middle East because leaders were asking their citizens if they wanted the 'democracy' offered by the Americans. There was genuine fear after the 2003 invasion of Iraq that Syria was next on the Bush administration's invasion list and Assad consolidated his power by arresting many democracy activists and journalists. Although it was unspoken, Moubayed seemed to enjoy expressing to me his love for the country but he was one of the few who remained sufficiently free to criticise the regime. It was a privileged position enjoyed by very few other Syrians.

Months after early 2002, when US President George W Bush labelled North Korea, Iran and Iraq as joint participants in an 'Axis of Evil', Under Secretary of State John Bolton (as he was then) nominated three more countries—Cuba, Libya and Syria—as being 'Beyond the Axis of Evil' and accused them of being equally determined to acquire chemical or biological weapons.[29] In late 2007, Bush said that his 'patience ran out on President Assad a long time ago'.[30] Assad's involvement with North Korea and assistance with its military program have only further isolated the Syrians.[31]

Wesley Clark, a retired four-star general of the United States, says that two months after the September 11 attacks, a senior general told him in Washington that then Defence Secretary Donald Rumsfeld had outlined a plan. 'We're going to take out seven countries in five years,' he said. 'And he named them, starting with Iraq and Syria and ending with Iran.'[32] Syria's paranoia has been justified and partly explains the often brutal behaviour towards opposition figures.

The Western and Arab perception of Syria shifted, temporarily at least, with its involvement in the 1991 US-led war against Saddam Hussein. The same decade saw a number of high-level meetings with archenemy Israel, but peace never eventuated. During my time in Syria,

I noted a keen interest in finally securing a peace deal with Israel, but one that fairly represented Syria's interest.[33] After Syria attended the November 2007 Annapolis 'peace conference'—with hopes that serious negotiations would be initiated between the two sides—a spokesman for Israeli prime minister Ehud Olmert simply said, 'We don't think it's feasible now with the present regime.'[34] Another missed opportunity for the Middle East, despite ongoing rumours of secret negotiations between Syria and Israel over the disputed Golan Heights.

The 2005 assassination of former Lebanese prime minister Rafiq Hariri in Beirut catapulted Syria back into the crosshairs. A United Nations probe found direct Syrian involvement and the international outcry resulted in Syrian troops being forced to leave Lebanon after thirty years of meddling. Damascus still plays a key role in the internal affairs of its small neighbour, with a number of assassinations of prominent anti-Syrian Lebanese politicians taking place in the last few years and the growing influence of the Iranian-backed Hizbollah. Washington also regularly accuses Syria of allowing foreign fighters to enter Iraq and fight the Americans (despite the fact that the vast majority of foreign insurgents, according to the US military, have come from Saudi Arabia, a key American ally).[35] The threat of an American attack has hovered over Damascus since the September 11 attacks.[36]

Unlike Moubayed, who appears to astutely traverse the country's red lines, Ibrahim Hamidi, a dark-haired and well-groomed Syrian journalist with *Al-Hayat*, the pan-Arab newspaper based in London, told me he regularly faces troubles with the authorities.[37] Having worked for more than seventeen years in Damascus, Hamidi has had his journalistic license confiscated seven times and been thrown into jail for publishing 'false' information. In fact, he had dared suggest before the 2003 Iraq invasion that Syria was preparing 'itself for the war, building refugee camps because they were expecting more than one million refugees', adding: 'That's correct now, of course.' I met Hamidi in an upmarket cafe with over-priced orange juice and female patrons who dressed like they were relaxing on the French Riviera. Hamidi told me that he regularly met contacts there, but he cautioned against talking too loudly. The ears of the security services were everywhere.

He remembered how when Syrian officials were given computers in the late 1990s they simply put them on their desks as décor without any connections. Even today, the government's major websites are poor, with little useful information. When we spoke, Hamidi said that the Ministry of Foreign Affairs still had no website (at the time of writing, a site existed but could not be accessed without a username and password.) His own newspaper website is occasionally blocked if the authorities don't like a particular story, but it always becomes available again within a few days. He had heard of the Iranian embassy complaining about certain websites and the Syrians censoring them as a courtesy.

Not unlike Moubayed, Hamidi sensed a feeling among Syrians before the Iraq War that some kind of change was necessary, 'regardless of what the alternative was'. Today, he says, 'after what they've seen in Iraq, people are more hesitant. The price of safety and stability is becoming much higher.' He also claims that the Iraq War has in fact helped consolidate Assad's rule. Hamidi argued in *Al-Hayat* in early 2006 that 'Syria is departing from a secular socialist past and witnessing increasing signs of an Islamist future.'[38] The Iraq War has undoubtedly intensified the rise of religious and fundamentalist forces opposed to secularism.

Despite the popularity of the Muslim Brotherhood in Egypt and Palestine, Syria's Islamists remain an isolated force. The regime decrees that membership in the organisation deserves death—though this is usually reduced to around twelve years in prison—and these factors have made a strong Islamic party a virtual impossibility in the short to medium term.[39] Isolated militant cells may exist in the country but they hold little influence. Islamist bloggers are not as ubiquitous as in Iran for the simple reason that the government views them as a threat to their rule. However, the last few years have seen a growing uncomfortable alliance between secular opposition groups and the Muslim Brotherhood, a realisation that only through unity can the regime be seriously challenged.

Democratic Russian roulette

'Bashar is not simply a Ba'athist thug,' argues Ammar Abdulhamid, a Syrian author who moved to the United States in 2005 after being threatened for criticising the regime in print. He was one of 219 people who voted against President Hafez Assad in a 1998 national referendum and was the first Syrian to publicly co-write an article with an Israeli in 2004 that called for the renewal of Israeli–Syrian peace talks. 'Bashar is a member of a family that has imposed itself on the country and that conducts policy for its own purposes.' He says that 'mafias of the ruling elite' are tasked to co-opt any reformers. 'We're talking about the Internet, but the same rules apply for any reformers,' he said. 'Either you get neutralized, you get destroyed, or you get sucked into the game.'[40] Abdulhamid currently works at a think-tank run by a former Israeli lobbyist.[41]

According to *Time* magazine in December 2006, Abdulhamid was at the centre of a plan to undermine Assad and institute election monitoring throughout the country during the March 2007 election. The Bush administration was allegedly investigating the viability of covert action with 'anti-Assad activists' to provide 'internet accessible materials [and] voter education campaigns'.

Shortly after the *Time* article, Abdulhamid, responding in the Jewish weekly *Forward*, denied being at the centre of the plan.[42] He reminded American officials that Syrian elections were 'quite staged and inconsequential' and 'perhaps the American officials who concocted the classified plan for regime change believed they could make it appear more credible by assigning a primary role to a dissident like myself'. Abdulhamid was a one-time member of the Washington-based, Syrian opposition group National Salvation Front (NSF) and allegedly attended the White House for two meetings, including in late 2007 with a Kurdish opposition activist and a Syrian MP.[43] Hence his relationship with the Bush administration remained unclear, but he rightly wrote that Syria's relationship with Iran 'dates back to the early days of the Iranian revolution' and Assad was unlikely to change his behaviour simply because of some internal American meddling.

Aside from Syrian bloggers both inside and outside the country, Abdulhamid remains one of the most quoted opposition figures in the West. Like many reformers in a non-democratic society, his support within the country is probably minimal, due to a lack of media coverage and grassroots campaigning. For this reason Abdulhamid's pronouncements should be treated with caution—as indeed should those of all dissidents who claim to speak for an unspoken constituency—but I have no doubt that he is a voice worth listening to. When, in early 2007, he told the Israeli news service Ynet that there were around 100 active dissidents in Syria and only fifteen to twenty with name recognition, the monumental challenge facing writers, dissidents and bloggers to institute change became clear.[44]

In many ways, Abdulhamid represents the quintessential dissident contradiction: critical of the status quo and keen for change but equally unsure how to mobilise popular support and unseat an autocratic leader. He explained on his blog in June 2007 that the goal of his fellow reformers was not 'a revolution, but it will be a serious grassroots effort to challenge the increasing mismanagement, corruption, and arrogance of the regime, even now, in these inauspicious and dangerous times'.[45] If he received funding from the US Government—and it's unclear whether he did—this would certainly undermine his project in the eyes of most Syrians and tie him to the worst excesses of the Bush years.

Syrian blogger Abu Kareem articulated a similar challenge to reformers in mid-2007 by urging caution. Reform was vital, he wrote, but the timetable had to be set by Syrians themselves:

> If there seems to be unanimity in Syria about the need for reform, there are great differences about what to reform, how much to reform and how fast. The unprecedented regional instability is being used effectively by the entrenched authoritarian government as an excuse to pushback against calls for political reform. There is also reluctance among the people, for different reasons, for rapid, radical political change. The source of this reluctance, beyond Syrians' penchant for caution, is clear. If independent opinion polls cannot tell us what Syrians want, we can safely surmise what they don't want: any change that will cause the type of implosion that is currently occurring next door in Iraq.[46]

During my travels across countries in the Middle East, Cuba and China the same question kept challenging me: How truly representative were all the dissidents, bloggers and writers that I read and met? Was I ascribing undue influence to their role in nations where they were largely marginal at best or irrelevant at worst? I didn't think so. Opposition inevitably starts with a trickle—take the dark, Soviet days or the monk-led protests in Burma. Attaining mass support takes years of often fruitless labour. 'Even under the most crushing state machinery,' said Burmese Nobel Prize winner Daw Aung San Suu Kyi, 'courage rises up again and again, for fear is not the natural state of civilised man.'[47] Hoping for change is often all a citizen has, and the internet has provided a unique forum for these thoughts to be expressed. The challenge to censorship can be beautifully poetic or brutally matter-of-fact. Or simply humorous. Syrian blogger Abu Fares writes:

> I would not go purposely on a quest to find pornographic sites. However, I stand by their right to exist and the right of any adult to browse these sites till he or she drops. Is it not strange that in a city like Dubai, where soliciting the services of a prostitute is as easy as ordering a pizza by phone, internet sites are blocked because of their morally unacceptable content? ... Through search engines and from behind firewalls, these maverick browsers were looking for a 'smooth ass'. Who has the right to deny these poor souls their right to see an ass? I have previously made a joke about this particular incidence but now I repent.[48]

The refugee equation

The United Nations refugee chief António Guterres has said that the four million-plus Iraqi refugees internally and externally displaced since the 2003 invasion is 'the biggest movement of displaced people in the Middle East since the Palestinian crisis in 1948'.[49] Syria has taken in at least two million refugees and the country is struggling domestically, religiously and politically under that burden. Revealingly, Syrian officials acknowledged only 700 000 Iraqis were supposed to have entered their country in early 2005.[50] The number has skyrocketed in the years since, to the point where it is now one of the key challenges facing Syria.

This is the issue that I heard talked about incessantly during my time there. Journalist Ibrahim Hamidi told me that many Syrians resent the massive Iraqi presence in their country and the Assad regime milks their discontent. 'The government can blame the Iraqis for all the problems,' he said. 'They are like scapegoats. When the Syrian people on the street complain that everything is expensive, the level of criminality is high or security feels compromised, the Iraqis are blamed.'

Years before I arrived in Syria I had been reading a blog by an anonymous Iraqi woman, Riverbend (http://riverbendblog.blogspot.com/). Her writings, an eloquent voice in English that detailed the gradual deterioration of her society, had become famous in the blogosphere since the 2003 invasion. Due to the parlous security situation in Iraq,

her family moved to Syria in 2007 and her occasional blogging continued. A post from late October 2007, written after she was forced to
obtain a visa to stay in the country—a relatively new requirement of the
regime—sensitively articulated the emotional cost of fleeing Iraq and
living in Syria:

> We live in an apartment building where two other Iraqis are renting. The
> people in [*sic*] the floor above us are a Christian family from northern
> Iraq who got chased out of their village by Peshmerga and the family on
> our floor is a Kurdish family who lost their home in Baghdad to militias
> and were waiting for immigration to Sweden or Switzerland or some such
> European refugee haven.
>
> The first evening we arrived, exhausted, dragging suitcases behind us,
> morale a little bit bruised, the Kurdish family sent over their represent-
> ative—a 9 year old boy missing two front teeth, holding a lopsided cake,
> 'We're Abu Mohammed's house—across from you– mama says if you need
> anything, just ask—this is our number. Abu Dalia's family live upstairs, this
> is their number. We're all Iraqi too … Welcome to the building.'
>
> I cried that night because for the first time in a long time, so far away
> from home, I felt the unity that had been stolen from us in 2003.[51]

The Middle East refugee crisis is the hidden trauma of war. Aside
from the occasional news story about Iraqi women and girls working as
prostitutes in Syria to support families because the regime wouldn't let
them work in most jobs[52], bloggers were the key source of information
about the crisis.

What is clear is that Syria's position as the main recipient of Iraqi
refugees has signified a profound shift in Arab nationalism, a rupture in
decades-old identity. The mass movement of refugees has forced many
to reassess where they belong. The sectarian strife unleashed by the war
has caused ethic tensions that lay dormant, or at least relatively stable,
to radically challenge the Arab sense of self. Furthermore, the racial bias
inherent in many Middle Eastern nations towards some groups over
others has been exploited.

I met Caesar (an online pseudonym) in downtown Damascus.[53] He
is a blogger (http://pentra.blogspot.com/) and a student of computer
engineering who moved to Syria in October 2006 (and returned to Iraq
in September 2007). His story, told in fairly fluent English, was painful
to hear. At twenty-three years old, he had amassed experiences like

those of millions of other Iraqis, some of whom initially welcomed the Americans in 2003.

Voices like Caesar's are important because they represent a liberal perspective on matters routinely ignored in the Arab world. Caesar's online identity is simply one of many in a growing number of young bloggers determined to challenge both Western perceptions of the Middle East and taboos in their own region. Despite the dire state of his home country and the dangers faced by his family, he remained both optimistic and at the same time desperate to return and finish his studies, and his attitude was infectious. He felt compelled to blog to tell the world about a young Arab refugee who remained sceptical, but not hateful, towards the United States.

Caesar's father was an officer in Saddam's navy forces and fought the Americans in the 1991 Gulf War. Although he was stationed in Basra in 2003 and initially tackled US forces—'my father wasn't fighting for Saddam, he was fighting for his country'—he soon left his position. Caesar and much of his family supported the invasion, hoping it would 'end wars', but they soon realised that the Americans had no intention of implementing democracy. He worked for the Americans as a translator in the early days of the occupation before fearing for his life from militants who were targeting any 'collaborators'. His neighbourhood was soon controlled by al-Qaeda and his family had little choice but to flee. 'They are jobless and they don't mind killing people. It's a piece of cake for them.' He couldn't have long hair or wear shorts, as this would have virtually guaranteed his murder. His best friend was killed by a bomb blast when he stopped to buy an ice-cream by the side of the road. When he returned to Iraq in 2007, he wrote on his blog that the security situation in his Baghdad neighbourhood had improved and that his fears about returning to university were unfounded. 'I'm enjoying the college with my friends whether they were Sunnis or Shiites,' he said.[54]

It wasn't hard to understand why somebody like Caesar would desperately want Saddam deposed. 'Imagine there was no internet, no satellite channels, no cell phones. Media was under Saddam's control and life was boring.' Starting a blog was almost inevitable:

In 2003 I was chatting on the internet with some girl from the US and she asked me about my ASL (age, sex and location). I said 19, male, from Iraq and she said, 'You are from marines' and I said, 'No, I am an Iraqi.' She said 'Oh come on, do they have computers?' I thought they received a bad image, a misconception about us, so I try to give a real image about our society [on my blog].

Caesar's blog—under the heading 'In Iraq, sex is like snow'—is a mixture of the personal and sometimes political. His focus on sexual issues and women's rights has created many enemies in the blogosphere but undoubtedly challenged myths about allegedly boorish Arab males. His post in April 2007 on sexual experiences was remarkably frank:

> I know very well the amount of troubles for any girl—in our society—who loses her virginity before getting married. She becomes a slut according to some people's viewpoints and her sin that she gave her heart and body to the wrong person. That's why I chose to have oral sex with my relative. No intercourse was allowed for both our own good. I didn't even disclose my genitals in front of her. However, I still feel bad about that incident.
>
> I heard many stories about relationships from pals, and I found that some couples choose to do it orally—and anally sometimes—in order not to deflower the female. As far as I'm concerned, I find hugs, kisses and caresses are quite enough. Oral is fine too, but it comes when the highest levels of love and trust are approved for that couple. Unfortunately, my relative chose the 'wrong person' = me.[55]
>
> You know why I like to try the pre-marital sex? First of all, I don't have a girl friend. Secondly, I'm 23 years old virgin. I can't marry a girl before at least 5 or 6 years from now (2 years to finish my studies and 3 or 4 years of work to establish a comfortable level of living). That's if I was so lucky to accomplish all that in this period. I don't come from a wealthy family or drive my own car. I don't wanna be just like others who entertain themselves by paying for sex.

Caesar was comfortable talking about his virginity with me, though I was more interested in discussing the political troubles in his homeland. His online reputation as a 'sex maniac' was an understandable distraction from a troubled daily life. He wanted his blog to show the world the 'liberal' Iraq, the non-political Iraq and the social Iraq. Although he worked in an accountancy firm in Damascus, he was one of the many middle-class Iraqis who desperately wanted to return to Iraq, despite the obvious dangers. Warm, curious and animated, he was keen to know if my musical tastes were similar to his. (I had to tell him that nu-metal bands like Green Day and Linkin Park weren't rocking my boat.)

We walked through the streets of Damascus for at least two hours, watching the day draw to a close. For a short period a power outage caused an eerie blackness to descend over a poor neighbourhood. Shop owners used candlelight to continue trading while others cranked up booming generators to assist the making of kebabs and fresh fruit juices. Caesar said it was refreshing to be away from his family for a few hours because he shared a very small house with them. He was the only one with a job.

At times it felt like we were old friends, talking about sex and girls as one usually does only in closer friendships. He despaired that Iraq would remain in chaos for the foreseeable future and even longed for the return of Saddam because life was at least safer under his rule. When he asked about the presence of Australian troops in Iraq, I meekly looked for an answer, mumbling something about the inability of successive Australian prime ministers to refuse requests from Washington.

Blogging was almost invented for people like Caesar. It is unpretentious, revealing and transparent about daily life—and thankfully doesn't require a tentative editor to censor the explicitness or rawness of the material. Hearing about his displacement in Syria and longing for his homeland made me feel ashamed of our own culpability in the Iraq disaster. Those in power in the West have taken no responsibility for the effects of their actions, as if the tragedy was a natural disaster over which they had no control. Without his blog Caesar's eloquence in the face of such horrors would never have been seen or heard.

At the crossroads

Like most countries where a growing internet culture exists, online debate will not be the catalyst or primary reason for political change in Syria. Assad's rule seems solid, insulated from possible internal threats thanks to the Iraq War. Although many neo-conservatives would like to depose the Syrian regime and implement a succession plan, there appears little appetite or ability to do so internally. Diplomatically, argued Joshua Landis in August 2007, 'Syria must decide what strategy it will pursue towards a post-American Iraq. Will it side with Iran in supporting a Shiite government or will it side with Saudi Arabia in supporting the Sunni resistance?'[56]

The Syrian blogosphere can be seen as a microcosm of Syrian life. It is small, though growing, and represents an encouraging sign of a space opening up to writers outside the privileged elite. Syrian blogger Yazan Badran articulates it perfectly:

> It is one of the few places that extends through the many shades of the Syrian society, whether at home or Diaspora. Politically, religiously and socially it has grown to represent most of the colours that make up the Syrian identity. Whether it is the far left, the liberal centre or the conservative right. Be it pro-Arabism, or pro-Syria, religious or atheist, the collective efforts of these fine bloggers writing their day-to-day life on their blogs has come to paint the collective image of Syria, through blogging.[57]

In Iran I was struck by the vigorous political debate on the web. This wasn't the case in Syria, although opposition was stirring. Syrians seemed moderately content with the status quo, afraid of rapid change, regime change or foreign intervention. Despite the wishes in many Western capitals, President Assad was relatively popular and dissent was solely on the margins. The blogosphere offered opposing views, but many of the key writers lived in the diaspora. This is not to underestimate the shifts that are undoubtedly occurring within Assad's Syria. Islamist leaders have started to modernise their message and the secular left are now embracing notions of individual liberty. Like any society suffering decades of autocratic rule, the internet was merely providing a space for incremental change. New voices are emerging in the media, however. Madina FM is a popular, Damascus-based station that plays Western pop music and hosts US-style talk shows though avoids religion and politics. The regime tolerates this non-threatening outlet, despite it debating sex, domestic abuse and child molestation, because it never challenges its rule.[58] This is surely a sign of progress.

Many dissidents are unable to articulate a clear vision for Syria's future, and various opinions compete for limited internet and satellite television coverage. The country is not ready for or interested in Western-style reform. The US relations with the Syrian opposition were non-existent until the 2003 Iraq invasion, and even then it was only with Washington-based dissidents.[59] As in Iran, the failed Iraq War has made the job of opposition groups even harder, granting legitimacy to autocratic strongmen.

I met countless intellectuals who believed that only a regional peace settlement that included Israel could bolster the prospects of locally driven change. Blogger Caesar told me that many of his friends in Iraq and Syria believed that one of the major insights the internet had provided since September 11, 2001, was a realisation that the West distrusted Muslim sensibilities. He expected that Islamophobia would have 'infected' Australia. He was right, of course, but his friendship with bloggers in the West had made him realise how much he didn't know about the non-Arab world.

Of course, some bloggers prefer to simply use the new technology to mock the restrictions of the regime. Anti-authoritarianism has never had a better friend. And yet Syrian blogger Mohammed has expressed his frustration:

> Sites are blocked and the net is so slow it brings a heart attack. Why do you need the Internet? For emails? I have a solution for you. We can go back to using carrier pigeons. At the least, they are more guaranteed and faster than the Internet we have.[60]

Saudi Arabia
Blooming Online in a
Fundamentalist Desert

'50 years ago, Saudi Bedouins were riding around on camels and now they're using mobile phones and the best technology. It will take time for society to catch up with this technology.'

Mohammad al-Qass, actor[1]

WHEN SAUDI ARABIA's King Abdullah visited London in October 2007 for meetings with Gordon Brown, British Foreign Office minister Kim Howells claimed that both countries had 'shared values'.[2] The King was feted at a state banquet at Buckingham Palace and a Foreign Office spokesman said that 'Saudi Arabia is one of the UK's most important international partners'.

The liberal media reacted with outrage at the visit. The *Guardian* editorialised that 'Realpolitik is supposed to produce results. As Britain's royal and political elite pay homage to the ruler of an intolerant, brutal and theocratic regime, it is worth asking exactly what those benefits are.'[3] Those so-called benefits included arms trade with a multibillion-dollar annual value[4], oil wealth, growing exports and counter-terrorism.[5] One commentator simply stated that King Abdullah was the 'leader of the most morally repugnant regime on earth'.[6] The *Independent*'s Robert Fisk was more blunt: 'The sad, awful truth is that we fete these people, we fawn on them, we supply them with fighter jets, whisky and whores.'[7]

The major Western powers have for decades been content to tap the Kingdom of Saudi Arabia's vast energy reserves and remain silent in the face of gross human rights abuses. There are no recognised political parties or national elections, though limited local elections were held for male citizens in 2005.[8]

With fifteen of the nineteen hijackers in the September 11 attacks coming from Saudi Arabia, the country's extreme interpretation of Islam, Wahabism (the eighteenth century reform movement of Sunni Islam adopted by a number of countries in the region) was slammed in every Middle Eastern country I visited. Across the region there was little affection for the country, its government or its people. I was constantly asked throughout the Middle East why I wanted to visit a regime that produced 'fundamentalists' and perverted Islam. Perhaps my paranoia got the better of me, but it wasn't helped by the fact that I hadn't met any journalists who actually achieved entry and I hadn't received any responses from bloggers or journalists until a few days before I landed.[9] A few bloggers and writers warned me of the profound distrust of foreigners. A Human Rights Watch worker in Cairo confirmed this by saying that Saudi Arabia was the only country in the region where his organisation had virtually no contacts.

Before I landed in Jeddah[10], I quickly discovered the vagaries of Saudi bureaucracy. Obtaining a visa required months of hassling the relevant authorities in Australia—and six hours of frustrating negotiation with Saudi officials in Damascus to actually obtain the relevant documentation, after stating that I was Christian, not Jewish (on recommendation of colleagues who told me that admitting I was a Jew could complicate, even bar, my entry). It was the only country that gave me pause to consider my personal safety—although terrorist attacks against Western targets and visitors were not commonplace they were hardly unknown. I booked a room at a hotel that I thought had decent security or bomb-proofing but soon discovered that there was nothing of the sort, just smiling foreign workers at reception.

Travelling from Syria via Jordan, I immediately noticed the exclusionary nature of the place. As I checked in my backpack at Amman's international airport, I asked the Jordanian worker at the Saudi Arabian Airlines counter if she had been to Saudi Arabia. 'Oh no,' she said, almost looking relieved, 'you know single girls can't get in there.'

Jeddah, allegedly the most liberal city in Saudi Arabia, is located on the Red Sea and has a population of over 3.4 million people (the country has an estimated 27.5 million citizens with more than half under twenty-one years old[11]). It is considered the commercial capital of the country and remains the gateway to the nearby Muslim holy city of Mecca.[12] I flew into the city expecting a modern airport—after all, Saudi Arabia is the world's leading oil exporter—but discovered drab infrastructure like other Arab airports. Most men were dressed in the traditional ankle-length shirt, the thawb, with a keffiyeh on their head. Most Saudi women must wear a veil and abaya, a long cloak, to protect their modesty when they leave the house. The women were like walking shadows, almost invisible in the bustle. One day I sat in a taxi and watched an abaya-clad woman begging from car to car and receiving nothing. It was a pitiful sight, made worse because she was faceless. It was only in early 2008 that women were legally permitted to stay at some hotels without male accompaniment.[13]

Thankfully, the last years have seen a loosening of restrictions over women's dress. It's not unusual, especially in Jeddah, to see multi-coloured abayas rather than the standard black version, and some women have started to ditch the abaya altogether, preferring head scarves and knee-length coats over jeans.[14] Lamsa, one of Riyadh's abaya manufacturers, hand-stitches its garments in the city but is forced to use men for most of the beading and embroidery because women are not allowed to drive, or access transportation, to the factory.[15] A Human Rights Watch report in 2008 found that women in the Kingdom were forced to live like children, were denied basic rights and relied disproportionally on men. For example, women are unable to open bank accounts for their children or take them to a dentist without written permission from their father.[16]

I was struck by an extreme, humid heat as soon as I arrived in the country. As the temperature approached 45 degrees Celsius, sweat started pouring down my back. A dusty haze covered the skyline where decrepit buildings and the odd glittering structure sat in uneasy company. My driver, a Bangladeshi, had lived in Jeddah for twenty-five years and visited his family back home only every two years.

There are roughly one million Bangladeshis in Saudi Arabia. Along with many other South Asian migrants, they mostly work in the service industries and are underpaid and often abused as third-class citizens without rights or protection. The driver told me, only half jokingly, that South Asians kept the country afloat. The manager of my hotel was a camp Filipino, as were many of his staff. A Sri Lankan man served me dinner that night and the workers at the mobile phone shop where I bought a local SIM card were Indians. The owner was Indonesian.

During my brief airport stopover in Amman on the way to Jeddah, I had read an article in a magazine for the Jordanian elite. It reminded readers to treat their domestic staff well and not abuse them, as so many Jordanians clearly did.[17] Stories of humiliation, rape, bad pay and psychological torture suggested an underclass in the Middle East not unlike sections of the Hispanic community in America.

The religiosity of Saudi Arabia was striking. In this absolute monarchy where the Koran is the constitution, the call to prayer must be observed by everyone five times a day. While in a mobile phone shop I was suddenly ushered out because the workers had to walk to the nearby mosque and pray. It was strange being told in internet cafes that I could stay inside during prayer time if I didn't mind the shutters coming down outside and working by the light of a few hanging globes.

The lack of social options in Saudi Arabia means that young people spend their time inside shopping malls or outside trying to get in. Fifty-seven young men were arrested in February 2008 for simply 'flirting' with women at shopping centres in Mecca.[18] The flashiest street in Jeddah, Tahlia Street, was like Las Vegas on speed. Kilometre after kilometre of massive malls were overflowing with the world's most expensive brands, such as Prada and Chanel and a host of other equally recognisable ones, such as Billabong, Quicksilver, Body Shop, Guess, MAC and the Virgin Megastore. Women aren't allowed to work in shops—there was a move in 2006 to replace male workers with women at lingerie shops but the idea was shelved by authorities after complaints from conservatives.[19] I found it slightly absurd seeing men offer advice to women at make-up counters. One blogger with whom I came to spend a lot of time, Fouad al-Farhan, told me it was a sign that globalisation was the ultimate equaliser. 'We could be anywhere in the world,' he sighed. I don't think he was too pleased with this importation of mall culture.

These mall palaces were where the elite played. Hummers, BMWs, Mercedes Benzes, Ferraris and Jeeps took their time rolling slowly down the roads, enough time for the men to check out the heavily made-up women, many of whom were not wearing the abaya. It seemed somehow unreal, removed from the lives of most Saudis.

Saudi Arabia has not had cinemas since conservatives in the 1970s deemed these to be un-Islamic venues.[20] Without a movie industry or thriving entertainment scene, many young Saudi Arabians are desperate to express themselves in ways that articulate their hopes and fears and simply pass the time. Unsurprisingly, computer games have been massively popular, although a Saudi conference in early 2008 expressed concern that 'juveniles' were mimicking actions they saw online.[21] YouTube has exploded in popularity, featuring videos of everything from young Saudis joyriding to women having egg thrown at them if they refuse advances from men.[22] The capital city of Bahrain, Manama, has become a Mecca for wealthy Saudi men to unwind, drink alcohol, go clubbing, mingle with women and even pick up prostitutes.

The Arab Internet Channel, started in early 2007, was a project between friends who wanted to show the Arab world that Saudis were capable of laughing at themselves by making short films about daily life and posting them online. Since its inception, more than two million people in Saudi Arabia and the region have downloaded the films and watched them on mobile phones, iPods or computers.[23]

Co-founder of the channel, Mohammed al-Qass, told the *Washington Post* that the internet is a medium that finally allows him to create, rather than just consume, culture. 'Ever since we were young,' he said, 'it's been one-way traffic of entertainment and drama from the West. We know America and how Americans think because of television shows and films. With the Arab Internet Channel, we want to open a window into our brains and reveal the way we view the world.'[24] Qass has played a buxom motherly figure and George W Bush with satirical intent, his team regularly traversing the sensitivities of Saudi society and avoiding the glare of the religious police. Finding advertising and sponsorship is challenging because most Saudi businesses remain afraid of advertising on new technology.

I met Qass, a thirty year old of solid build with jet-black wavy hair and a beard, in Riyadh, the Saudi capital. Qass liked to talk and articulately explained why his society welcomed the internet (though he wasn't a blogger). I liked him, a warm and critical man who revelled in talking about a world outside Saudi Arabia that he didn't know but was curious about. He craved the chance to visit Greece, especially so he could see 'how women really should dress in public'. He constantly said that he loved the opportunity to converse with a Westerner who didn't blindly embrace Washington. He wanted to hear about life in Australia and whether it was easy to find a girlfriend there. I said that greater freedom didn't automatically mean more dating opportunities. Qass clearly believed that Western women were, in his words, more 'up for it'.

During one of our many conversations, we were interrupted by his mobile phone ring-tone: the Eagles song 'Hotel California'. I burst out laughing and Qass looked at me with a combination of shock and amusement. For this Saudi man to chose the daggiest tune from the 1970s signalled a moment of exquisite irony—the song's lyrics could easily be interpreted as describing a country such as Saudi Arabia where, 'you can check out any time you like, but you can never leave'—but Qass said he simply liked the 'cool' melody. I asked him not to turn off his phone during our time together; I never tired of hearing the Eagles.

For Qass, the internet was revelatory. Issues like sex, politics and religion, rarely engaged with by state-run media, were now being openly discussed in chat-rooms, allowing men and women to relate, something virtually impossible to do in public. Qass had met many women this way. He told me about attending a lesbian party with strippers, cocaine, hash and alcohol. Like Iran, life below the surface is thriving, partly due to social suffocation.

Qass told me about a recent Saudi TV drama series that showed rich women sleeping with their drivers. I wanted to know if he was turned on by the premise, but he laughed at the suggestion. The series was too tame and unrealistic, he said; and besides, he could see the real thing online or on American programs. The show was controversial but, with the use of strategically placed shadows covering kissing and female body parts, issues were raised that were impossible only a few years before.

Qass loved Michael Moore's documentary *Fahrenheit 9/11* because it was 'an alternative way of seeing the world'. His enthusiasm for works that criticised the Bush administration was unsurprising, but he was no rabid anti-American. He merely saw the effects of the calamitous Iraq War and didn't trust the American government's claims about spreading democracy. Many Saudis seemed to agree; the vast majority of foreign insurgents discovered in Iraq are Saudi born.[25]

Though born in Syria, Qass had spent twenty-seven years in Saudi Arabia and was optimistic that Saudi society was progressing and opening up to the world despite the best efforts of the conservatives. He said cinemas would exist within five years. To prove his point, he had recently read a best-selling book about a lesbian in Riyadh. Written by a Saudi woman in the style of a diary, the book (which Qass said he found pretty dull) had upset the establishment and was initially banned but was eventually published. Acknowledging that women, let alone gay people, have sexual desires is an undoubted revolution in Saudi Arabia.

In the Kingdom, getting engaged is like dating in the West. It's perfectly normal for a man and a woman who recently met to be engaged, but this might not necessarily lead to marriage. In fact, one can get married without initially having a wedding ceremony.[26] We talked about women's rights and he remained sceptical towards so-called Western progress. He said if things were so much better in the West for women, as many Saudi women claimed, why was there still so much sexual harassment in the workplace? Months after I left, a Saudi court more than doubled the number of lashes suffered by a female rape victim after she was sentenced in 2006. Her lawyer appealed the original sentence[27] and the punishment for the woman was eventually quashed after international outrage. Months later a married university professor in Mecca was sentenced to 180 lashes and eight months in prison for simply having coffee with a female student.[28]

Managing change in a fundamentalist land

One night as I sat in the empty large dining room in my hotel eating an oddly cooked hamburger—a welcome change from months of kebabs—the waiter told me that most Saudi guests had room service because women had far more freedom in the privacy of a hotel room. Life for women in the Kingdom is notoriously difficult and the 'Commission for the Promotion of Virtue and Prevention of Violence'—a group of uniformed thugs who roam the streets—has wide powers to discipline females who break the law by driving, working in shops or leaving the house without a male guardian. A manager of a local Riyadh office of the religious police told the *Christian Science Monitor* that 'the main target of this organization is for the country to live in safety ... We are concerned about religious safety.'[29] The extremism of this policy was exposed in 2002 when the religious police blocked fourteen schoolgirls who were not wearing the appropriate Islamic dress as they tried to escape a burning building.[30]

Although their presence has decreased in the last years, the religious police have always been untouchable and seemingly above the law, but two cases in 2007 suggested a small improvement in accountability and a public no longer willing to accept its infallibility. Three policemen stood trial for their involvement in the death of a man in their custody—the man had allegedly invited a woman into his car; he was later arrested and found dead in the commission's office soon afterwards. For the first time the mainstream media covered the controversy by condemning the extra-judicial powers of the police.[31] A week after the announcement of the first trial, another member of the religious police was charged over the killing of a man in Riyadh whose house was raided after he was suspected of hoarding a large amount of alcohol. The man's father said the police beat his son to death in front of him.[32]

Walking the streets in Saudi Arabia was not dissimilar to doing so in many other Middle Eastern cities, except, of course, for the extreme gender divide. In Riyadh, for example, the sign 'Young Men Not Allowed' is displayed at the entrances of many supermarkets and shopping malls across the city and aimed at all men over the age of 16. (The same law applies in other parts of the country but is not enforced.) One exasperated man told *Arab News*: 'Is everyone walking in a mall out to molest women? Sometimes shops are crowded with women so we prefer to stay outside to not annoy them.'[33] Also in Riyadh partitions were often seen in restaurants, to complement the existing tradition of having separate men's and families' sections in cafes, Starbucks and other public places.[34] One diner told *Arab News* that he requested partitions when his family ate in public because 'my wife and three daughters don't appear modest when eating (in that they are uncovered)'.[35]

Women speak

I soon discovered that it was virtually impossible for me, as a Western male, to speak to a Saudi woman. I had read reports of Saudi journalists, writing for Western news services, interviewing Saudi female bloggers, but I had no such luck.[36] However, during my visit I was encouraged to read a report in *Arab News* about a woman-only lecture on blogging in Riyadh that aimed, according to the convenor, Saudi writer Hadeel Al-Hodhaif, 'to educate the women in the audience about the importance of blogging as an efficient medium that can greatly influence the public opinion'.[37]

Many Western women who are married to Saudi men blog about their lives to challenge the Western perception of female oppression (though most of them live in lavishly appointed compounds, therefore avoiding some of the most challenging dictates of Saudi law). I spent a few hours with an American woman and blogger, Carol, who worked in a hospital in Riyadh and had married a Saudi man.[38] She was a 'patriot' who became disillusioned with the Bush administration and had previously coordinated defence contractors in Iraq. We met in her office at the King Faisal Special Hospital and Research Centre, the largest hospital in the country. The medical sector is the only space where doctors and nurses of both genders work alongside each other. Carol was in her late forties and had converted from Catholicism to Islam around ten years ago. She was a typical big-haired and smiley American, keen to be friendly, although I noted that her CV said she was 'firearms qualified'.

Her blog, American Bedu (http://delhi4cats.wordpress.com/), was initially started to keep her family and friends in America informed about her life but soon morphed into an attempt to demystify what she called the Western misconceptions about the Kingdom. She believed that changes for women must come from within the country and not be imported from the outside. She said not being allowed to drive wasn't a big issue for her, but her blog regularly focused on women's education, principally because her step-daughter wanted to study journalism but was unable to do so in the Kingdom (women were finally allowed to enrol in law school in 2006).[39] Although 58 per cent of university graduates are women, they represent only 7 per cent of employed workers. For this reason alone, many Saudi women are pushing for greater opportunities to enter the workforce. Some praise King Abdullah for including several women in his entourage when he travels overseas, but others claim that the bureaucracy in the ministries is resistant to change.[40] He told female participants at the 2008

National Dialogue Forum to be 'patient and we will deliver' reforms for Saudi women. One guest was nearly overcome with emotion in the King's presence. 'The fact that he is meeting us is a message to the world that he is the greatest supporter of Saudi women,' she said. 'The feeling is unbelievable, I am so nervous and so excited.'[41]

Carol's blog was often insightful about a world that many Westerners find hard to fathom, asking why would a Western woman choose to move to Saudi Arabia and become a second-class citizen? Carol didn't see it that way, of course[42], because she felt able to traverse both the traditional side of Saudi life and a privileged existence. She lived comfortably. She was quietly critical of the regime's restrictions on women's rights, but not in a way that openly defied its rule ('Carol' is a pseudonym adopted for her blog). Carol was happy to complain about certain taboos, but she acknowledged that she wanted to avoid being portrayed as an American meddler, a dangerous situation in the Kingdom.

Carol consistently blogged about the realities of Westerners living in the Kingdom and the cluelessness she often discovered among new arrivals. A post from January 2008 expressed astonishment that many Western women, who wanted to come to Saudi Arabia for a well-paying job, had done little research on the daily realities of life there:

> Okay, I can accept how financial issues can drive and motivate many individuals but to allow those factors to take one to a place so vastly different without the least bit of research on the life? It still astounds me. So not surprisingly there were a number of individuals (women in this case) in the lecture who were devastated and having a difficult time on what they were learning was the reality of the life here. They could not yet accept they were unable to drive, had to wear an abaya, could not meet members of the opposite sex and date, there were no clubs and the list went on.
>
> One woman in particular stood out. She claimed that due to no one informing her of the need to have an abaya she was forced to remain in her apartment for a period of time until someone was kind enough to deliver an abaya to her.[43]

One of the country's most prominent female journalists, Faiza Saleh Ambah, is the Saudi correspondent for the *Washington Post*.[44] She was born in Los Angeles and previously freelanced in Egypt, where she also worked for the *Christian Science Monitor* and the *San Francisco Chronicle*, and in Dubai she had been with Associated Press. She has been married twice (once to a Muslim, once to a Christian) and is currently living alone with her two children. An attractive forty-seven year old with long black hair and thick-rimmed glasses, she was dressed like a Westerner and told me she often felt like a Westerner looking at Saudi Arabia, even though she was a Saudi Arabian who had spent many years in the Kingdom trying to inform Western readers about a country she clearly loved. When she returned soon after September 11, she discovered that the mood had shifted and become more amenable to public debate. International attention on the Kingdom had an effect on the perception that the Kingdom was a hotbed of anti-Western radicalism needing to be challenged. She was now allowed to use words like 'Wahabi'—'it used to be a four-letter word'—and discuss female driving. Local media started covering issues like child molestation and other sensitive issues. 'When I left in 2000 … this was a "perfect" society,' Faiza told me, and according to the media then, 'there were no paedophiles in Saudi Arabia and men did not beat their wives'. The terror attacks had unleashed a period of self-reflection in the Kingdom, spurred on by the huge international outcry. Faiza said that King Abdullah had recognised, perhaps superficially, that his society had problems that needed to be addressed.

A sign of change was highlighted in the *Saudi Gazette* by a column during my visit by a man who wrote that 'women-related items used to be a taboo for men. Traditionally, a husband would hesitate buying menstrual pads for his wife.' He said that men would have been deeply embarrassed 'if somebody he knows sees him in that aisle in the supermarket' selecting the pads. 'Now, I see people walking freely in that aisle, choosing the desired brand and even the appropriate size of pads, and bringing them to the cashier to pay without a hint of awkwardness.'[45] I doubt you would see many Australian men up for that particular challenge.

Faiza and I met in a cavernous, two-storey restaurant and bar in the wealthy part of Jeddah, adjacent to Starbucks and Burger King and down the road from the heavily fortified American embassy, which was attacked in 2004 by a militant group linked to al-Qaeda. Pizzas and many-flavoured shisha (water pipe) were on offer. Faiza's appearance initially shocked me: she dressed differently to virtually every woman I saw. She looked like a fashionable Westerner. As I looked around, however, I noted that most women were liberally dressed, their heads often fully uncovered. One contact told me that Faiza's fame in Saudi Arabia made her untouchable. She was the first female reporter to work at the Saudi news organisation *Arab News* and now worked for a respected American media group. The authorities probably viewed hassling her as too much trouble.

Faiza said that, although the internet had undoubtedly opened up public debate, 'to me it's like you're able to vent but I don't see it as a movement forward'. Faiza did, however, believe that one of the main benefits of the net was its empowering of youth:

> I think it's given young people a sense that they should have an opinion, can have an opinion and they can express their opinion. I mean, that might not seem like much but I think it's very important. Previous generations would not have had a political opinion necessarily about anything. If you're online and motivated it can give you more of a sense of yourself, a sense of what you think counts.

Faiza explained that Saudi Arabia's tradition of media coverage was radically different to that in the West and it would take a long time before the internet could truly challenge decades-old practices. (King Abdullah directed the country's newspapers in May 2006 to stop publishing pictures of women because it was supposedly leading young men astray.)[46] When Faiza was writing a story about the fifteenth anniversary of the 1990 protest that started when middle-class women were arrested for driving, local colleagues said she would have to find women who didn't want to drive, 'to be balanced'. 'It's like if you interview someone from a concentration camp, they say make sure you get the other side of the story from a Nazi. They go out of their way to be fair.'

Faiza was amazed to find a number of Saudi women, often with a PhD, who didn't want to drive because, as one woman who had lived in America and driven there told her, 'my husband takes for granted that I drive and then I become the maid and the driver and everything. This way he keeps some of his responsibilities.' A woman wrote an opinion piece in a local paper that argued that decriminalising driving would 'strip women of their femininity'.[47] Growing Western influence, including the internet, is seen as a threat to a stable way of life for some Saudi women, including the most highly educated. One woman told a reporter from the *Los Angeles Times*, after agreeing that the 2005 elections were a positive development even though women couldn't vote, that she didn't feel any need to participate. 'I don't need to,' she said. 'If I have a father or a husband, why do I need to vote? Why should I need to work? They will take care of everything.'[48]

The 2007 formation of the Committee of Demanders of Women's Right to Drive Cars, however, was an indication that a growing number of Saudi women would no longer accept discrimination. An electronic petition sent to King Abdullah in September 2007 had gathered over 1000 signatures thanks to spreading the word through email and text messages and called for the 'stolen' right of free movement to be restored. The statement, published on an Arab website, read: 'This is a right that was enjoyed by our mothers and grandmothers in complete freedom, through the means of transportation available.'[49] The group's co-founder has been agitating for women's rights for years and protested on the bridge between Bahrain and Saudi Arabia during the 2006 Lebanon War, holding a sign to King Abdullah that read 'Give Saudi women their rights'. She was arrested and interrogated but had to wait until her male guardian, her brother, could come to pick her up before being released. 'The whole Arab world was inflamed at what was happening in Lebanon,' she said. 'And I wanted to say: Yes, that's bad, but why don't you look closer to home and see how bad our lives are here?'[50] In early 2008 a Saudi woman posted on YouTube a video of herself driving as a way to pressure the authorities to allow her gender to drive. Her sister was the camera operator. The woman spoke as she drove: 'For women to drive is not a political issue. It is not a religious issue. It is a social issue.'[51]

Surreally, Saudi women are now allowed to sell cars in all-women showrooms but remain barred from driving (though many people told me it was not unusual for a wealthy Saudi woman to drive in a heavily tinted Mercedes or BMW.) When a female employee at the dealership arranged a women-only private viewing in 2005 the religious police arrived hours before the presentation and demanded it be moved to a private home.[52] The showroom is adjacent to a dealership owned by men, with over 100 cars on display, where women can watch a live feed of the showroom in a viewing area and ask to have a particular car brought into a separate female showroom.

In the middle of our interview, Faiza's young cousins arrived. One was in a death metal band and he told me that the metal scene in Saudi Arabia was small but growing. Both were dressed in American hip-hop style, spoke English pretty fluently and longed to travel the world.[53] They seemed bored with the lack of possibilities in Saudi Arabia and talked about their interest in graffiti.

A few hours later, a friend of theirs, Ahmed, arrived dressed like the others. He wanted to be a journalist and wasn't keen on the 'materialistic' West. He was a practising Muslim and believed that all Israeli citizens were legitimate targets and all peoples in Israel and Palestine should live in one state 'under our rule'. He appeared moderate in many ways, speaking calmly during our conversation, while condoning violence against civilians as sometimes necessary. He was in Lebanon at the beginning of the 2006 war between Hizbollah and Israel and wanted to fight in solidarity with Hizbollah because he believed in the group's cause and wanted to battle a country he deemed illegitimate. In the end he was too inexperienced to be accepted, lacking military skills. He craved fighting Israel on foreign, Muslim soil.

Saudi's most popular (banned) blogger

On the Friday day of rest, an eerie silence descended over Jeddah and virtually every shop was closed. In the morning a handful of men wandered the streets but little else moved in the oppressive humidity. It felt like a ghost town; only skinny cats scurried through the dusty streets.

In the afternoon I met Fouad Al-Farhan, an IT guru, popular blogger and political reformer.[54] At thirty-three, with two children from an arranged marriage with a woman from his tribe, he was highly Westernised, having studied in America in the late 1990s. Fouad was open about his views.

An observant Muslim, he believes in an Islamic democracy, but one inspired from within, not imposed upon it. He isn't interested in living in a secular society, but feels Islam needs reforming to be more tolerant and inclusive. He sincerely thinks that many Saudis are dissatisfied with the regime's interpretation of Islam and are craving an alternative view. Channels such as al-Jazeera had finally shown them what was possible in other Arab countries. His own family is a fascinating mix. His sister supports the government and believes talking about politics is pointless. His brother is a jihadist who wanted to fight in Chechnya, Afghanistan or Iraq but was convinced to stay in Saudi Arabia. I could only imagine the dinner table conversations.

Fouad was profiled in the *Washington Post* in late 2006[55], where it was announced that Kingdom of Saudi Arabia Bloggers had been established and an online charter was to be released which would make membership open to male and female bloggers. On the day the article was published, Fouad was visited at his office by an Interior Ministry official and told it was clear he had a hidden agenda. Although they didn't specify this 'hidden agenda', Fouad told me, 'they said you are steering these naïve young Saudis down the wrong path'. Reluctantly, he decided to shut the fledging group down because he felt they simply didn't have strength in the early stages to fight the authorities. He told me that he knew the high price paid by his friends who had been jailed and found their bank accounts frozen for at least two or three years, even after they were released. These individuals have to get handouts from friends and family. Fouad was detained in 2007 for allegedly campaigning online for the release of a group of detained activists.[56] It was the first known arrest of an online dissident in the country and there was an international outcry accompanied by demands for his immediate release.[57] He was released without charge in April 2008 after nearly five months in prison.

With nearly 20 per cent of Saudis online, the web has become an undoubtedly influential tool to challenge societal norms. The internet is gradually seeping into Saudi life. There are over 2000 bloggers, with women making up half of them, no doubt lured by the anonymity of the medium.[58] The Kingdom has cracked down on online dissent through the Kingdom's internet watchdog, King Abdulaziz City for Science and Technology (KACST), but has nothing like the filtering infrastructure in countries like Iran or China.[59]

I had read Saudi blogs, written in both English and Arabic, before I arrived, but wanted to discover the ways in which a truly repressive regime viewed the rise of new technology and how young Saudis were attempting to discuss their no-party Kingdom. Some pushed for political reform. Opposition activists have used the web to distribute material, often Islamist and anti-government, and the Kingdom has struggled to contain it. Monopolising the internet may be a fruitless task, but this hasn't stopped the regime continually playing catch-up against suspect sites.[60] Even being a democracy activist puts someone at risk of being charged with 'supporting terrorism'.[61] A prominent Saudi lawyer who has defended a number of activists won the 2008 International Human Rights Lawyer Award from the American Bar Association but, due to his previous work, was barred from leaving the country to receive it.

As in every country I visited, authorities in Saudi Arabia seemed oblivious to the nebulous nature of the internet and the inability to ever fully close a website down. It's like a game of cat and mouse with dissidents, as the regime wonders how the blocked websites appear soon afterwards at different addresses. It was revealed in 2001 that the Saudi Council of Ministers had issued internet rules to be followed by all users. These included refraining from viewing information that contained 'anything contrary to the state or its system', 'subversive ideas' and 'anything damaging to the dignity of heads of states'.[62] In its ineptitude the Saudi regime was not unlike many other countries in the world but was only cementing its image internationally as a dictatorship with oil revenue going to its head.

The Kingdom of Saudi Arabia Bloggers had ambitious plans. They wanted to vote for either a male or a female president and hold meetings online. When they hammered out their charter, the small group of twenty discussed whether there should be a clause banning criticism of the world's major religions. Interestingly, the majority agreed to this self-censorship because it was seen as too politically risky at such an early stage to allow unfettered and unfiltered discussions, but that was something many hoped was achievable in time. One blogger, King of Mac, asked whether they should intervene if fellow bloggers were blocked for publishing erotica (a famous female Saudi blogger, Mystique, had attracted controversy for writing erotic fiction and for describing police finding her and her boyfriend in a car about to have sex).[63] A decision wasn't reached but the consensus was that an executive committee should make decisions on a case-by-case basis.

As a devout, liberal Muslim, Fouad passionately believed that democracy and Islam could co-exist, but he consistently stressed that, despite the 'myths in a post–September 11 world', the idea of transforming the many Islamic nations to embrace the rule of law and human rights was little different to how America attempts to straddle the separation between a devout, Christian majority and secular laws. A small army of Saudi bloggers were trying to articulate this point, but he feared that at the present time only the jihadis were presenting a cogent alternative to the Kingdom's rule. This was the challenge he saw for liberals: articulating what an Islamic democracy would look like. He opposed these violent extremists but wondered if bloggers and opposition figures could provide as strong a narrative to generate public sympathy.

Wahabists thrive on stories that highlight America's alleged contempt for Saudis. When a well-known Saudi reporter for the Arabic satellite channel Al Arabiya reported in 2005 that an employee of the American embassy in Riyadh had called him and his colleague 'animals' when trying to apply for a business visa, it played straight into the hands of individuals who claim, not entirely without justification, that the West views the Kingdom as little more than an always-open petrol station.[64] It's not surprising that a poll of Saudis in 2007 found that only 12 per cent viewed US president George W Bush positively, lower than Iran's president, Mahmoud Ahmadinejad, and Osama bin Laden.[65] A Zogby International study in early 2008 found that a majority of Saudis believed if Iran acquired nuclear weapons it would have a 'positive' effect on the region.[66]

Fouad knew that many young Saudis were angry with the Kingdom's rulers but remained even more hostile towards Washington, making them prime candidates for embracing a fundamentalist, virulently anti-Western interpretation of Islam. This offered quick and easy answers and black-and-white morality. Fouad's Islam was more compassionate but he acknowledged it could take a generation or more to implement. When he articulated the challenges in this way it became clear that he was struggling not just with authoritarian intolerance but with Saudi impatience for change.

The complexities of reform were also highlighted by King Abdullah's announcement in October 2007 of a new graduate research institution near Jeddah, designed to modernise a region he acknowledged had fallen behind the West in innovation.[67] The King pledged to bar the country's religious police from the university and greatly liberalise the mixing of the sexes on the site. His gradual reformist agenda, praised by many bloggers I interviewed, has been met with great resistance by the hardliners in the country, men who believe that any change in women's rights undermines the strength of Islam. A Gallup Poll conducted in 2007 found that a majority of Saudi men and women supported greater female rights and their ability to hold leadership positions and meaningful employment.[68]

In Fouad's highly popular blog, closed down then re-opened in 2007, he expressed dissatisfaction with authorities that didn't listen to the country's youth and instead repeated old mantras that seemed irrelevant in the twenty-first century. Fouad told me that his country's identity was ill-defined:

> We need to find the common ground, really define who we are. Sometimes you think you are not a citizen at all. This is a country that belongs to a family. This family really believe this land belongs to them. It's part of their creed and it's part of their belief. They say all their actions show this. You minimize yourself or your alliances to become your real tribe. My country is my tribe. I have nothing in common with these people in Jeddah. We share only the citizenship, but actually the citizenship of what? We don't have rights. It's not even defined; you don't know your rights.

The inherent contradictions in Saudi society were highlighted by the popularity of TV programs such as *Oprah* and *Dr Phil*, American celebrities who talked about dysfunctional American families. Yet they resonated in the Kingdom. Fouad said that many of the large American television companies, such as ABC, CBS and NBC, were translating their major programs within twenty-four hours of screening at home. Although they weren't making money out of the process, he had heard, the Saudi authorities clearly believed, after urging from former US Secretary of State Colin Powell, that 'cultural imperialism' was one way to modernise the state.

Despite the shallowness and predictability of much Saudi state media, I was struck one night by a program called *On the Chess Board*. It spent one hour discussing the appointment of former British prime minister Tony Blair as the Quartet's Middle East peace envoy. The debate went far deeper into the issues than most equivalent shows in the West. It featured reports from London, Baghdad and Ramallah gauging average citizens' views on the Blair appointment, inter-cut with analysts in London, Baghdad and East Jerusalem. Channels like al-Jazeera have clearly had a major impact on Arab political debate, forcing rivals to emulate its style of less propaganda and more argument.[69] Despite this progress, al-Jazeera's fearless style has become less critical of many Arab states in the years after the 2003 Iraq invasion due to the fear of growing Iranian influence.[70]

Like many democracy activists I met around the world, who often felt isolated, I understood Fouad's desire to reach out to like-minded individuals in other countries. He remained suspicious, however, of foreign intervention. He said he would never accept American money, even if it were offered. Earlier in the year he had attended a Cato Institute conference in Morocco, a get-together of various democracy activists from around the world. He became particularly friendly with activists from Mauritania and was influenced by their methods of creating large-scale dissent against the country's dictator. Fouad was healthily sceptical of Cato's conservative and interventionist goals and recognised that the American foreign policy establishment was generally in sync with Washington's positions. Fouad was invited to a prominent Saudi scholar's home in 2005 to meet President Bush's then Undersecretary of State for Public Diplomacy, Karen Hughes. He wrote that 'it is rare to get the chance to meet someone who is close to the most human being I hate on earth [*sic*]'. But he left before the meeting started because the kow-towing of Saudi liberals convinced him that 'those people cannot represent Saudi society'.[71]

Despite our vast differences, I bonded quickly with Fouad, probably helped by the fact that he had lived for a number of years in America. One event had coloured his experiences of living there. He was studying in Oklahoma in 1995 and on the day of the infamous bombing there was immediately treated with hostility by fellow students because he was Muslim. It made him feel like an exposed minority. Fouad then casually mentioned to me that he knew one of the 9/11 hijackers; they came from the same tribe. When they were both growing up, the man wasn't especially different or violent but Fouad remembered that he never closed his bedroom window. The room overlooked a cemetery.

We had lunch at the 'best pizza restaurant in Jeddah'. The place was empty and cost US$60 for two large pizzas, Caesar salad and two 7-Ups. We spent the afternoon driving and walking along Jeddah's Corniche, the languid coastline near the centre of the city. Being a Friday, families were sitting and lying on mats on the waterfront as they watched rich Saudis cut up the water on jet-skis. All women were covered in black from head to toe and were segregated from the men. Fouad said he opposed segregation although he told me he would feel uncomfortable with me even taking a picture of his uncovered wife in their home. However, he believed that the country wasn't ready to even think about ending the gender divide and should instead focus on establishing democratic institutions.

As we drove around Jeddah, skyscrapers cast shadows over the poor suburbs and dusty roads, often situated in the same strip. Our conversation flowed effortlessly. Fouad represented the Muslim democrat, comfortable in the West but determined not to embrace the worst excesses of our society. He condemned the Iraq War, dismissed the *New York Times*'s columnist Thomas Friedman as 'delusional' (principally for his support of the invasion) and regularly derided the Kingdom's rulers. Ironically, he had just been awarded a US$300 000 contract to design the official website for the Hajj, the Muslim pilgrimage to Mecca and Medina.

As the day progressed, and we drove around Jeddah across smooth roads through a barren desert as far as the eye could see, Fouad asked if I wanted to smoke a shisha. It was a scorching hot day as he took me to the outskirts of the city in a run-down area that contained auto repair shops. We walked into a large cushioned venue with only a handful of men sitting and smoking. The white walls were bare. Bright, white neon lit the windowless room. Fouad said he came here regularly to relax. A man approached us and asked what we'd like and we ordered two shisha pipes, water and tea.

We then drove across kilometres of empty desert to visit the rich suburbs nearby, with gated communities for Westerners consisting of massive houses behind imposing fences, some lit by colourful lights. It was still close to 40 degrees at ten at night. Then, like a garishly appointed oasis, large structures appeared on the horizon. Saudi Arabia had never seemed more disconnected. The idea that bloggers either spoke for this wealthy class of Saudis or could claim to understand the needs of the people when being part of an elite was an interesting question.

Fouad was not rich and he obviously lived modestly. His dreams for the country were impossible to test in a public forum or within the mainstream media, but I was attracted to both the realistic optimism towards his people's desire for change and his understanding of the patience needed to achieve it.

Comfortable Saudi denim

One of the finest sources of unfiltered information about Saudi Arabia is the blog SaudiJeans.org, run by 23-year-old Ahmed Al-Omran. He was a founding member of the Kingdom of Saudi Arabia Bloggers with Fouad Al-Farhan and regularly appears in Western news features about the growing blogging community in the region. A pharmacy student in Riyadh, he runs two blogs, one in English and one in Arabic. His sites have been occasionally blocked by the authorities, but other bloggers, even those who disagreed with his liberal political stance, rallied to his cause.[72]

I met Omran in central Riyadh and we had dinner at a Texas-style steak house with a Sizzler-like salad bar.[73] With short-cropped dark hair, and wearing a t-shirt that read 'My Monkey Got Spanked', he told me he started his blog in May 2004 at a time when only a few local blogs existed. His family is Shia in a predominantly Sunni country and he grew up in the eastern provinces of the country. He was proud of his Shia heritage but 'my interest is first and foremost nationalist, for Saudi Arabia as a whole and for all Saudis'. He acknowledged that the majority Sunni population knows little about the Shia and that the exposed ethnic tensions in Iraq have allowed him to explore these fault lines on his blog. The Sunni Saudi press now routinely damns Shiite Iran, the new, perceived threat to its regional power.[74] King Abdullah urged a conference of Muslims in Mecca in June 2008 to speak with one voice and prepare for inter-faith dialogue with Christians and Jews.

Omran was one of the few Saudis who seemed unafraid to tackle the Shia and Sunni split. It was a radically divided society, he claimed, with little tolerance for the Shia minority. He told me:

> If you criticise something about the religious establishment in Saudi Arabia, they say you are criticising them because you are Shia. It's hard because I am not doing that. I am criticising them as a Saudi citizen. I have a right do to that … Sometime after the [Iraq] war started, the tension between

the Shia and the Sunni was getting more intense across the Middle East. There was a negative side to it, but on the other hand I think the war has been somewhat good for the Shia because it has put them more in the light. After the war many people got to know the Shia, to study them and understand them more. Now after the war the Sunni Saudis have come to see more Shia on TV and in the media, to get to know them and maybe to think they are not that different from us.

Omran has never been afraid to honestly depict the effect of Wahabi Islam on his country and personal life. In 2006, after having lived in Riyadh for nearly four years, he expressed profound unhappiness with the rigidity of Saudi Arabia's most conservative city:

> It [Riyadh] is a Mecca of extremism, and it is killing all the beautiful things inside me. Riyadh is a living hell for guys like me. There is nothing to do, and nowhere to go: no cinema, no theater, no clubs, no parks, no nothing. The segregation of sexes is way too extreme, and most people here think this is Islamic. I'm afraid it is not. In fact, it is psychological and social.
>
> The ban on entering shopping malls for young men makes it a challenge for those boys. So, sneaking in and hooking up with some girl has become an achievement to the boys to show off and be proud of. The result of such situation is that all males are viewed as hysteric sex monsters, or as [blogger] Farah once put it, 'werewolves'. In the same time, any girl is viewed as an 'absolute seductress,' Farah said.[75]

Although Omran initially started blogging only about his personal life, his readership became interested in his observations on current news. Despite many bloggers hiding behind anonymity, Omran recently decided to start using his real name because he felt it gave him greater credibility. He fearlessly covered taboo subjects—except the royal family because crossing this 'red line' would, he said, cause trouble for him and his family. I asked why he called his site Saudi Jeans:

> I'm Saudi and I like to wear jeans, clearly. The other thing is I think jeans can be a symbol for many things in Saudi Arabia. Things that we say are not part of our culture, not part of who we are. So this is the idea. This is something we say doesn't belong to us but at the same time it's part of me, of what I do, of what I wear and what we see in our everyday life.

Omran has advocated social reform since he started his blog and regularly focuses on women's rights and greater religious freedoms.

These attitudes have caused him to suffer virulent online attacks, and one conservative Saudi blogger started harassing him after he had somehow found his mobile phone number. But such threats are rare and his high profile in the Western media probably gives him a level of protection not enjoyed by his fellow bloggers.

Omran painted a Saudi blogging scene inhabited by both liberals and conservatives and men and women, though he told me that Arabic blogs are now the fastest growing group, conservatives generally being keener to tighten their grip to maintain the status quo. As the medium has developed, Saudi bloggers are less interested in reaching the Western world and convincing them that they have embraced the new technology, and prefer to talk with each other and across the Arab world. In 2008, in response to an anti-Islamic film made by a Dutch lawmaker, a Saudi blogger posted a video that featured Bible texts allegedly calling for violence against non-believers. Raed al-Saeed said, in a clear message to both the Muslim and Western world, that it was easy to take religious books out of context.[76]

As in Iran, Saudi hardliners have discovered the importance of spreading their message. A group formed in 2006 called the Official Community of Saudi Arabian Bloggers (OCSAB) said they would only accept members whose blogs were educational, cultural and beneficial, blocked immoral content, respected Islam and were not personal diaries.[77] Liberal bloggers claim that OCSAB has started to intimidate both liberal male and female bloggers in an attempt to silence 'un-Islamic' sites.[78] Other bloggers have praised the group for bringing bloggers together and providing support. Omran exposed the co-founder of the group who pretended to be a reporter in order to meet him. 'I feel that OCSAB is excluding so many people with their rules,' Omran told *Arab News*.[79] 'I don't see how they can build a community that way.'

A Saudi Jeans post from October 2007, called Love/Hate, encapsulates Omran's humour and mixed feelings towards his country's restrictive life:

Relationships

I love them because they can provide you with a sense of security and peace that you can't feel on your own. I hate them because in a society like ours they are risky, shaky and so complicated you usually have little or no control over how they progress.

Religious TV channels

I love watching them every now and then because they offer a form of entertainment rarely found anywhere else: laughing at something not intended to be funny. I hate them because in most cases they promote a very narrow-minded agenda that would actually hurt the religion they claim to represent.[80]

The importance of blogging in the Saudi context is to initiate the art of political debate, something virtually unknown before the rise of the internet. Days before I met Omran, he had written on his blog about an issue that the local media refused to cover. He was appalled that squads of the Commission for the Promotion of Virtue and Prevention of Vice, whose actions are endorsed at the highest levels of the Kingdom, had visited the offices of his friend who worked at the Saudi Hollandi Bank and informed the company that the 'commission were not happy about the mixed work environment there and demanded that the bank segregate men from women'.[81] Omran blogged that he couldn't believe that a bank would be willing to comply with an 'unwritten' law that demanded complete segregation in workplaces and was concerned that 'female bank employees said the decision would negatively affect their careers'.

Despite the staid political environment, Omran was quick to point out that the Kingdom, unlike Iran and Egypt, rarely imprisoned bloggers and didn't torture writers or journalists, merely banning them. However, without a mature political culture, parliament or accountability, liberal bloggers such as Omran were finding it difficult to institute major reform any time soon. 'One of my big dreams,' he said, 'is to wake up some day in this country and find that we have an elected parliament, an elected government, an opposition and a democratic political system and we all can live in a civil way.' Omran blogged because he didn't 'want to be forty and still struggling with the same issues as today'.

Cross-dressing plus no eyebrows equals progress

Years before I arrived in Saudi Arabia, in 2004, the *New Yorker* published a feature by American journalist Lawrence Wright about his experiences for three months in the Kingdom training young journalists at the English daily *Saudi Gazette*. His observations revealed a society quite foreign to Western sensibilities. The invisibility of women was, for Wright, 'the most unnerving feature of Saudi life'. 'It felt to me as if the women had died, and only their shades remained.'[82]

Wright recalled a striking discussion with a journalist at the paper, who had just married. While he was still a bachelor he had visited his cousin in Dubai and was persuaded to cross-dress at a Halloween party. The assembled women were intrigued by his flamboyance and 'they were, like, kissing me. They even let me come into the women's bathroom! But I hated myself in the morning. I woke up with no eyebrows.' It was the perfect example of the desire of many Saudis to taste the freedom of a more liberal society, however fleetingly.

Unlike Iran, where opposition and dissent are almost tattooed into the youth's DNA, Saudi Arabia remains in the early stages of reform. Full-throttled American support and the US addiction to oil fundamentally undermine the immediate prospect of serious change. However, the internet is playing a small but significant part as a catalyst for the necessary changes. Even during my short stay in the country, I felt stifled, unable to truly gain a representative picture of the Kingdom. I was frustrated that women played only a small role in my discussions, but I had little choice. I was more encouraged by the knowledge that, despite the repressiveness of the regime, China-style web filtering was ultimately counterproductive and not being implemented. Hearing from Ahmed Al-Omran of Saudi Jeans that the blogging community was growing by the week, and that he was being informed about new blogs on a regular basis, suggested that a space for civil debate was increasingly important for Saudi youth.

One of the strongest messages I continued to receive was that change had to come from within the Kingdom, and not be imposed or prescribed from the West. Jamal Khashoggi, editor of *Al Watan* newspaper, has said that although reform should be gradual, 'nobody wants to live in a ghetto, even a nice one. As a Saudi, I say, let's open up.'[83] With internet penetration steadily growing and contact with the outside world showing Saudis what they cannot do at home, the oil-rich nation should be at the forefront of innovation and development. Money is not the issue; the political will of the ruling elite to share power is.

Cuba
Blogging away the Castro
Blues

'If Karl Marx were living in Cuba today he would have been shot or imprisoned because Marx would have been saying the government needs to liberate the forces of production.'

Cuban dissident Elizardo Sanchez, 1998[1]

'Extremism in Miami and extremism in the White House ultimately serve to fuel extremism in Havana. Fidel must be laughing!'

Dissident Miriam Leiva, 2004[2]

O N THE OCCASION OF former Cuban president Fidel Castro's eightieth birthday in August 2006, Nobel prize-winning novelist Gabriel Garcia Marquez offered a positive appraisal of 'the Fidel I think I know'. The leader was faultless, he wrote, and 'has never refused to answer any question, however provocative it might be, nor has he ever lost his patience'. The Cuban people, according to Marquez, 'address him informally, they argue with him, they claim him'. [3]

Venezuelan president Hugo Chavez is equally incapable of seeing fault in his Latin American mentor and hero. In 2006 he said, 'I don't think in Cuba there is a lack of freedom of speech. There is no repression in Cuba.'[4]

Both men were either deluding themselves or lying. Castro's Cuba is neither the socialist paradise imagined by its most fervent supporters nor a 'tropical gulag', as described by US president George W Bush in October 2007.[5] I had heard for years from colleagues on the political left that the demonisation of Castro was false propaganda spread by successive belligerent American administrations determined to unseat a non–Washington-aligned country in its backyard. Western media often did little to challenge this narrative, preferring to portray Castro as an oppressive and petty dictator who punished dissenters and held on to power for far too long. There is truth in this, but the reality is far more complex.

When former United Nations weapons inspector Hans Blix was in Sydney in November 2007 to receive the Sydney Peace Prize, he was asked about his attitude towards the Iraq War. 'I can see one good result of the war and that was eliminating Saddam Hussein because he was a brutal and bloody dictator,' he said. If the war had not happened, he argued, Saddam would still be in power 'and that would have been as bad for the Iraqi people as having perhaps Gaddafi or Castro'.[6]

It was the sort of glib statement that demonstrates many of the gross distortions in both Western perceptions and media coverage. To suggest that Castro had killed hundreds of thousands of Cubans, akin to Saddam's massacres in Iraq, was not just factually wrong but it displayed a moral blindness all-too-common in some sections of the liberal elite. Castro has outlived countless American presidents, survived numerous assassination attempts and once desired to spread worldwide revolutionary change. His primary 'crime', in some eyes, was not submitting to Washington's dictates. Freedom of speech, freedom of association and freedom of the press are undoubtedly lacking in Cuba, but Castro's faults are far from total.

I discovered a small taste of the regime's pettiness. Near the end of my Cuban visit,[7] I returned to my hotel in Havana to be told by the receptionist (who spoke only a few words of English) that officers from the Ministry of Immigration had come to the hotel and wanted to speak to me. They had just left, saying they would return shortly. I had been warned before I arrived that Cuban intelligence services were notoriously suspicious of foreigners and although this tendency was partly explained by decades of American meddling, there was no justification for the ongoing harassment of Cubans who criticised Castro and his policies. A senior Havana-based American journalist had told me a few days earlier that, since Fidel had fallen sick and disappeared from public view, the authorities had tightened the screws on gaining information from sources. I had spent the previous days meeting various dissidents around the city and realised they were probably under surveillance. I raced up to my room and started madly transcribing information from my notebook to separate pieces of paper, thinking that I would at least have a decent copy if my original notebook was confiscated.

It was a typically steamy day. The officers returned, three short men in tight, neatly pressed green uniforms. They spoke no English but clearly wanted to ask some questions. I was led to a windowless room in the hotel and the door was shut behind me. They wanted my documents and passport and one officer, moustachioed and occasionally smiling, wrote down my passport number, visa number and flight details. The men seemed friendly enough. A hotel staff member suddenly entered the room. She was the 'translator', a young woman with silver eye-liner and a crooked smile. The officers wanted to know who I had seen, where I had been, where I was going next and why I had come to Cuba. Or at least that's what I think they wanted to know, because my translator's English was minimal.

I stayed calm and said I was in Cuba as a tourist enjoying the sun. When asked if I had seen anybody in particular, I responded that I was just wandering around the city. My answers seemed to satisfy the men, who left after forty-five minutes of repeating nearly identical questions. I was not overly worried, just slightly paranoid. I figured the worst they would do was throw me out of the country (something that was happening to a growing number of Western journalists at the time).

That was Cuba.

I had arrived in Cuba with mixed feelings. The country, superficially at least, almost felt familiar after Wim Wenders's stunning documentary on the country's aging but soulful musicians, *Buena Vista Social Club*. Havana is polluted, with power chords dangling in the streets, doorways teeming with movement and sensual music pounding over the pavements. There are pictures of Castro and Che Guevara[8] on every conceivable white wall (Castro encouraged the placement of Guevara's image on seemingly endless spaces but his own image is more sparingly displayed), women in high heels who walk with a feisty attitude (and men who stare and holler), and a diverse racial mix (over 11 million people live in the country, with a sizeable black and mixed-race population). Winston Churchill, arriving by sea in 1895, wrote of Havana: 'Here was a place where anything might happen.'[9] The city has intrigued invaders, colonialists and travellers for centuries.

My arrival at Havana's international airport in the middle of a work week was greeted by a handful of bored-looking customs officials. I could have brought in bags of cocaine and nobody would have noticed. I expected a more thorough examination. I had read that, from the late 1990s, officials searched the bags of incoming foreigners at the airport to note the serial numbers of laptops to ensure they all left the country.[10] A friend told me before I arrived that Cuban doctors in Venezuela were buying TVs, toasters and other electrical equipment there and had no trouble bringing them home.

One day I went to the Iranian embassy in Havana, seeking some documents. I failed miserably, my only gain a mountain of paperwork. But when the heavens opened and the muggy heat was briefly 'cooled' by warm rain, I started talking to one of the guards working at the embassy. Felix was in his fifties, with slicked back hair, and had spent most of his life teaching English at a local university. He left a few years ago because the pay was poor—he said the Iranians, with no hint of irony, paid him more than his former employer, principally because it was in US dollars—and he needed to better support his family.[11] Felix lamented the lack of a free press in his country and the ways in which the internet—something he had seen a few times with former university friends—was routinely blocked and restricted. 'Life for us is very tough,' he told me. He resented the ruling elite who dictated policy to the masses while enjoying complete personal freedom themselves.

Felix said that freedom in Cuba was illusory and a change in the system was long overdue. He lamented that he would never have the opportunity to see the world, the cost being simply out of his reach. His eyes lit up at the chance to speak English. 'I never really have the opportunity,' he said mournfully. Cautious signs of openness heralded the late 2007 screening in Havana of the acclaimed German film *The Lives of Others*, about the former East German Stasi, or secret police. Cubans waited in line for hours to enter the packed cinemas.[12] I wondered if Felix would have seen Cuba reflected in the failed Stasi methods of repressing an entire society.

The sex, colour, faded glamour, determination and creaking Cadillacs showed a Cuba that thrived in an earlier age but today struggles to enter the modern era, not helped by the collapse of the Soviet Union, a key former backer. Hugo Chavez's Venezuela is trying to fill the gap (along with China), both financially and ideologically, with Castro even becoming a father figure to Chavez. Both Castro and Chavez started out as anti-imperialist nationalists, writes Venezuelan expert Gregory Wilpert, 'and only once in power did [they] move towards socialism'.[13]

An open and free democracy has been Castro's Achilles heel since the beginning of his rule and continues to this day, including the limited availability of computers, the internet and a robust media, even if the former leader was known to surf the unfiltered web.[14] Blogging is not universally utilised and modern communications remain a plaything of the elite in many countries, including Cuba. Castro's regime wants to keep it that way, though this will inevitably fail. I was consistently told in bars, in interviews and even on the street that the regime was fearful of any kind of Western influence, including new technology.[15] A number of young Cubans wanted me to tell them why and how I blogged and whether I truly believed my voice made a difference. I expressed cautious optimism. Even the concept of self-expression in a medium that could reach anybody in the world was an idea that remained foreign to many Cubans.

The 1959 Cuban Revolution saw the overthrow of US-backed military dictator General Fulgencio Batista by Castro's guerrilla revolutionaries.[16] Batista ruled for Washington and the Mafia, who owned hotels and casinos on the island. Castro and a small group of armed men had failed to seize a barracks in 1953 and during his trial, where he defended himself, he uttered the immortal words: 'Condemn me. It does not matter. History will absolve me.'[17] Although ridding Cuba of Batista was a major goal of Castro's, the Cold War almost inevitably pushed him into resisting American domination and subversion. The newly born country needed support and the Soviets were willing partners. Socialism, in conjunction with the Soviet Union, was the desired goal, even if Castro too liberally borrowed many of Moscow's authoritarian ways. Chile's first envoy to Cuba in 1970–71, Jorge Edwards, has written that Castro's repression was largely ignored or forgiven by the world's global left.[18]

Fidel Castro ruled Cuba for nearly fifty years, passed partial power to his brother Raul after sickness in 2006[19] and resigned formally in early 2008. Although Fidel has not been seen in public again—he appears irregularly on TV in a colourful tracksuit meeting sympathetic leaders such as

Brazil's President Luiz Inacio Lula da Silva and Chavez—during my visit Cuban state media irregularly insisted on parading a clearly shaky and sick Fidel in front of the cameras.[20] It was a pitiful sight, akin to imagining an embalmed Stalin or Mao performing in public. Although elements of the global left have become fierce critics of the Cuban Revolution, many were slow to recognise the brutality of Castro, Mao and Stalin.

A Cuban-born, left-wing American writer, Saul Landau, who travelled with Castro in the early years of the revolution, visited Havana in 1960 and wrote that he immediately saw the desperation and poverty of the Cuban population and was told by his guide in one shantytown that 'under the old regimes no one cared to do anything about such conditions. This is why we're showing it to you, so you'll understand why we had to make a revolution.'[21] Massive strides in public education and health care remain one of the great legacies of the revolution, though services have started to deteriorate in recent years.[22]

Cuba's political development was a constant struggle under American siege. The continuing US embargo was imposed in 1962 and the US State Department's senior advisor for Latin American affairs argued in 2007—after the United Nations, for the seventeenth year in a row, condemned Washington's immoral stance—that 'the embargo was caused by Cuba in its denial of freedoms of its people'. Subsequent presidents in Washington feared that Cuba would be a 'contagious example' and inspire other nations around the world to subvert America's imperial designs.[23] Cuba was added to the official list of Washington's terrorist states in 1982, replacing Saddam so that he could be given US aid.[24] This obsession with opposing Castro was revealed as late as 2004, when a body tasked to investigate financial transfers in the 'War on Terror', the Treasury Department's Office of Foreign Assets Control, revealed that of its 120 employees, four were tracking Osama bin Laden and Saddam Hussein but nearly two dozen were enforcing the embargo.[25]

The fall of the Soviet Union brought Cuba to the brink of collapse as desperately needed aid suddenly disappeared. Liberal Democrats in Washington even urged further punishment of the island.[26] The so-called 'Special Period' of economic crisis (1990–2000) forced the regime to reorientate its priorities due to necessity and by the end of the 1990s had brought closer relationships with the European Union and Latin America. Food and services were initially sparse at a time when the failure of the

Soviet-led socialist revolution forced the leaders to liberalise the economy and appease angry citizens. Ideology would often come second to getting food on the table. Cuba regularly sends doctors to various countries around the world, including Venezuela, in exchange for much-needed oil.

The elevation of Raul Castro to the presidency in early 2008 heralded small but significant reforms designed to 'liberalise' the economy and society but maintain the path of socialism. The campaign has been compared with the reforms instituted by Soviet leader Mikhail Gorbachev in his 1980s Glasnost program. The European Union lifted its diplomatic sanctions against Cuba in June 2008 but pledged to monitor the ongoing human rights abuses on the island. The agriculture sector was decentralised to allow farmers more freedom in land use and resource allocation.[27] Virtually all death sentences were commuted to terms ranging between thirty years and life.[28] People were allowed to acquire titles to houses they rent from the state. Wage restraints that had kept sugeons and taxie drivers on similar salaries were dropped. A 24-hour television channel with foreign content was available. Citizens were finally able to purchase prescription drugs from pharmacies not owned by the state, and electrical goods such as home appliances, computers and DVD players became more widely available (though officials cited improvements in electricity supply as the reason).[29] The restriction on mobile phones was lifted, reversing a policy that allowed them to be owned only by employees of foreign firms or senior members in the Communist Party.[30] The vast majority of Cubans, however, were financially incapable of taking advantage of the changes.

The Cuban Revolution is likely to survive the eventual death of Fidel Castro. Eugene Robinson of the *Washington Post* has written that the regime's repression is not the only way it has held on to power for so long. 'In my visits to the island,' he argues, 'I've been struck by how Cubans can be bitterly critical of the hard-line restrictions the regime imposes on speech, assembly, movement, commerce and other activities, and in the next breath speak with pride of the government's achievements in providing free health care and education.' Riding the bus across Havana or on longer distance travels revealed similar sentiments. Perhaps some people were afraid to share their thoughts with a stranger, but Fidel Castro seemed mostly liked, if not sometimes tolerated. However, criticisms of his methods, rather than of the man himself, were openly made. I remember one man in Havana asking me what I thought of Australia's then prime minister, John Howard, and his decision to join Washington in the invasion of Iraq. He was amazed to hear that I had expressed public opposition for years and suffered no personal consequences as a result. Wasn't I scared, he asked?

As I walked around Havana's outskirts, smelling the burning corn, people would sometimes stare and point at the Westerner with the dark beard. I wanted to engage with them, and some were more forthcoming than others. Women popped their heads out of small windows as they tied up washing to wispy ropes while muscly, shirtless men stood around talking to friends on uneven concrete paths. Children played baseball with balls made out of plastic refuse. Neighbourhood after neighbourhood looked and felt decrepit, with faded, coloured revolutionary murals on large and small walls. Many of these areas shared one telephone in a hallway. An entire floor of people had to make do (though I noticed modern landline and mobile phones for sale in a Havana communications centre).

Not unlike Wim Wenders, with his Cuban love letter, film-maker Oliver Stone made a 2003 documentary about the island. *Comandante* was a glowing portrait of Fidel Castro. It made for fascinating viewing but avoided the daily realities of Castro's Cuba. As I walked around the dirty but lively neighbourhoods, I wondered how the residents would honestly view a film that admired Castro primarily for his defiance of Washington. Stone was too smitten to see past his admiration.

Confused communism

When I travelled around the country away from Havana, it soon became clear that the countryside was no less vibrant. The landscape often reminded me of Sri Lanka, with lush greens enveloping wooden houses, ramshackle highway general stores and horse-driven ploughs on massive farms. I remember speaking to a man in the small northern town of Varadero who told me that he rarely travelled more than a few kilometres from his home, but he felt he knew about everything that transpired in Havana from the state-run newspaper. For him, Fidel Castro was the best thing that had ever happened to Cuba. This man was seventy years old.

The desperation of average citizens was apparent everywhere. In central Havana, many people with whom I spoke were calling not for a revolution or the overthrow of Castro but for political reform and a chance to improve their economic lot. On a number of nights thousands of Cubans gathered in major squares to watch baseball on massive screens, drinking, flirting, screaming and dancing unlike in any other one-party state I have visited. Perhaps it was a welcome escape from the stresses of daily life, but a number of older Cubans told me that they prayed for Fidel Castro's health and hoped he would reappear in public soon.

A couple once approached me and asked me to drink mojitos with them in a local outdoor bar. I agreed, curious as to their motives, and the young woman, with long, braided hair, gold-capped teeth and hairy arms, started looking at me seductively, holding my hand, rubbing my arm and asking, 'You like to salsa?' These were her only words of English. Her male partner then led me to a local kiosk and asked me to buy some milk powder for his baby. I suspected he was lying, and I refused to purchase the milk, but I wondered afterwards whether I was being wilfully blind to the country's hardships, even if the whole scene felt like a setup. Other Cubans approached me while I walked around Havana, keen to talk with an Australian. Their two constant questions were: What do you think of George W Bush and what do you think of Hugo Chavez?

A United Nations envoy praised Cuba in November 2007 for adequately feeding its people—'We cannot say that the right to food is totally respected in Cuba, but we have not seen a single malnourished person,' said Jean Ziegler[31]—though he urged reforms to reduce the country's dependence on food imports. Many young Cubans, watching illegal satellite channels like MTV and dressing like American hip-hop stars, told me that they simply wanted the freedom to engage with the world. Away from the dissidents, I met very few people who expressed strong feelings of admiration towards Castro, though they wondered what would happen the day after he died. Sitting in a central park in Havana one day, a pasty-looking unshaven man in his sixties sat on a bench beside me. He was wildly gesticulating. I soon noticed he was unable to speak due to a gaping hole in his neck, I presumed from smoking. 'I need a machine for talk,' he wrote in my notebook. He started whispering, in broken English, about the need to find a new direction for the country. When I asked him his thoughts about Castro, he just shrugged and started feeding the birds gathering around us. He almost begged me to visit his home and continue our conversation.

Castro biographer and editor of *Le Monde*, Ignacio Ramonet, claims that 'the loyalty of the majority to the revolution is unquestionable'. While he rightly chastises Washington for its 'devastating commercial embargo', he refuses to acknowledge the legitimate desires of young Cubans who bristle at their government's restrictions on freedoms and liberties enjoyed by comrades in countries like Venezuela, Brazil and Bolivia.[32] Unlike many Latin American countries, however, Cuba is still widely respected across the region because Castro survived half a century of American meddling and fared far better than the US-backed dictatorships of Chile and Argentina.

Economic prosperity is not the only benchmark by which one can judge the effectiveness of a regime. For example, Ramonet conveniently ignores the regime's brutal repression of gays, lesbians and transsexuals—the 1980s onwards saw a gradual loosening of social restrictions on gay people, including representations in state-produced cinema[33]—though Castro's niece, Mariela Castro, director of the National Centre for Sex Education, attempted to rectify this stain in 2007 by proposing legal reform to recognise sexual difference.[34] The Cuban Parliament was likely to pass a law in mid 2008 to give gays, lesbians, transvestites, transsexuals and transgender people the same rights as heterosexuals, allowing unions between same-sex couples and funds for gender reassignment treatment. Havana saw the country's first public gay community meeting in May 2008, with Mariela Castro joining leaders in a conference to mark the International Day Against Homophobia. Cuban state television allowed a screening of the acclaimed gay cowboy film, *Brokeback Mountain*.[35] It was a small sign that Raul Castro was less dogmatic in old age than his brother.

The dissident life

I arrived at the home of Elizardo Sanchez in the outer suburbs of Havana.[36] He lived alongside a wide boulevard and his house was the personification of 1970s kitsch, with multiple, various-sized figures of Mary Magdalene and John Paul II scattered throughout the modest abode. On his walls hung photos of a younger Sanchez meeting former US president Jimmy Carter, US senator Ted Kennedy, former Spanish president Jose Maria Aznar and former communist dissident and president of the Czech Republic Vaclav Havel (who urged Europe in early 2008 to be more forthright in its condemnation of human rights abuses on the island and support its 'democracy movements').[37]

Sanchez was a university professor in Marxist philosophy in the early years of the revolution but he soon became a political activist, founding the Cuban Human Rights and National Reconciliation Commission, an advocacy group for political change. (Because the government controlled all levels of employment, he lost his post soon after 1968 as 'there was small-scale "cultural revolution" ... against thinkers who questioned the orthodox, Stalinist approach of the time'.[38]) He has spent years in prison for defying one-party rule. Sanchez, relaxed and chomping on a cigar, remained disarmingly laid-back during our interview. Dressed in stylish brown loafers, ironed shirt and pressed pants, he seemed in good physical shape. He was the snappiest dressed dissident I'd ever met and was able to converse in a language and tone that Western journalists would understand. Although this was refreshing, I wondered if I was getting the sanitised dissident view.

We were joined by fellow dissidents—including journalist Ana Leonor Diaz, and Hector Palacios, recently released from prison and on probation (he told me that he was an early 'comrade' of Che Guevara before disagreeing with his methods). During my visit, a delegation from the Japanese embassy arrived to speak to Sanchez and Palacios, the latter looking frail and needing a walking-stick, his time in jail having taken a noticeable toll on his health. Other dissident friends wandered in and out throughout the day and I was informed that virtually all of them had spent years in jail for speaking out. Leading Cuban–American writer Samuel Farber argues that most of the Cuban dissidents 'across the board ... all assume that the market is a force of nature. It's not even discussed, it's taken for granted.' Although he called Sanchez a 'moderate social democrat', he claimed many others in the opposition were 'centre-right'.[39]

These dissidents were neither revolutionaries nor recipients of American funds (so they said).[40] Diaz was a large and vivacious woman, her English translations pushed out between sucking on multiple cigarettes. The others looked worn down, fighting a lonely path of resistance against Castro and lacking the basic tools of the modern activist—a broadband internet connection and a mobile phone. Sanchez had said to *New Internationalist* in 1998 that 'despite the peaceful nature of our work the government refuses legal recognition of our group'. 'We're prohibited from having a computer, a fax machine, a photocopier and other office equipment.'[41] He told me his home had been raided countless times over the years. Sanchez believed that the government would lose if free and fair elections were held, but 'personally, I believe we shouldn't have elections in the short term. We need a gradual and orderly transition.'

All three dissidents were highly critical of Castro and his leadership—dubbed the 'Taliban style of totalitarianism'—in Cuba. Sanchez argued in 1998 that the country had developed 'a hybrid between the totalitarian model of Eastern Europe and the *caudillismo* (strong-man) model of Latin America. This explains the strength of the Cuban government and its enormous capacity for social control.'[42] Sanchez showed me posters of detention centres both before and after the 1959 revolution. There has been an explosion of repression, literally hundreds of prisons for a variety of 'crimes'. All three were against the crippling US embargo and the Bush administration's clumsy attempts to isolate Castro.[43] They were equally wary of Chavez, fearful that he was providing the regime with a new lease of life.[44]

As I spoke with the dissidents it became clear that they received Western journalists fairly often. I felt comfortable around them. I was asked about Australia, though little was known except that the Melbourne-based publisher Ocean Press printed books about Castro and Che Guevara. They were unimpressed with this and wanted to know why a country on the other side of the world would embrace a 'dictator'. I was offered glasses of water and nuts and everyone present answered questions with a familiarity that often predicted my questions. None of the dissidents drank anything harder than chilled water, though it was only early afternoon when we met. I sensed no arrogance or presumptions on their part, nor claims that they spoke for the Cuban people. They were angry, passionate and even reflective. Diaz said they felt abandoned by the West, Europe and America especially. She under-stood why Washington had maintained a futile embargo for so long—political posturing and appeasing the extremist Miami Cubans—but she told me that the 2003 Iraq War had given the Castro regime the perfect cover to increase repression 'while the world was focused on destroying another country'. Dozens of journalists and dissidents were imprisoned in 2003 and sentenced in one-day trials for 'destabilising the country'. Many remain behind bars in atrocious conditions, their drinking water contaminated with faecal matter.[45]

The internet was an important, though largely untapped, resource to challenge the regime but access was both prohibitively expensive and restricted. Of over 3000 journalists who work openly for the government, Diaz said, only 150 regularly used the web. 'They belong to the government party and they are allowed to get access to the internet at home with a server that is provided by the Cuban Government,' she said.[46] Some sites were inaccessible and an internal intranet was widely used by the authorities. (I was regularly surprised during my visit how many Cubans used email, but it was usually a Cuban address, and not Yahoo, Hotmail or Gmail.)

A growing number of young, elite Cubans are covertly surfing the web, passing sensitive information to friends via flash drives and down-loading the latest American television shows.[47] The Cuban Union of Writers and Artists opened an internet forum to gather opinions about its annual congress in April 2008.[48] An internet phone link in early 2008 allowed students in Miami and Havana to converse as they railed against 'tyranny' and 'repression'. Such events, while undoubtedly important in any democracy, did not indicate that widespread discontent existed on the island but highlighted the desire of some Cubans to discuss issues ignored by the state media. One young man articulated the challenge: 'We, the youths of Cuba, want change. The gerontocracy is in power and the other side is youth, each time more powerful.'[49]

Washington has undoubtedly contributed to the country's inter-net difficulties, however. In December 2006, according to the regime, America sent a message to all the US internet service providers naming six countries that they were instructed not to deal with—including Cuba[50], whose government has been forced to use satellite links with regional countries.[51]

Dissidents were now able to use the internet at some foreign embassies, but Diaz said it often took up to one month to secure a place, such was the demand. She was simply unable to pay the US$6-plus per hour that many internet cafes at hotels charged Westerners for painfully slow, dial-up connection (and Cubans are not allowed to use some of these terminals). Even foreign media is difficult to obtain, with the exception of a few American newspapers and magazines at hotels, though they also remain highly priced. For Cubans outside the main cities, especially in small towns, the internet remains largely unknown and Diaz said many of her colleagues simply had to rely on fax machines to get the word out. Listening to her talk about the internet and its possibilities reminded me how I felt in the late 1990s after I had first discovered the new tool. She spoke at times almost like a child filled with wonder.

Diaz works as a journalist—after spending many years in America as a reporter for a news agency and the United Nations—but is unable to publish in Cuba. She tries to sell her Spanish articles via email and fax to news services in Miami, Madrid, Prague, Amsterdam and throughout Europe. She noted that China, with over one billion citizens, has many journalists in detention, while Cuba, with over 11 million people, has twenty-five reporters in detention. She said that in 2006 she wanted to write about an outbreak of dengue but 'in Cuba, everything is a national security item and therefore you cannot write about that'. She also couldn't write about house evictions, problems in schools, prostitution, brutal treatment in police stations, why Cubans can't be guests of Westerners in hotels (Raul Castro reversed this ban in early 2008 and finally allowed Cubans the right to stay alongside foreigners, though they had to pay in hard currency) and of course anything critical of Castro. Diaz told me, in one of her only periods of optimism, that the internet was in its infancy in Cuba but the youth craved information about the world and wanted to engage with American culture, especially hip-hop. 'The government can't stop progress,' she said.

Her observations mirrored comments I received from a senior American journalist based in Havana who told me that 'the two main security issues for the regime are cell phones and the internet'. The authorities were scared not so much about the web's political content, he said, but the fact that they were no longer able to control the primary method of delivery.[52] 'Why do you think most houses have government-purchased TVs,' he asked, 'and not many other appliances?' Despite the rise in the possibility of debate, the reporter said he 'basically ignored the Cuban dissidents because they have zero support among the people'. It was a necessary perspective when meeting dissidents—who, to be fair, never claimed to represent public opinion, except a belief that Castro's regime would lose in open elections. This American journalist, a gruff and chain-smoking cynic, had married a Cuban woman and raised a child with her. He said he imagined leaving the island soon after Fidel died and many colleagues thought similarly, 'because this story will come to an end'.

Unlike in every other country I visited, the internet currently plays no major role in organising opposition. I had arrived in Cuba looking for bloggers but found it extremely difficult to contact the handful that existed. They rarely used their real names, and they remained wary of Westerners. A combination of censorship, state control and poverty restricted the options for Cubans to agitate for change. The universality of blogging was not even on the radar for most Cubans (though state-run media pronouncements were greeted with the required scepticism, I was constantly told). Most Cubans I met weren't craving internet access, however; they merely wanted better services and jobs. But the kind of protest we take for granted in the West was unimaginable in Cuba. A country such as Egypt regularly oppresses dissidents, but the introduction of the internet has facilitated new conversations there. Under Castro, new technology has always been viewed not in a benevolent light but merely as a threat to be managed. The Cubans who knew about the internet seemed more interested in accessing information about entertainment and music stars than serious political commentary.

Dissidents blame limited access to the state media and repression for their lack of popular appeal. Most dissidents I met seemed to accept their fate, more celebrated overseas than at home. Most of their demands, however, seemed reasonable, not least the chance to speak freely and conduct free elections. As in any opposition movement, there were factions and disagreements, but their primary focus was the ability to publicly discuss the country's problems and shortages. I sensed similar desires from average, young Cubans, too, increasingly frustrated that what they saw on satellite television was unavailable to them. Revolution was no longer the name of the game; social and economic perestroika was. American interference in the island was also cited as a reason for the dissidents being marginalised. The Western media's obsession with framing the Cuban dissidents as the only voices of opposition in Cuba is mistaken, though unsurprising. Many are articulate, anti-Castro and Westernised. I look forward to the day when Western reporters can gauge public opinion by comments posted on popular blogs in Havana and Trinidad.

There was little optimism that a new generation would liberalise the country. Palacios told me that he wasn't sure they were more democratically minded. Diaz said that her son, who worked as an officer in the regime, is a 'Taliban member', seemingly opposed to full democracy, proving that many Cubans still believed in the system and its benefits. Diaz said she constantly fought with her son about why she opposed Castro. 'He believes it's much easier just to accept,' she sighed. Palacios articulated that the strength of globalisation, and the rise of the internet, would inevitably increase pressure on any new leader to address what for him was a key issue: the release of political prisoners. But he remained fairly pessimistic, largely because Chavez would, in his opinion, simply prolong the worst elements of the revolution even after Castro died.

When I spent a day with Diaz and visited her apartment in central Havana—a small space with crumbling ceilings—it was clear that turning against Castro was a lonely and often futile choice. Despite her large size and health troubles due to the humidity, she endlessly smoked cigarettes in a rocking chair. Her tools for journalism, as she proudly displayed, were simply a pen and paper, though she desperately wanted a laptop and a mobile phone. An old Cuban friend, now living in Italy, had wanted to send her these items, but negotiating the Cuban authorities was no easy matter. She asked if I could help her obtain them. Diaz spoke longingly for a day when the country and the internet were opened up for all, 'when the government trusts us'.

At a rare press conference in Havana in September 2007, Palacios and other dissidents urged opposition groups to lay aside their differences and unite in the face of a 'vulnerable and disorganised' government. The group, Liberal Unity, demanded the release of political prisoners and the abolition of repressive laws used to imprison Castro's opponents.

'We do not have to wait for Fidel Castro to die to grow,' Palacios said. 'We are growing every day.' Al-Jazeera English acknowledged after the event that the dissidents 'are not well known in Cuba, where they have no voice in the government-controlled media'.[53] There was no mention of utilising the internet to rally support, as penetration in the community remained negligible. After the sham January 2008 election, Palacios stated in Warsaw that 'Cuban society is ready for change and there are people among the dissidents who are ready to take power'. One hoped he meant only if they were democratically elected. Joined by Poland's legendary Solidarity leader Lech Walesa, Palacios was defiant. 'Every Cuban who lives at least a year will see a free Cuba,' he said.[54]

When *Observer* journalist Ed Vulliamy visited Cuba in early 2008 to gauge the direction of the country, he noted that it was virtually impossible to discover the heart of the opposition, due to its tiny size and influence. He met Yoani Sanchez, the owner of website Generation Y, a space where the handful of connected citizens could express views forbidden by the government. She was a thin 32-year-old woman who wore baggy surfer shorts and a T-shirt. She said that her hope was that Cubans would not be 'dazzled' by capitalism 'like they were in eastern Europe'. 'Here,' she said, 'if you see somebody wearing an American flag, they're probably Cuban. If they wear Che Guevara, they're probably a tourist.'[55] Sanchez recognised the thrill of American culture and knew many of her fellow countrymen and women simply wanted the option of choosing their future.

Life at dial-up speed

Less than 2 per cent of the Cuban population have access to the internet, the lowest figure in Latin America.[56] It is particularly revealing considering the country has one of the world's highest levels of education. Despite this, in Cuba I met no bloggers; a lack of technology, fear of censorship, poverty and other priorities made the expression of ideas seem futile to many. Most people I met had never heard of blogging, and this included the dissidents. The internet was yet to percolate seriously into their thinking. For others, even the thought of being able to express themselves, away from the prying eyes of the state censor, was still foreign. Unlike in a country such as Iran, where blogging is utilised by the mullahs and reformers, the ruling regime has deliberately withheld the necessary tools to empower its citizens. At some point soon, however, the information floodgates will open—but China, rather than America, may be the economic saviour.

The 2007-released Latin Technology Index found Cuba had Latin America's lowest internet, broadband and wireless penetration rates. Chile topped the list.[57] The regime has utilised many methods to block access to the internet and although the authorities blame the US embargo for the country's communications problems, there are other, more ominous, reasons for the technology deficiency. A thriving black market in computer parts has been the result, such is the desperation of some Cubans to connect with the world (and supplement meagre salaries). Many stories have surfaced of IT workers stealing web access codes while repairing the computers of foreigners.[58] In early 2004, Castro enacted a law that tried to block 'unofficial' internet usage, in yet another futile attempt to insulate his people from the digital revolution. Raul Castro's easing of restrictions on computers will inevitably lead to a growing online scene, though Fidel Castro's estranged daughter, Alina Fernandez, said in 2008 that Raul would 'make all kinds of economic changes except those that could affect the political system'.[59]

As I discovered when I entered internet cafes around the country, staff members require a passport number before granting an access code and only US dollars are accepted. Many commercial licences of the cafes allow only foreigners and Cuban nationals married to foreigners permission to log on. I met many young Cubans who were studying IT at university but were unable to access the internet, instead having to rely on a heavily restricted intranet.[60] Rider, a twenty-something Cuban dressed in skater clothes, with cropped hair and a furry beard, was sitting around playing chess in the street with his friend when I spoke to him in the centre of Havana. He said he resented having a government that still spoke of revolution when most of his friends loved rap tunes and wanted to speak to the Americans as normal people. His paranoia of being seen with foreigners was depressing but understandable. 'If the police stop us,' he said, 'please say you've known me for a few years.' Rider took me to a nearby restaurant where, after traversing a few flights of narrow stairs, we were served a hot lunch. The chicken was bony and virtually inedible but the rice and vegetables seemed healthy.

A senior Cuban official expressed the regime's sentiment towards the internet in early 2007. Communications Minister Ramiro Valdes defended his country's restrictive policies as a response to American aggression. 'The wild colt of new technologies can and must be control-led,' he said, arguing that Washington in a post–September 11 world was determined to destabilise smaller nations.[61] At a United Nations conference in Athens in November 2006, Juan Fernandez, a spokesman for the Cuban Commission for Electronic Commerce, told the global meeting of IT experts that the US embargo blocked Cuba from purchasing the latest technology and it was therefore forced to purchase the required equipment elsewhere. 'I'd like to remind you here,' he said, 'that the main obstacles to access to [the] internet [are] hunger, lack of education, discrimination and exclusion.'[62]

The undoubted and multiple attempts by America to subvert the sovereignty of Cuba over the last decades have allowed officials to justify ongoing repression against dissent and web access. At the turn of the century, the regime regarded the internet as 'an influence from the North', the land of 'the enemy'.[63] However, Cuba was relatively quick to realise that the new technology was an ideal tool to promote itself to the world, strengthen its economy[64] and assist the burgeoning tourist industry.

My camera was stolen one humid afternoon as I watched a raucous parade pass near my hotel after a local baseball team had secured victory. Hundreds of men, women and children danced, ran and walked through the streets holding banners and playing what sounded like an entire brass section in celebration. A man suddenly tapped me on the shoulder, I turned around and another man ripped my camera from my hand. It was over in a split second. Reporting the robbery to the police was a slow and painful experience—when I arrived at Havana's central police station I was greeted with looks of incredulity—but I was soon led into a small room and asked to wait. An officer entered, laughed at my few words of Spanish and sat down in front of a computer. There was no internet cable connected. Windows 98 opened and he used a dot-matrix printer to hand me an English-language police report form. I was reminded of reporting a stolen backpack in Krakow in 1998. There was a period of nine years between the two incidents but both states were at a point in their histories where they seemingly wanted to welcome tourists and the US dollar but still feared the cultural consequences of doing so. The Cuban police officer asked whether I used 'the email' but mumbled that he 'hadn't seen it'.

In 2000, the Cuban regime wasn't 'purifying' internet material because, according to conservative commentator Taylor C Boas, 'those with internet access are already sympathetic to the government's point of view'.[65] Today, however, there is evidence that the regime is actively employing a deliberate policy of censoring websites (Yahoo was blocked during my visit), but it appears to be ad hoc at best. Claire Voeux, a freelance reporter working for Reporters Without Borders[66], discovered in late 2006 that 'internet surveillance seems to be fairly haphazard, with the level of vigilance varying from hotel to hotel and from computer to computer'.[67] Voeux discovered that typing in certain words and names triggered a government-installed filter. Trying to read reports about Castro's failing health resulted in a warning on the computer screen and the website closing down.

Reports in 2007 suggested that Google Earth and Google Desktop were made inaccessible by Google itself and apparently not by the authorities.[68] Google was adhering to Washington's 'export restrictions' and taking the liberty of blocking access to many of its products in countries such as Cuba, Iran, North Korea, Sudan and Syria.[69]

Although the issue of internet access barely rates a thought in most Cuban minds, the case of independent journalist Guillermo Farinas is notable. A resident of the provincial town of Santa Clara, 320 kilometres from Havana, Farinas, in his mid-forties, went on his first of many hunger strikes in early 2006 to protest his inability to access the web freely. The authorities refused entry to an internet café in Santa Clara and Farinas issued a letter to Castro that said he would not eat 'to the death' unless he and his fellow journalists had unfettered access to the web. 'If I must be a martyr for internet access, so be it,' he said.[70] The authorities said he could have 'limited' access to the web after he had spent months in intensive care suffering from heart and kidney problems, but he refused, demanding uncensored access or nothing at all.

A one-time employee of the Cuban Government, Farinas became disillusioned when he saw that the leadership enjoyed what most Cubans did not: good food and fancy cars. His health suffered terribly during his hunger strike—Ana Leonor Diaz told me that he had nearly died during his multiple hunger strikes and his life remained in danger—but his wish was simple. 'I want pluralism in Cuba,' he said, 'not only internet access.'[71] Farinas faces continuous intimidation by the authorities, having been placed under house arrest in October 2007 after calling for a boycott of municipal elections. I was planning to visit him in Santa Clara with Diaz, but on the day of our proposed trip from Havana his health took a turn for the worse. Diaz constantly cited Farinas as a source of inspiration for her struggle. Eating lunch one day together as we sat overlooking a grimy waterway, she told me that her decision to dissent against Castro was an easy one when she saw how they treated Farinas. I bought the food for us both—tough chicken with rice and potatoes—and she said it was the most food she'd eaten in days. She couldn't afford to eat properly.

While Cuba has few bloggers of its own, Miami is home to many Cuban bloggers—most of them against Castro's regime. A number of prominent Cubans train publicly in Florida to violently overthrow Havana's rule, yet Washington ignores these 'terrorists'.[72] In early 2007, one anonymous blogger, Cuban of the Island, said that it was virtually impossible to discuss openly the fading health of Fidel Castro, principally because it implied political uncertainty. 'By having a blog,' he told BBC News online, 'you are daring to talk about certain themes openly, so it makes it quite risky.' He noted that it was now possible to 'say whatever you like in the street without anything happening to you', adding: 'People have lost that political fanaticism. But that is only in the street, among the ordinary people. Questioning any official policy or leader in front of an official or policeman is classified as subversion. There is no middle ground—you are either with the government or against it.'[73]

A read through the writings of many of Miami's Cuban bloggers reveals a pathological hatred of Castro and an inability to recognise that Washington's pig-headed policies have only entrenched his regime. One blog, Kill Castro (http://killkasstro.blogspot.com/), believes that 'there is ZERO tolerance for anyone who thinks KaSStro can be handled through diplomatic means'. It goes on: 'KaSStro may only be referred to as KaSStro or The Beast assassin, murderer, thug and any other sobriquet that denotes this animal's true nature are highly encouraged.' Despite the fact that many younger Miami Cubans no longer subscribe to these kinds of tactics, the strongest voices from Republican-friendly Florida remain obsessed with overthrowing Castro. After the 2003 Iraq invasion, some Cuban émigrés actively campaigned for Bush to 'liberate' Havana in a similarly brutal way.[74]

While many government employees write blogs, and simply republish Castro's recent speeches or diatribes against America, a small but growing number of individuals are using the anonymity of the medium to express the disappointment and frustration caused by Cuba's economic decline and repression. Yoani Sanchez has written about the high number of policemen patrolling the streets of Havana and their obsession with searching for black-market goods or documents. Because it is illegal for her to use internet access at Western hotels, and the hourly fee is prohibitively expensive, Sanchez has to write fast and avoid being caught. Some island bloggers are forced to dress as tourists, feign accents and covertly enter hotels to get online. For funds, Sanchez offers tourists tours of Havana. Unsurprisingly, most of Sanchez's readers are out of Cuba.[75] She received four million visitors in March 2008 and was awarded the Ortega and Gasset prize in Journalism, the Spanish language equivalent of the Pulitzer by the newspaper *El Pais*.[76] When the authorities refused Sanchez permission to travel to Madrid to receive the award, Raul's daughter, Mariela, told a Spanish newspaper that she believed the regime 'should grant permission to all those who want to leave'. She said that her father wanted to 'slowly' usher in reforms. 'We do not want to install a consumer society, but to produce the goods and services that people need.'[77]

Soon after Raul Castro's rise to power in early 2008, Sanchez's blog was initially blocked by Cuban authorities then allowed painfully slow access from inside the island. 'This breath of fresh air [of the internet] has dishevelled the hair of bureaucrats and censors,' she said.[78] A generation of officials clearly had no idea how to manage the new technology. Raul talked of greater openness but his regime didn't know what that truly meant. One anti-Castro blogger in Texas, El Café Cubano, wrote that the regime was using 'the Chinese model [of internet censorship.] Wow, computers are available now, but no one can afford them and as you can see the internet is restricted.'[79]

Although many Cuban bloggers avoid politics altogether and prefer to focus on cinema or literature, a columnist for the Communist Youth newspaper *Juventud Rebelde* issued a stark warning in 2007 on a blog: 'Without public criticism, mistakes will continue to hurt our country.'[80] Since Raul's elevation to power, the newspaper has begun, for the first time, to investigate what is not working in the country, including troubles in agriculture and youth unemployment.[81] Other blogs are gradually emerging, including one called Sin EVAsion run by a woman with the pseudonym Eva Gonzalez who has described herself as being part of a 'generation that came of age in 1980', the year Castro gave permission for Cubans to leave the country. Some 125 000 Cubans took advantage of his offer.[82]

Opposing Fidel

Dissidents, although routinely discussed in the West, represent only a tiny proportion of the Cuban population. Barry Carr, director of the Institute of Latin American Studies at Melbourne's La Trobe University, tells me that 'it's clear that Cuba does not conform to the Soviet and Eastern European model of the 1970s and 1980s' and the dissidents who opposed the Soviet Union.[83] Although Carr is one of Australia's leading experts on Latin America, he doesn't personally know any dissidents in Cuba and says that the dissident label 'is almost always applied only to people who are part of the Bush administration's' plans. Dissident may not be the only word to describe Castro's opponents, but I didn't meet anybody who refused the label. (Sanchez and Diaz were both happy to be referred to as 'dissidents'.)

'All the intellectuals and academics who I know are critical of the Cuban system would never regard themselves as dissidents,' Carr argues. The biggest player in the 'dissident' scene, says Carr, is the US Interests Section, located in central Havana. As I heard from many Cubans, America's blatant interventions in Cuban affairs have largely neutralised or weakened oppositional groups by association. Cuba's official Communist organ *Granma International* reported in June 2008 that a meeting in Washington in May discussed using USAID to 'promote the clandestine dispatch of electronic materials to the island via European and Latin American intermediaries'. The aim of the US$45 million was to distribute 'propaganda pamphlets, cell phones and modern communications equipment' and 'train Cubans resident in third countries.'[84]

George W Bush has publicly stated that he wanted to use the internet to destabilise the Cuban Government. In May 2001, Bush gave a
speech in which he advocated the internet as just one tool to weaken
Castro[85], and the 2006 Commission for Assistance to a Free Cuba Report
stated that US$24 million was being spent on 'efforts to break the Cuban
government's information blockade and expand access to independent
information, including through the internet'.[86] The deep involvement of
the American intelligence establishment is one of the key reasons, says
Carr, that 'most Cuba watchers have concluded that the Cuban dissident
groups have so little purchase on Cuban society.'

The Cuban community in Miami, fundamentally opposed to Castro's
rule, has worked unsuccessfully for decades with the CIA and successive
Americans to unseat the regime. It was revealed in 2006 that a number
of prominent Miami-based journalists had been paid by the Bush administration to air anti-Castro propaganda that was broadcast into Cuba.[87]
It also emerged in late 2006 that the vast majority of American funds
given to Miami's anti-Castro groups had been issued without oversight
and been wasted.[88]

Miriam Leiva and her husband, economist Oscar Espinosa Chepe,
have remained opponents of Castro for decades.[89] I met them in their
tiny apartment in Havana, filled with thousands of papers, books and
notes. The bedroom, a darkened room with the blinds drawn, had little
floor space due to the clutter. When I went to the bathroom, there was
a bucket of water under the basin to catch the drips. The kitchen and
lounge room were poky but clean. Blackened pots and pans perched
on the stove and a tiny TV sat in the corner. The place was radically
different to the almost luxurious home of fellow dissident Elizardo
Sanchez, a clear sign that Miriam and Oscar had to survive on meagre
handouts from the government. Miriam was a fierce woman, probably
hardened after years of campaigning for her husband. Oscar seemed
more mild-mannered.

Both were diplomats in the former Yugoslavia and Miriam used
to work for the Foreign Ministry (she even showed me a picture of
herself at the United Nations in New York with Castro beside her) but
was fired in 1992 for being married to a 'counter-revolutionary'. Oscar
also used to work for Castro—and 'that's why', Miriam said, 'many prisoners in Cuba are really Fidel's personal prisoners. He never forgives

or forgets.' Both initially supported the 1959 revolution but soon grew disillusioned with its restrictions. Oscar was inspired in the 1980s by Mikhail Gorbachev's reforms in the Soviet Union.

They also both opposed the US embargo and successive administrations' attempts to support dissidents. 'The regime's best friends over the years have been the Soviet Union and the US,' Miriam said, because the former funded the regime and the latter allowed Castro to maintain a permanent state of siege. They were equally sceptical about Venezuelan president Hugo Chavez, for 'completing the Latin revolution that Fidel wasn't able to do himself', and Noam Chomsky. 'He comes down here, appears on state TV, and then goes back to the US and says what he wants,' Miriam said. The Miami Cubans were 'hardline and didn't really know what was happening on the ground'. I sensed that these dissidents felt pretty isolated, unwilling to associate themselves with the US-backed solidarity movements, and were frustrated by the constant criticism of Cuban opposition groups from the West. 'Nobody says this about opposition parties in the West,' Miriam said.

Oscar and Miriam were also deeply critical of fellow Cuban intellectuals. From the 1990s, Miriam said, the regime recognised that many intellectuals wanted access to the internet so they were essentially bought off and given raised living standards and sometimes cars. 'It is a pity,' wrote Oscar in his 2005 essay, 'that Cuban intellectuals and journalists lend themselves to this shameful and undignified task which, immobilised by the fear or with the aim of pursuing privileges, remain blind, deaf and mute before our national tragedy. They are quick to serve as ideological sepoys of the government.'

Oscar has spent time in jail, including in isolation, and during this period Miriam, along with other wives of political prisoners, formed Ladies in White in 2003, an opposition group that regularly marches through the streets of Cuban cities protesting the regime's imprisonment of dissidents.[90] The group issued a statement to the European Parliament in June 2007 that stated they were 'immensely thankful for the solidarity of parliaments and governments who can greatly contribute so the Cuban government modify its intransigence and its use of prisoners, their families and opponents as hostages, to be selectively and restrictively interchanged according to its interests'.[91] During our conversation, the phone rang and Oscar spoke to a trade union leader friend who was calling from a prison hospital. He later said that many such figures contact him regularly for updates on the political situation.[92]

Miriam told me that when police came to take Oscar away, they confiscated a laptop, a newly purchased fax machine, a radio, a tape recorder and money stored in a safe, funds Oscar 'always thought we had to save for the future'. Oscar was jailed in Guantanamo, but in the Cuban section. He was sentenced to twenty years' imprisonment from March 2003, but received a provisional release in November 2004 'until it is considered that he has recovered his health'.[93] 'I don't want power,' he told me. 'I'm only a writer.' He writes books and articles in Spanish, though not always on Cuban politics and sometimes about the situation in Latin America. Oscar is not permitted to leave Havana without government permission.

In August 2005 Oscar penned an essay titled 'Anatomy of the Cuban Information Apartheid'.[94] In it he cited figures from the Report on Human Development published by the United Nations Development Program in 2005. Cuba had 64 telephone lines per 1000 inhabitants, far below many other nations in the world, such as Mexico (160), Botswana (75), El Salvador (113) and Panama (122). With respect to mobile phone subscribers and the internet, Cuba was also far below most nations, with only 3 and 9 per 1000 people respectively. Even Haiti was higher. Oscar wrote that 'the current and unbelievably low level of telecommunications and computer technology in Cuba—one of the most mediocre in the world—is a direct consequence of the restrictive policies regarding current information for the interior of the country'. The sale of computers was until recently prohibited to nationals, even when paid in convertible currency (one of the two currencies in Cuba, a curious monetary duality).

Oscar acknowledged that the government had provided computers to schools for studies in computer science and assisted in the establishment of computer clubs, but the restriction of internet access was nothing more than 'fear that information ... could threaten its absolute power'. This 'information apartheid', Oscar lamented, also extended to the restriction of cable and satellite television 'reserved for tourist hotels and foreign residents [and] the sale of video cassette recorders and photocopiers in foreign currency stores is strictly prohibited by special regulations'. After the collapse of the Soviet Union, Cuba was forced to establish relationships with foreign telephone companies—ironically, principally from America—but the cost of calls remains extreme.

I was listening to a determined couple who wore on their deeply lined faces the hardship of ongoing harassment. Despite the limited ability of the internet to thrive in Cuba, Miriam tries to send regular emails to various international human rights groups about the political situation in the country. Rather than accessing the internet at the US Interests Section, however, she 'spends most of her money going to two hotels nearby, which are owned by an enterprise belonging to the military'. Sadly, her work in the era of Raul Castro still generates hostility. During a weekly Ladies in White protest in Havana in April 2008 they were roughed up by government supporters and some were thrown into a bus and driven home. 'They are dying, they are dying,' one woman screamed with tears in her eyes, describing their imprisoned husbands.[95] The regime predictably accused the women of doing the bidding of America.

Miriam's strength lies in her determination to deny the authorities the opportunity to remove her dignity. When she used to visit Oscar in prison for her monthly visit, the guards told her that she wasn't allowed to kiss her husband. She refused to comply. 'They were trying to depress Oscar, trying to take him away from reality.' She knew many friends who had lost hope after years of campaigning against Castro, especially women whose husbands were either imprisoned for years or lost their will to live. 'Make no mistake,' wrote Miriam in Salon in 2004, 'the Cuban people are exhausted by the rule of one leader for 45 years.'[96]

There are small signs that the Cuban regime is listening. A group of university students asked Parliamentary Chief Ricardo Alarcon in early 2008 tough questions about Cuban society, and a video of the event, taped clandestinely, was made public on the internet. One student, Eliecer Avila, asked, 'Why don't the Cuban people have the real possibility to stay at hotels or travel to different places around the world?' Alarcon answered lamely—an indication that he wasn't used to being challenged on the country's inequalities—that 'If everybody in the world, all six billion inhabitants, were able to travel wherever they pleased, there would be a tremendous traffic jam in our planet's airspace'.[97] Days after Avila's question, anti-Castro blogs in America started circulating information that stated he had been arrested for asking pointed questions. In fact, Avila said, he only wanted to better socialism and berated the Western media for so quickly believing he had disappeared.[98]

The resignation of Fidel in early 2008—initially announced on the regime's official newspaper website Granma—allowed the Western media to herald the new president, Raul Castro, and his possible plans to slowly liberalise the country. Latin American scholar Aviva Chomsky wrote that the vast majority of commentary 'disparaged Castro, glossed over US aggression against Cuba and idealised capitalism'.[99] Most of the Western media welcomed Fidel's official departure from the scene—even the left-leaning UK *Independent* said that his reign was 'cruel and stultifying in many ways'[100]—and the regime responded with a few signs of greater tolerance, such as pledging to the Vatican that it would open up the country's media to the Church[101] and signing United Nations human rights treaties on civil and political rights, not signed by Fidel for more than forty years.[102] A number of Cubans told Western news services that they expected change in a post-Fidel world but remained unsure exactly what kind. Havana-based blogger Yoani Sanchez wrote that 'in general there is a sense of frustration, because we had expected more. There is talk of change, but he [Raul] puts off defining those changes.'[103]

But the country's youth are stirring, no longer willing to accept regime excuses over lack of freedoms and disposable income. One Cuban blogger, Ivan Garcia, wrote after Fidel's retirement that, 'after almost 50 years of material poverty and dearth, patience is running out,' adding: 'Internal surveys by the communist party reveal that the popularity of the Castro brothers and their political system is supported by less than 25 per cent of the population.'[104] Such figures were impossible to verify, but they matched my experiences on the island. In the early years of the twenty-first century, the thought of revolutionary fervour felt like an anachronism to many Cubans. After the lifting of restrictions on electronic goods in early 2008, Andrea, a 44-year-old technician, welcomed the changes. 'Finally the government is listening to us,' she said. 'This is stuff we've been asking for for years.'[105]

After Fidel's resignation, Time.com's senior editor Tony Karon explained why many people around the world 'revere' him— 'People ... who would not be comfortable actually living in Castro's

Cuba, much as they like the idea of him sticking it to the arrogant yanqui, his physical and political survival a sure sign that Washington's awesome power has limits—and can therefore be challenged.'[106] Karon was right, but this only proved that the often deafening silence in the West about Castro's cult of personality had adversely affected his people.

Being a Cuban Jew

There are about 1500 Jews in Cuba—1100 live in Havana—although their stories are rarely told in the West. In the years after the revolution religion was officially banned, as in the Soviet Union, and books by Jewish writers were censored, though Castro ensured that religious groups were protected and did not suffer violence.[107] I thought of these Jews as dissidents from birth, forced to assimilate at a time when they had no choice. Ninety per cent of Jews fled soon after 1959 and it wasn't until 1992 that the country changed its constitution to recognise religious freedom. Not unlike in Iran, where the Jewish population is much larger, openly practising one's faith required more than a touch of bravery. Castro's regime opened guerrilla-training camps for Palestinians in the 1960s and supported former leader Yasser Arafat.[108] After Fidel's resignation in early 2008, Moises Asis, a Hebrew teacher in Havana and general secretary of Cuba's B'nai B'rith lodge, said that the former leader was hostile to Israel but never to Jews, because 'they weren't a challenge to his power [due to their small numbers]'.[109]

New York Jewish newspaper *Forward* made note in September 2007 of Jewish New Year celebrations taking place in an atmosphere of growing liberalisation. 'Many of the worshippers were converts who came to Judaism as recently as last January,' it wrote. 'For the first time since the Cuban revolution, the Jewish community is growing.'[110] As in most countries that I visited, I wanted to connect with the local Jewish community and determine how they lived in an officially secular nation. 'To be a Cuban and Jewish is to be twice survivors,' says Cuban historian Maritza Corrales.[111]

I visited Havana's Adath Israel, the country's only Orthodox synagogue—one of the three active in Havana—and met the youthful, heavily bearded, quasi-Rabbi Yacob Berezniak Hernandez.[112] He spoke English and as an Orthodox Jew wore a yarmulke (skull cap) and tefillin (black boxes worn on the arm or forehead containing parchment with verses of the torah). The synagogue was basic but clean, with an Ark and Torah, silverware, an open eating area, kitchen and donation box. The synagogue was situated in a dusty street near the central railway station.

Yacob told me that the Cuban Jewish community never suffered anti-Semitism and any government attack against Israel was 'purely political because my country, in trade, is still close to Israel'.[113] The synagogue was a cultural centre, held daily prayer sessions and provided free daily meals to the hungry. Yacob told me that they imported kosher food from Israel via Panama (especially during Passover). Canadian Jews also send an annual kosher food package.

Yacob seemed open to debate on realities of life in Cuba, so I asked him about the use of the internet. 'The government does not allow it and maybe in time they will,' he said. He was unwilling to discuss the possible reasons for the regime's restriction of the web. 'I don't want to talk about that, but hopefully in time it will be easier.' He gave me his card, which contained a local Cuban email address.

Unlike many Cubans I met, Yacob had travelled overseas, visiting Israel, Britain and America in 2000 thanks to an Israeli and American organisation. He had especially liked Israel and seemed enchanted by the kibbutz. He said Cuban Jews were strongly supportive of Israel because 'Israel won the war' against the Palestinians. Yacob thought that Israel 'was surrounded by countries that wanted its destruction'. I sensed that Yacob, in his modest way, was a dedicated Zionist because that was seen as the wisest position for an isolated community.

Jewish community president Andela Dworin, who has spent nearly forty years promoting Jewish life in Havana, met Castro in 1998 and asked the leader why he had never visited the community. He replied: 'Because I was never invited.' He was then asked to a Hanukkah celebration and Castro enquired about the significance of the holiday. 'It's a holiday commemorating the revolution of the Jews,' she said. Castro was impressed[114] and arrived at the event, eventually addressing the congregation in a long speech.

The future may not be American

A Gallup Poll taken in late 2006—interviewing 1000 people in two of Cuba's largest cities, Havana and Santiago—found that 40 per cent disapproved of the performance of Cuba's leaders but the majority were satisfied with their personal freedom to choose what they did with their lives.[115] They praised the country's health and education system and hoped that commercial ties would be increased to America, China and Venezuela.[116]

The survey was a rare piece of non-government research into the views of the Cuban people. There was hardly a mood for radical change or foreign intervention. Dissidents remain marginalised, although the internet is starting to play a growing role in rallying like-minded opposition groups.[117]

In many ways I found Cuba a contradictory country, far removed from the clichéd images of languid living, socialist paradise or Castro adulation. Instead, I saw many young Cubans who said they felt literally cut off from the world, due to information apartheid and the US embargo. I was inspired by their stories and efforts to rail against the tired rhetoric of the regime. It is not unrealistically optimistic to argue that the internet has the potential to challenge the government even further but any changes must be directed from the Cuban people themselves. Raul Castro may provide some of these necessary charges but his reign, as a man in his seventies, is unlikely to be long-term. Cubans are eager for change but ignorant of democratic problem-solving. Many simply feel that the hopes of the revolution were never fully realised.

However, the impact of new technology on Cuba was more minimal than in any other country I visited. Poverty, fear, poor communication, the US embargo and regime repression all contributed to a lack of public dissent, despite the best efforts of Castro's opponents. There remains a disconnect between the general public and the dissidents, something the internet could possibly bridge. It's possible to imagine this situation changing soon, though it's hard to predict the possibly transformative effect of a post-Castro Cuba. Blogging is neither a universal craving nor the automatic response to life in an autocratic regime. I don't doubt that blogging and online agitation will prosper in years to come, but a Western-friendly stance may not emerge. Freedom of expression is just one natural outcome of democratic reform, though the internet's facilitation of this process could lead Cuba in a direction that aligns itself with the world's new 'socialist' superpower, China. Washington will only have itself to blame.

In October 1996 authorities heralded the arrival of the internet and declared it a 'fundamental right' of the Cuban people. Computer clubs waited in anticipation. Soon afterwards, though, officials made it nearly illegal for citizens to buy a computer.[118] Such difficulties with accepting the rights of people to access information revealed a profound contempt for human rights and a lack of trust in citizens' rights. Were they afraid Cubans would question Castro's rule and his alleged benevolence? I constantly heard students complain that they studied the internet but couldn't access it. Others told me they wanted to see a world outside the Cuban intranet.

These voices stay with me because their requests are so simple and achievable, but Cuban democracy, in whatever form it may take, needs more than internet cables and vibrant bloggers. Dissidents, as no more than a small section of Cuban society, could not claim to represent the hopes and fears of the average citizen. The future of the island should be written only by the Cuban people themselves—in a form that empowers more than the tiny elite that has thrived after years of one-party rule.

China
Punching through the Great Firewall

'We don't have software blocking internet sites. I'm not sure why people say these things. We do not have restrictions at all.'
Chinese diplomat Yang Xiokun, 2006[1]

'We don't have the ghosts our parents had. We don't have the fanatical idealism our older brothers and sisters once had. So what do we want? Nike shoes. Lots of free time to take our girlfriends to a bar. The freedom to discuss an issue with someone. And to get a little respect from society.'
Student rebel leader Wuer Kaixi, 1995[2]

THE BEIJING OLYMPIC GAMES were an opportunity for the Communist Party to present a welcoming face to the global community. The complexity of this position was highlighted by global protests in 2008 over China's repression of Tibet. Violent uprisings took place in Tibet and China and caused the deaths of over 100 Tibetans and Han Chinese. The Dalai Lama was accused by Beijing of being a 'monster with a human face' who craved independence from the motherland (even though he has long stated he only craves meaningful autonomy). The Chinese warned it would increase its 're-education' campaigns against Tibetans, with the state-run *Tibet Daily* calling on Tibetan monks to become Chinese patriots.[3] The regime was also faced with mounting protests across the world towards the torch relay, with pro-Tibetan activists causing disruption to the route in London, Paris, Canberra and San Francisco.[4] One leading Chinese dissident warned that, 'if the games fail, human rights will suffer'.[5]

The Chinese media and local bloggers reacted with near-uniform outrage at the perceived anti-Chinese Western coverage.[6] 'For a long time now,' one wrote, 'certain Western media, best represented by CNN and BBC, in the name of press freedom, has been unscrupulously slandering and defaming developing nations.'[7] CNN.com even bowed to the pressure and changed an online poll from, 'Should the Olympics in China be boycotted?' to 'What do you think of a website that gives dolls breast implants?'[8] Although public opinion was difficult to gauge, one woman expressed the sentiments of many: 'The [Chinese] government is worried; we're all worried. We've been preparing for these Olympics for eight years.'[9] Nationalism flared across the country, though only a partial picture of the situation was transmitted to the people.[10] Websites were temporarily blocked—including Google News, Yahoo, the *Guardian*, the *Los Angeles Times* and YouTube—and bloggers reported that countless sites and SMS messages from Tibet were heavily censored.[11] Chinese hackers proudly stated their desire to disrupt the websites of Western 'enemies'.

After only being shown images of violent anti-Chinese riots in Lhasa and beyond by the state run media, it was unsurprising that Chinese bloggers rounded on the Tibetans: 'The Western media see nothing about those thugs with knives in hand who killed innocent people, but tried to confuse people by saying that our government is cracking down on a "peace demonstration".'[12] This sentiment was common. One Tibetan author was found to denounce the Dalai Lama as 'ruining' Tibet in the name of religion and human rights. The Buddhist leader had 'never done anything good', he said.[13] Chinese citizens protested in China and across the world to defend the motherland against perceived Western bias and racism.[14] Despite pledging to improve rights in the years before the Beijing Games, pollution, press freedom and human rights remained far below global expectations.[15] Many global leaders agreed to boycott the Olympic opening and closing ceremony in protest. Virulent nationalism was unleashed but the Chinese leadership was determined to maintain an iron grip on public opinion.

The devastating earthquake in Sichuan in May 2008 temporarily changed the rules of the game and allowed greater openness. Users of mini-blogging tool Twitter, bloggers and journalists were initially allowed relative freedom to report firsthand accounts of the crisis, despite government orders not to send reporters to the scene. 'Never before have we shown a person go from living to death on live Chinese television', said Zhang Kaipei, deputy director of Sichuan Television's Channel 4.[16] The live questioning of China's Housing Minister over the thousands of schools that collapsed in the quake led to a tightening of media rules, though some bloggers continued to campaign against corrupt officials. There was a massive outpouring of global aid—the regime even allowed foreign assistance, including from former enemy Japan—and countless Chinese citizens donated blood and travelled to the quake zone to help. An American teacher in Beijing wrote, 'I'm hoping events can dispel another false impression: that young Chinese are xenophobic nationalists who cheer for their country, good or bad.'[17] The Olympic torch relay was temporarily suspended after online campaigns urged authorities to respect the disaster victims.

Despite the apparent openness of the regime, Geremie Barme, professor of Chinese history at the Australian National University, urged caution. The Communist Party, he said, historically liked to stage, 'performative revolutionary humanitarianism.' He went on: 'People have responded generously to this vast human tragedy but many are also aware that the Party is *zuo xiu*, that is "putting on a show" for mass consumption. There's a tradition reaching back into dynastic times in which power-holders display their virtue through great shows of munificence through disaster relief.'[18]

I arrived in China a year before the Games at a time when the Western media both lavished praise on the regime's remarkable economic growth and expressed disquiet over its authoritarian stance towards 'liberal' ideals.[19] Hundreds of Western and local journalists still reported harassment from the authorities despite the regime's public claims of greater liberalisation.[20] Western human rights groups and Chinese intellectuals pressured Beijing to uphold its pledge to improve citizens' rights before the Olympics[21]; they included film-maker Steven Spielberg, who withdrew as the event's artistic director citing China's collusion in Sudan's Darfur genocide. A coalition of Nobel laureates, athletes, celebrities and politicians issued pleas for Beijing to consider Khartoum's conduct but the Chinese dismissed the concerns and accused the critics of having 'ulterior motives'. It was the most politicised global sporting event in my adult life and provided a unique moment to experience a collision between Chinese nationalism and a Western world that preached about human rights. An Australian journalist who worked on the Sydney Olympic Games told me that she resented foreign news crews focusing on the country's indigenous population and its problems. This was probably how many Chinese citizens felt.

When I landed at Shanghai International Airport I felt as though I had been dumped on a conveyor belt. Masses of people surged from various planes and rushed towards the spotlessly clean and brightly lit immigration halls. Signs heralded the upcoming Games and welcomed the tourists with enticements of friendliness and Western products. The taxi ride into the city was a drawn-out affair, despite being made late at night. A video screen attached to the back of the front passenger seat paraded under-fed female Chinese models in various states of undress and car magazines lay across the backseat. Girls and fast cars. Through the thick haze I must have seen hundreds of advertisements for Japanese electronic brands and billboards advertising high-speed wi-fi access, the latest fad. China was open for business.

I had been reading for years about the collusion of Western multinationals in Chinese censorship of the internet and the extraordinary lengths to which the authorities would go to monitor websites, chat rooms and blogs. In a country with a staggering growth of internet usage—roughly four million people are going online every month[22] and 300 million people are expected to be online by the end of 2008[23] —could the web provide the impetus for revolutionary change and democratic participation?

During my first visit to China in 2000, I noted an apparent reluctance of many citizens to welcome foreigners, as if they were still a relative oddity. Seven years later the situation had unquestionably changed, the country's face firmly turned towards the outside world while still maintaining distinctly Chinese characteristics. There was still little time for patronising Western preaching. One blogger, commenting on Beijing's major pollution problem in late 2007, resented Westerners complaining about the country's air quality because 'these foreigners protect their own countries and environment and move all the environment-destroying industry over to China, make their money, use their products and then they still say China's environment is bad!'[24]

Travelling around the major cities reveals a singular policy of dividing the rich and clean from the poor and grubby. I rarely noticed the sight of rubbish in the wealthy areas but in the outer suburbs a toxic combination of rotting food and dog urine wasn't uncommon. I actually preferred these areas, because here a visitor wasn't completely insulated from how the majority lived. Construction across Beijing was also ubiquitous, the scale of new buildings reminding me of Berlin in the late 1990s, a time when development was a key indicator of proving to the locals and the world that a city was serious about looking forward.

There is no country on the planet more paranoid and repressive towards the internet than China. 1996 was the 'Year of the Internet' in China—and there were still only 150 000 users online out of a massive population of over 1.2 billion people; 1.6 per cent of Chinese families owned a computer and 86 per cent of citizens had never touched one.[25] The Communist Party initially toyed with establishing a China-only intranet, therefore closing China off to the world in an infernal feedback loop of its own devising, but they eventually realised the practical impossibility of doing so and the adverse effect it would have on economic development even if it could be done. *Wired* magazine published a report in June 1997 that foreshadowed the issues surrounding Chinese internet censorship and culture and the ways in which the technology had the potential to seriously challenge the grip of the communist regime.[26] By November 2007, the China Internet Network Information Centre (CNNIC) said that there were a staggering 72.82 million blogs and 47 million bloggers.[27] One out of every 30 Chinese had become a blogger. By March 2008 it was claimed that China's internet users had risen to 228.5 million, compared with 217.1 million in America.[28]

Writers Geremie Barme and Sang Ye wrote in *Wired* that one story in the mid 1990s catapulted the new technology to the masses. A science student at a Beijing university fell ill and distraught friends sought help on the net. A diagnosis was quickly found and the media informed the public. They were enthralled. A marvellous new device, capable of reaching the corners of the globe, had arrived in the Old Kingdom. Today internet users must register with the police one month after opening an account and the regime has instituted a website that allows citizens to report 'subversive' websites.[29] The regime, however, has made itself more accessible to its citizens by means of the web. It was revealed in early 2008 that millions of people had posted questions, comments and advice to Premier Wen Jiabao on the country's leading news agency in the lead-up to new sessions of the National People's Congress. One netizen wrote: 'I wonder if Premier Wen can provide pension for peasant workers above 65 years old. We only need one yuan (about 14 US cents) for one meal … to be happy in our later years.'[30]

The desire to restrict information has deep roots in recent Chinese history. 'The Chinese movement itself was born in China of surreptitious gatherings, cell meetings in gloomy garrets and covert exchanges of information—plus a large dose of mass dissatisfaction and oppression,' wrote Barme and Sang. 'Mention the information revolution and the instinctive overreaction is to clamp down.'[31] 'Comrade X' told the writers in 1997 that he was involved in building a 'firewall' to block 'problem' websites and material that would undermine Chinese unity, such as Tibetan and Taiwanese independence. 'People are used to being wary,' he warned, 'and the general sense that you are under surveillance acts as a disincentive. The key to controlling the net in China is in managing people.' Despite these restrictions, a study by Middlebury College in June 2008 found that blogs were far more likely to carry criticism than Chinese newspapers. Many blogs were more likely to carry multiple viewpoints and shun outright propaganda.[32]

'For many Chinese writers and thinkers,' wrote Linda Jaivin and Geremie Barme in their 1992 collection of Chinese dissent writings after the 1989 crackdown, 'coming to terms with such concepts as democracy and personal freedom … is tantamount to a struggle to be released from Mao's hold over them.'[33] During both my trips to China, I was astounded at the reverential tone in which young Chinese people spoke about Mao, in what seemed a collective amnesia about his bloody history. He was praised as a strong leader, a uniting leader and a forward-thinking leader because, despite his barbarity, Mao was believed to have partly forged the economic conditions for China to enter the modern age. I noticed a similar tendency in Russia in 2000 towards Stalin (though not in Germany towards Hitler or Cambodia towards Pol Pot).

More than a decade later, the regime has virtually perfected the art of internet censorship and Western companies such as Yahoo, Google and Microsoft have happily invested in the country and abided by the censorious restrictions imposed by Beijing. Human rights are playing second fiddle to the bottom line. China remains the world's biggest jailer of journalists[34], with online and print reporters regularly being imprisoned for 'subversive' material. Premier Wen Jiabao said in early 2007 that China would have to wait for at least 100 years before becoming a liberal democracy. Only 'mature socialism' would allow independent courts and elections.[35]

This concept didn't seem to concern most Chinese. Democracy activists are a minority in a country that thrives on success through order. One day, at my Beijing hotel, which was built by a Mongolian general during the Qing dynasty and backed onto an historic hutong (one of the city's traditional narrow lanes), I asked the receptionist to help me buy credit for my mobile phone. He happily assisted, but made a point to ensure I would only call people who would 'give me good news'. I was initially unsure what he meant, but later his colleague told me that he had recently served a Western journalist who told him he was speaking to 'alternative' individuals. It had clearly bothered him that somebody would want to even engage with such people, considering the possible consequences. It was a tiny example of how average citizens worked actively to ensure 'social harmony'.

China today has a population of nearly 1.4 billion people, one in every five people on the planet. Even though India's population is likely to surpass China's in the next decades—principally due to a much higher fertility rate[36]—the country currently manages a booming economy with little political freedom. China has advanced extraordinarily fast. For example, there were no MBA graduates in 1998 but an estimated 30 000 ten years later.[37] The 'China Model' boasts 'economic freedom plus political repression', writes journalist Rowan Callick, describing a regime with an almost obsessive need to improve the lives of the country's middle class to avoid significant political opposition.[38] This has worked relatively well and dissent is limited and disorganised. Other countries are increasingly borrowing this model, ensuring economic freedom but maintaining tight political control.[39]

Communist web surfing

Insights into the highly secretive world of Chinese web censorship are occasionally leaked. 'Working instructions' issued by the government propaganda unit emerged in early 2008 and were posted on some Chinese blogs,[40] which displayed an extraordinary degree of control and almost Nixonian paranoia. Some examples:

—On the assassination of [Pakistani politician Benazir] Bhutto, only report on the objective occurrences and reactions from various parties, do not associate the event with Pakistan's internal struggles, or with Pakistani terrorist forces, thus avoiding attracting fire onto ourselves and getting involved in Pakistan's internal problems.[41]

—Web sites should only republish information from the Xinhua News Agency about the leadership reshuffle at the General Administration of Civil Aviation, and should not open forums, blogs and interactive columns to discuss this.

—Keep a good schedule of shifts for the 24 hour period between Dec. 29 and 30. The New Year period should also be adequately monitored, ensuring a positive public opinion.

Another report, allegedly written by a Chinese technician in an internet company, was released in October 2007 by Reporters Without Borders and detailed the multiple level of relationships between web corporations and authorities.[42] 'Mr Tao' revealed the departments in each company specifically tasked to censor and monitor content; the first line of control came from the companies themselves. Executives of the companies had to attend weekly meetings with the Internet Information Administrative Bureau. Authorities, in an attempt to prevent distribution of the document, issued a directive that included keywords to be blocked. These featured phrases such as 'control of the Chinese internet network' and 'searches aimed at suppressing website content'.[43] The Ministry of Public Security issued directives in early 2008 to 'regulate online order' and were tasked to clean out naked pictures and 'unhealthy' adult literature.[44]

Whereas ten years ago the bulk of net users were white-collar elites in urban areas, rural area users such as farmers are today's greatest growing enthusiasts for the new technology. CNNIC announced in early 2008 that 'as the popularisation of village informationisation continues and policies such as every village has access to the Internet and every village has a website are going smoothly, the rural internet market will certainly be promising'.[45] The Western image of city-dwelling elites in developing nations embracing the internet is seriously challenged by these figures and remains largely ignored by the Western media. The idea of relatively poor farmers using email and surfing the web hasn't yet seeped into the consciousness of foreign reporters.[46]

While authorities keep a close watch on the system—keen to spot any organised opposition to the Communist Party—in truth bloggers embrace entertainment far more often than politics, as do technology users in general. The majority of Chinese bloggers are the post-1980s generation. On their wish lists, a Nintendo Wii comes far ahead of democracy. Free pirated films, television shows and music are their primary concern. A study by advertising firm JWT found that the vast majority of Chinese netizens agreed that they lived some of their life online—more than double the figure for Americans—and most Chinese also said they lived a 'parallel' online life.[47] Chinese youth seem even more obsessed than their Iranian counterparts—typically passengers on trains, bent over mobile devices—with the possibilities of communicating while on the move.

Shanghai feels like a city with boundless energy. In 1985 there was one skyscraper; today there are over 300. Spending long periods in various 24-hour internet cafes was a revealing experience, for me and no doubt for the cameras mounted in every corner.[48] Hundreds, if not thousands, of terminals filled massive rooms while young men and women sat hunched over their computers, playing games, chatting online, surfing the web and smoking what smelt like the most pungent cigarettes on the market. Some young boys were scrolling through soft porn, watching giggling girls in their underwear spraying water on themselves. People shouted out periodically, presumably when they had won a game. Staff paced the lanes taking soft-drink orders. It felt like an insulated fishbowl where time and days could pass unblinkingly. Police in Beijing, desperate to monitor the web, utilised animated cartoon cops in 2007 to pop up on a user's browser, biking, driving and walking across screens every thirty minutes to warn netizens to avoid 'illegal internet content' and 'bad websites'.[49] The system was active on the country's leading portals, including the largest blog-hosting services. I was bemused to see cute figures parading across computer screens in what looked like an elaborate dance.

After discovering a plethora of censored websites in Iran, I wanted to test the 'Great Firewall of China' or 'Golden Shield', the infamous filtering system blocking thousands of problematic sites. Sites like BBC News and Wikipedia[50] were inaccessible—though the English versions of these sites were inexplicably unblocked in early 2008—but it was difficult to discover many others.[51] Leading Western newspapers such as the *New York Times* and the *Guardian* were viewable, as were many American news and analysis sites that regularly criticise the Chinese regime. A handful of well-known Iraqi blogs, including those supporting the US occupation, were blocked. Israeli newspapers were available some days, then censored the next. The regime has never published a list of banned websites or the ways in which guidelines are established. After advocacy group Reporters Without Borders released its list of the worst global culprits of web censorship in late 2006, a Chinese Foreign Ministry spokesman denied there was any censorship at all. 'The Chinese enjoy free access to the internet,' he said, 'and they can have the information they need. Currently, the information the Chinese people get is far more than before the introduction of the internet in this country.'[52] While this is undoubtedly true, the regime believes it has the right to prescribe a user's viewing abilities.

Despite its censoriousness the Chinese leadership has encouraged the growth of the internet and recognised its economic and cultural worth. President Hu Jintao called on government officials in early 2007 to 'actively and creatively nurture a healthy online culture'. He urged the net to assist 'the development of socialist culture' and 'spread more information that is in good taste and promote online products that can represent grand Chinese culture'.[53] Ahead of the 2008 Beijing Olympics, President Hu encouraged officials to 'perform well the task of outward propaganda [and] further exhibit and raise up the nation's good image'.[54]

The regime has employed around 40000 technocrats to trawl the internet daily and watch user content.[55] Applicants for the positions are offered lessons in Marxist theory, internet development and propaganda techniques. An official in Nanjing said that the roles didn't have to be full-time. 'They don't need to give up their current jobs … All they need to do is spend some time every day monitoring internet discussion.'[56] The focus isn't just on deleting material but on trying to guide public opinion. An editorial in the *People's Daily* (the main organ of the Community Party of China) in mid 2007 even praised the internet as a way to assist democracy. 'People should note that developing internet policies well will enrich the development of socialist democratic politics,' it wrote.[57]

Chinese web users received a taste of these 'socialist' policies in the run-up to the Communist Party congress in October 2007 when thousands of websites were blocked with no explanation and internet data centres were simply shut down. Many bloggers complained and ridiculed the congress itself ('the most pre-arranged press conference in history,' one wrote).[58] An employee of an internet company directed to block access explained to Radio Free Asia's Mandarin service that 'They told us, "We'd rather wrongly close 1000 websites than let a single website post illegal information"'.[59]

Li Dongdong, vice-minister of the General Administration of Press and Publication, said in early 2008 that his country's newspapers were free to criticise, but reports had to avoid 'false news, harmful information or irresponsible reports'.[60] Another senior official told a conference in London in 2008 that 'any attempt to use internet issues to interfere in China's internal affairs is definitely opposed'. The regime, he said, understood the importance of the net but 'traditional values' had to be incorporated, including 'good will' and 'self-discipline'.[61]

As I discovered in China, and confirmed by a Pew Internet and American Project study in 2008, a majority of Chinese netizens supported their government's censorship. Nearly 80 per cent of those polled said that the government should be responsible for doing it; a majority claimed they didn't trust what they read online and 'an influential and highly informed group of elite Chinese bloggers continues to test the limits and vigilance of censors'.[62]

There is, however, dissent within President Hu's cabinet information office. Vice-minister Wang Guoqing told the *London Times* in mid 2007 that the internet and mobile phones had made China's traditional rules on secrecy redundant. He accused local government leaders of being 'too naive' and blocking information about disasters or corruption and encouraged party members to move towards greater transparency.[63] 'It has been repeatedly proved that information blocking is like walking into a dead end,' he said. Governments before the internet believed they could block 90 per cent of negative news, he argued, but the internet age proved that managing and controlling information, rather than covering it up, was the only way forward.[64] Wang's position was a voice of moderation but were the upper echelons of the regime listening? In late 2007 the National Bureau of Corruption Prevention launched a website that asked citizens to denounce corrupt officials. Such was the demand that the site crashed within a few days of opening.[65]

I wanted to know the attitude of Chinese bloggers towards authority. Were they mostly, as I had read, keen to engage and vent about rules, regulation and corruption or willing to accept the doctrines of a one-party state? A number of people started talking to me around the major cities and seemed willing to praise, without encouragement, their government's skilful management of the nation. Then there was one blogger who, once prodded about her views, seemed to crave some political engagement but didn't know where to find it. Shanghai-based freelance writer and blogger Mica Yushu told me that most Chinese didn't feel they had the power to affect daily life 'because we use the internet mostly for entertainment, sharing information, earning money or other fun'.[66] The Starbucks store where we met was just one of hundreds, as was the formulaic coffee, though she said she couldn't now imagine her life without it.

We met through a Shanghai contact and initially the conversation was a little stilted. She and a friend had just come from an arts exhibition and wanted to know if I could name any Chinese artists. I had to admit that I couldn't immediately recall any Chinese writers or artists. Embarrassed, I partly redeemed myself by praising the work of film directors Chen Kaige and Zhang Yimou and actress Gong Li. My lack of knowledge about younger and probably far edgier figures was something I pledged to rectify. Mica looked slightly exasperated with my response, though I was pleased she also couldn't name any Australians. But I was in her country.

Mica wasn't optimistic that Chinese blogs could bring about political change because of what she ascribed to public apathy. She said she never spoke to her friends about politics and preferred to discuss stocks, property and cars. They were part of China's ever-expanding aspirational middle class. She didn't seem overly perturbed by this; she just accepted the reality. 'Chinese people don't really know much about how politics works,' she said, while acknowledging that there was far more political debate in Beijing than in Shanghai.

She was highly critical of the regime's filtering of websites—'It's absurd … they're trying to be overprotective,' as if officials were benign and paternalistic rather than controlling and censorious—and gave the example of the photo-sharing site Flickr, blocked because somebody had uploaded a handful of photos of the Falun Gong. Her cynicism towards anything the government said was something I noticed in many other Chinese. During the SARS epidemic, particularly in 2002 and 2003, Mica said she eagerly read the online media for information 'but we didn't know the truth'. She seemed more curious than seriously interested in current events, out of a belief that the average citizen could have no discernable effect on government policy. The Communist Party either wants docile citizens or rampant capitalists who don't agitate for political change. I sensed Mica was neither and wanted to criticise somebody, somehow, but for this 30-something generation social and economic aspiration doesn't necessarily equate to political aspiration. She said her parents were far more interested in politics than her generation—'my father reads the newspapers and loves to discuss politics, and that's a very typical Chinese old male thing'—and allegedly believed what they were told by the authorities. When she mentioned to her parents years ago that she wanted to pursue a writing career, they tried to persuade her otherwise because, for their generation who had experienced the Cultural Revolution, a writer's life was a dangerous, often fatal pursuit.

She told me a story about interviewing a successful man for an article in 2005 and how he told her that the original reason for his interest in becoming rich was to 'change somebody else's life'. It was the first time, Mica said, that she had heard a Chinese person talk about an interest in bettering society. She blamed the ways in which Chinese children were reared—'in China we have the Communist Party and when we were in school we had to learn information, word by word, whatever the government said. We hated it, of course.' Life was what it was. Who was she to try and change it? The irrelevance of the individual in a communist community couldn't be starker.

We met again a few days after our initial meeting and Mica said she had been thinking about our conversation and her inability to speak proficiently about politics. It clearly troubled her. She said she wanted to better use the internet to search out information that would inform her but it was difficult because none of her friends seemed to care. They wanted to live the capitalist lifestyle and tune out completely. It wasn't that they trusted the government, Mica said, it was that they simply trusted them enough to keep the economic boom prospering.

She asked me why Westerners protested about an issue when our governments rarely listened. I said it was because we believed we had the right to demand change and accountability, even if it was rarely delivered beyond polling and election-day assurances.

As Mica and I walked around central Shanghai talking about political protest and activism, we were surrounded by shops selling items for staggering amounts of money. Louis Vuitton handbags for US$5000 and Prada dresses for US$10 000. In the space of a few blocks, every leading Western clothing brand had established itself in buildings of glittering opulence. I had never seen anything of that size in New York or London. Mica said she sometimes wanted to talk to the Chinese people buying the over-priced items and ask what they thought about the millions of peasants in the countryside. She lamented that it would never have crossed their minds. But there was an inevitable logic to it. An expanding middle class and an insatiable appetite for luxury goods allowed the population to disconnect from thinking about the realities behind the country's prosperity. State-run media helped this delusion, focusing on celebrity and trivia at the expense of social justice stories. Self-censorship has become the primary form of control in China, with most netizens ignoring political issues or democratisation. Public apathy with politics has become a way of life because economic success has supplanted most other desires.

Westerners have gained an invaluable insight into these changes thanks to sites such as Danwei.org. Founded by South African Jeremy Goldkorn in 2003, the Hong Kong–hosted site discusses Chinese culture and translates articles from local media. We met in the company's Beijing high-rise office, a 1970s-style building in the embassy district.[67] The view from Goldkorn's office was hazy and polluted. Goldkorn talked with a Chinese cigarette permanently attached to his lips. He said that China was certainly opening up politically and it would have been unimaginable even a few years ago to stage online protests against corruption. When he first arrived in China in 1995, he said the country felt like a grey, communist outpost but by 2000, and with the massive growth of the internet, the Chinese people began having their own voice for the first time.

Goldkorn told me he generally avoided discussing politics on Danwei, but I couldn't determine whether this was because he was personally uninterested or simply accepted the rules of the game.

I suspected the latter. He found the government's censorship of the web frustrating and short-sighted but believed it would lessen its grip in time. The authorities had never tried to censor the site, probably because it's in English.

Goldkorn's Danwei colleague, Joel Martinsen—an American-born media junkie who had been in China for seven years—also believed that the internet was having an irreversibly positive effect on Chinese society but was unlikely to lead to anything politically significant.[68] He knew a number of older journalists, who had spent decades reporting the party line for state media and were now complaining that younger journalists out of journalism school were even less likely to ask questions at press conferences. 'It's like press releases,' Martinsen said, with no critical edge at all. Fan Jingyi, a former editor of the *People's Daily*, the Communist Party's official newspaper, told students at the Research Centre on Marxist Journalism and Journalistic Education Reform in Tsinghau in 2007 that the role of reporters in a country such as China was to 'guide public opinion' because the general population wasn't educated enough to understand events.[69] It was encouraging to see staff at the small Danwei office determined to counter the often factually inaccurate and biased interpretations appearing in the Western media. Both Goldkorn and Martinsen suggested that too many Western reporters in Beijing and Shanghai were content to amplify the suspicions towards China led by Washington and London.

How can our products help your repression?

The explosion of the Chinese internet has revealed an insatiable appetite by Western internet multinationals desperately looking for new markets. China has the highest number of internet users in the world and the behaviour of companies such as Google, Yahoo, Microsoft, Skype[70] and Cisco suggests that protecting human rights has taken a back seat to maximising profits.[71] It's a wonder that anybody thought the democratising potential of the web would infuse internet companies with a sense of obligation towards users living under dictatorships. Google's informal corporate motto is 'Don't be evil' but the company's 'chief internet evangelist', web founding father Vint Cerf, reveals the real meaning in a country like China. 'There's a subtext to "Don't be evil",' he says, 'and that is "Don't be illegal"'.[72] Whatever the Chinese government asks, Google is clearly happy to comply with.

Cisco Systems is also a model of complicity. The company acknowledged in 2005 that it sold networking and telecommunications equipment to China's Public Security and other law enforcement departments. Terry Alberstein, the company's director of corporate affairs, told Rebecca MacKinnon, CNN's former Beijing bureau chief and assistant professor at the University of Hong Kong's Journalism and Media Studies Centre, that his company was not breaking any American laws and Cisco wasn't tailoring its products for the Chinese market. In other words, what the purchaser did was up to them. A press release issued in 2005 by Cisco's senior vice-president, Rick Justice, stated that the company 'adhered to the laws and regulations of each country in which it operates'.[73] This was of course technically true, but what did it say about the company? MacKinnon argues that America:

> should change the law to make it illegal for companies like Cisco to sell networking and telecommunications equipment to police agencies in countries like China where the practice of law enforcement includes things like beating up little old ladies who demonstrate peacefully for religious rights in Tiananmen Square, routine torture[74] of people jailed without due process and ongoing crackdowns against political dissent of all kinds.[75]

Author Ethan Gutmann has claimed to have attended a Shanghai trade fair and seen Cisco advertising its ability to coordinate legal and police networks and border security.[76] A quarter of the sellers at the Security China 2000 trade show were selling products to enhance the 'Golden Shield'.[77] By 2008, the situation had worsened. A Beijing China International Exhibition on Police Equipment, sponsored by the Ministry of Security, saw Western multinationals, such as DuPont and Motorola, selling items for security and crime prevention.[78] The Bush administration even approved the export of security equipment and expertise to China's military and police units in the run-up to the Beijing Games, in a possible breach of the Export Administration Act.[79] Writer Naomi Klein investigated the rise of the Chinese police state and discovered that the assistance of US defence contractors was essential to the system. She explained that, '"market Stalinism"… a potent hybrid of the most powerful political tools of authoritarian communism—central planning, merciless repression, constant surveillance—[is being] harnessed to advance the goals of global capitalism'.[80]

With the assistance of Western computer hardware, the Chinese regime has constructed a system that allows it to monitor virtually all traffic into or out of the country. There are three major geographic points where fibre-optic cables enter the country through 'international gateways'—devices that mirror information and gauge whether it needs to be stopped—and the regime then decides what action to take against a user.[81] One of the latest advantages in the system is the ability to scan actual pages of content for 'subversive' material. Searching for external information can be painful, however, leading many Chinese to remain in the familiar environment of social control.[82]

Cisco, like other Western companies operating in China, claimed that if it didn't do business there, its competitors would. But weren't Chinese consumers worse off with Cisco's involvement? Unlike the more famous internet companies, its role remains relatively hidden—with a degree of secrecy it probably seeks to protect. Senior Vice-President Rick Justice compared dictatorships using its technology to 'the same functionality that libraries use to block sites in accordance with policies that they establish'. However, a document emerged in May 2008 that revealed the true aims of the company. An internal marketing presentation from 2002 appeared to show a willingness to assist the Chinese Ministry of Public Security in its aim of 'combating Falun Gong evil cult and other hostile elements'.[83]

The imposition of human rights considerations into corporate decisions was virtually unheard-of until fairly recently. There is little evidence to suggest attitudes have changed in the boardrooms of America's Fortune 500 companies, but the rise of human rights organisations such as Amnesty International and Human Rights Watch as well as persistent activists has forced corporations at least to answer critics and defend questionable practices.[84]

Microsoft launched a free blog service, MSN Spaces, in China in 2005 but agreed to censor 'sensitive' words from the service. Terms such as 'freedom', 'human rights', 'democracy', 'Tiananmen', 'communism', 'socialism', 'Dalai Lama' and 'Taiwanese independence' were blocked.[85] Users who tried to include them in subject lines were warned: 'This topic contains forbidden words. Please delete them.' Defending the move, an MSN sales and marketing director said that, 'even with the filters, we're helping millions of people communicate, share stories, share photographs and build relationships. For us, that is the key point here.'[86] The company continued to defend its practices in China in early 2006 by claiming that its services 'have increased the ability of Chinese citizens to engage in free expression'.[87]Microsoft shareholders voted down a proposal in late 2006 to limit the company's activities in countries with serious human rights violations, such as China.[88]

Microsoft has also helped the regime monitor Chinese users in real time, accessing blogs, email and chat rooms.[89] Founder Bill Gates was nonplussed by the regime's authoritarianism, stating that the country had adopted 'a brand new form of capitalism, and as a consumer it's the best thing that ever happened'. Gates further embarrassed himself by claiming that, 'there's really no way to, in a broad sense, repress information today, and I think that's a wonderful advance we can all feel good about ... This [the internet] is a medium of total openness and total freedom, and that's what makes it so special'.[90] Presumably his Gates Foundation's generosity to various causes around the world is his mea culpa for his own company's collusion in human rights abuses.

The company incurred international condemnation in late 2005 for shutting down and deleting the website of a Chinese blogger who used MSN Spaces. Michael Anti, a leading investigative journalist who wrote about matters concerning press freedom and the rights of protesting journalists at the *Beijing News*, had upset the Chinese regime, and Microsoft happily obliged when the authorities claimed the company had broken laws by hosting him. Anti wrote soon afterwards that he believed Microsoft's behaviour, without warning him, 'destroyed the trust I had in [them]'. He lamented the fact that the Chinese people were unable to punish the company for its action. 'We have no means in China to protect our own freedom of expression,' he said, 'which is precisely the fundamental rationale for why our generation must continue striving'.

Anti's long-term goal was the establishment of legislation by the Chinese National People's Congress to protect freedom of expression in his homeland.[91] His calls were largely ignored within China but he highlighted one of the key challenges facing the country's internet community and its ability to subvert establishment rule. He bravely pointed the finger at Western multinationals: 'for the sake of an opportunity to enter the Chinese market … at least in the short term Chinese netizens will not have more freedom'. His belief in the democratising power of the internet has waned since this incident: the internet, he argues, is turning China into a country like Singapore rather than a Western democracy.

It was revealed in 2007 that Microsoft was conducting research in China on software that would analyse a user's online behaviour and design a profile for them (based on sex, age, location and so on).[92] The company claimed it wanted to better know its users to deliver targeted advertising. *New Scientist* reported that a software engineer in Microsoft's research lab was beginning to understand the ways in which a person's browsing history revealed many things about them, such as the fact that 34 per cent of women surf online for information about religion while only 25 per cent of men do the same thing.[93] Privacy issues were raised by critics—especially in China where the private lives of web users are ignored—and advocacy group Reporters Without Borders expressed concern that the technology could be used to identify 'subversive' citizens.[94] MSN China's homepage was utilised by Chinese netizens in 2008 to allow them to display their patriotism and anger towards perceived anti-Western media coverage over the Beijing Olympics. Millions of users placed on their MSN IDs comments such as 'Tibet in China' and 'Peaceful Olympics'.[95]

A rare exception to the capitulation of most leading internet companies has been the behaviour of WordPress, popular open-source blogging software with millions of users. American founder Matt Mullenwag acknowledged that around a quarter of its traffic was coming from China but the authorities blocked his site unless he behaved similarly to Microsoft, Yahoo and Google. 'We found out if we were willing to forbid certain words, track people and give up their information if asked, we could be turned back on,' he said. 'It was tough. We decided that being there under those circumstances isn't worth it—we'd rather not be there.'[96] WordPress sites are supposedly still unavailable in China. It was refreshing to hear about a leading internet company arguing for a principled stand and suffer the inevitable financial consequences. Imagine if all the leading companies joined Mullenwag's call and stood firm against

China? I suspect the regime would budge on some issues and refuse on others, but at least it would be delivered a message that it would not be able to simply snap its fingers and find receptive Western executives.

Google has followed a more predictable path. The launch of Google.cn in early 2006 signalled an expected capitulation to the Chinese regime.[97] After claiming that its US-based search service was inefficient, the company decided to filter politically sensitive material from the Chinese version. Mention of 'the three T's'—Tibet, Taiwan and the Tiananmen massacre—were forbidden. Not unlike Microsoft, the launch incurred the wrath of critics, but Google shareholders refused to force the company to adopt an anti-censorship proposal that would have required its products not to engage in filtering.[98] Google co-founder Sergey Brin, speaking in early 2007 about the company's decision to compromise its principles in China admitted: 'On a business level, that decision to censor ... was a net negative'.[99] He recognised that its reputation had suffered in the US and Europe. Months earlier, in Washington, Brin had indicated that, 'perhaps now the principled approach makes more sense'. He changed his view, however, telling Google shareholders in May 2008 that, 'I say at the outset that I'm pretty proud of what we've been able to accomplish in China ... Google has a far superior track record than other ... internet search companies in China.'[100] A study released by Citizen Lab in June 2008 found that the sites censored by Yahoo, Microsoft and Google were 'often the only sources of alternative information available for politically sensitive topics.' Moreover, the companies appeared to be selecting themselves the sites to be blocked. [101]

Google's senior policy counsel Andrew McLaughlin wrote on the Google blog that the company was 'not happy' about the Chinese rules but hoped 'that over time everyone in the world will enjoy full access to information'. He claimed that engagement with the regime would ultimately bring better results for users, though provided no evidence to back this up.[102] The company said its commitment to transparency meant it would inform users that particular webpages had been censored on government orders. This key fact, many Chinese web users told me, made them reluctantly admire Google more than any other internet company. In comparison, Microsoft has removed the censorship notification from every search page and buried it in a separate 'help' page.

In a less than convincing performance with the *New Yorker* in June 2008, Google CEO Eric Schmidt said that he never anticipated countries such as China would implement router-level censorship. Considering his company contributes to the regime's filtering, Schmidt's naivety was absurd.

During testimony to the US House of Representatives in early 2006, Google's vice-president of Global Communications and Public Affairs, Elliot Schrage, argued that the company had found a 'different path, a path rooted in the very pragmatic calculation that we could provide more access to more information to more Chinese citizens', and pledged not to maintain services such as email on Chinese soil because it couldn't guarantee privacy.[103] Executives conveniently didn't mention that the company was losing the economic battle to China's leading search engine, Baidu.com—the CNNIC released a report in September 2007 that found Baidu with 74.5 per cent market share[104]—and wanted a larger piece of a massively growing internet market.[105]

Leading Chinese blogger Isaac Mao wrote a letter to Google's founders in early 2007 telling them that Chinese web users still loved their products—'a hope for many people around the world to open their thinking'—but expressed concern that its capitulation to the regime's dictates over censorship was ruining its image. Mao recommended three ideas to improve its China strategy. Firstly, to 'set up a US$1 billion corporate venture fund to invest in China's internet pioneer sites and cutting edge companies'. Secondly, 'develop anti-censorship tools and service for global internet users'. Finally, 'increase the incentive to Chinese Google Adsense users'. He warned that 'compromise' was a sure way to ruin Google's long-term viability.[106] It was a warning equally relevant to every other internet company operating in China.

Yahoo's behaviour has been the most problematic. Evidence emerged in 2005 that the company had supplied Chinese authorities with information about a journalist, Shi Tao, and allowed the regime to link his personal email to an anonymous message that allegedly breached government secrets. He was sentenced to ten years in prison for sending foreign websites the text of a 'top secret' message that was given to his publication and which warned Chinese reporters of the risks involved in the return of dissidents on the fifteenth anniversary of the Tiananmen Square massacre.

Yahoo founder Jerry Yang admitted the act of complicity. 'I do not like the outcome of what happens with these things,' he said in 2005, 'but we have to follow the law'.[107] By 2006, it emerged that at least four Chinese journalists were in jail thanks to Yahoo. Li Zhi, Wang Xiaoning and Jiang Lijun also suffered because the internet company had placed its email servers in China with local partner Alibaba.[108] Despite the vast press these cases received in the West, there was little about the activities of the dissidents themselves. Their use of the internet was often incendiary. For example, Wang Xiaoning had edited and contributed to e-journals calling for open elections, a multi-party system and a separation of government powers. He called socialism a 'totalitarian and despotic system' and argued that the Chinese regime was 'outwardly democratic but inwardly despotic'.[109]

Yahoo was soon under international pressure to explain its actions, its reputation in tatters.[110] A 'statement of beliefs' issued by Yahoo—an attempt to express 'deep concern' over government internet censorship—did little to appease the critics[111] (though Yahoo shareholders refused to vote for a proposal that would have forced the company to adopt tighter controls when working in non-democratic countries).[112] Further evidence of Yahoo's collusion emerged in late 2007 with the revelation that an organisation called the Beijing Association of Online Media—comprising some of the world's leading technology companies, including Ericsson, Nokia, Intel and Yahoo—had used a 200-strong team of 'volunteers' which reported more than 20 000 examples of politically prohibited web content since mid 2006.[113]

The families of two imprisoned journalists sued Yahoo for contributing to the torture of jailed dissidents.[114] When the lawsuit was filed in the US under the Alien Tort Claims Act and the Torture Victims Protection Act, this was the first time an internet company was forced to answer charges against its behaviour in a court of law.[115] Yahoo insisted the charges be dropped—a spokesman said 'every sovereign nation has the right to regulate speech within its border'[116]—but released a statement to appease the critics. 'Yahoo is dismayed that citizens in China have been imprisoned for expressing their political views on the internet,' it read. The company claimed it had told the Chinese authorities that it condemned 'punishment of any activity internationally recognised as free expression'.[117]

The US Congress was eventually brought into the debate in 2007 when it announced it was investigating whether Yahoo had lied during testimony in early 2006, denying it had any knowledge of the Chinese regime's intentions towards Shi Tao. The company soon apologised for failing to inform lawmakers of what it knew, and when, and it settled the lawsuits with the Chinese families.[118] The late US Democrat Tom Lantos admonished Yahoo. 'While technically and financially you are giants,' he said, 'morally you are pygmies.'[119] By early 2008 it looked like Yahoo was starting to slowly respond to years of public pressure: it asked the Bush administration to request that the Chinese release the dissidents imprisoned on account of its complicity.[120] It was revealed that the company had spent US$1.6 million in 2007 lobbying the US administration on issues related to China and the rights and responsibilities of US companies in the international market.[121] Yahoo's major sponsorship of the 2008 Beijing conference 'One World, One Web' however, which aimed to track the changing behaviour of web users and their involvement in current affairs through social networking sites, suggested that the corporation was still willing to turn a blind eye to repression.[122]

Similar sentiments were expressed by Congressmen and -women in early 2006 when representatives from Yahoo, Google, Microsoft and Cisco Systems were interrogated over their collusion with the Chinese. An Iowa Republican, James A Leach, challenged Google's Elliot Schrage to justify his company's actions. 'So if this Congress wanted to learn how to censor,' Leach said, 'we'd go to you—the company that should symbolise the greatest freedom of information in the history of man'.[123] The fact that China is starting to threaten America's political and economic dominance should not be discounted as a factor behind some of these critics' stridency.[124] In early 2008 China rightly challenged the US's annual human rights report, which was critical of China, and branded its position as hypocritical. The US invasion of Iraq, the regime argued, was the 'greatest humanitarian disaster' of the modern world.[125]

A number of senators in 2006 proposed establishing the Global Online Freedom Act, rendering illegal American companies doing business in repressive countries such as China. It would ban corporations from filtering certain political or religious terms and disclose any filtering to users.[126] The European Union followed suit, passing a proposal in early 2008 to treat internet filtering as a trade barrier and discussed establishing a European version of the American-inspired Global Online Freedom Act.[127] Another US Senate investigation in May 2008 pressured Google, Yahoo, Microsoft and Cisco to better protect user privacy in China or face stronger regulation. Democrat Senator Dick Durbin compared the 'intolerably slow' negotiations over a code of conduct for companies working in repressive regimes to the behaviour of corporations in apartheid South Africa.[128]

While it sounded like a positive development in corporate transparency, leading Hong Kong–based academic Rebecca MacKinnon told me in a phone conversation that there were fundamental problems with it.[129] 'It seeks to divide the world into good countries and bad countries,' she said, 'and it regulates the behaviour of these internet services in the bad countries but does not allow for the fact that governments in all countries overstep their power and are constantly pushing the boundaries of what they can do.'

MacKinnon argued that the Act would hold the United States 'as the gold standard for freedom of speech ... and creates a structure for how these companies would be regulated directed by the US government'. Many Chinese would find this hypocritical, patronising and interventionist. After all, why should only Washington be able to determine which countries are democratic and which are not? MacKinnon reminded me of the ever-growing censorship of websites in India, the world's largest democracy. She advocated an agreed voluntary code of conduct between the major internet players, though their hands are inevitably tied by shareholders.[130]

'The broader problem is that American business executives have little training in how to deal with ethics in a corrupt and totalitarian global business environment,' wrote Peter Navarro, a business professor at UC Irvine.[131] MacKinnon argued that the only positive that could come out of the experience was that Yahoo and all internet companies are now being forced to consider the human rights implications of their business decisions before launching in a new market. The price could be steep later if they refuse to do so.[132]

There is only an issue with Yahoo's behaviour if one believes that companies should operate with human rights in mind. Most do not. Rupert Murdoch's News Corporation, one of the great opportunists in China, has long tried to appease the Chinese authorities in its attempt to capture the market, including killing stories in its Western newspapers that might upset Beijing.[133] The outlook at News Corp doesn't look brighter if the baton is passed to Murdoch's son and likely successor, James. He chastised Western media in 2001 for their focus on human rights and insisted that 'these destabilizing forces today are very, very dangerous for the Chinese government'. He also labelled Falun Gong as 'dangerous' and an 'apocalyptic cult', which 'clearly does not have the success of China at heart'.[134] Former Murdoch lieutenant Bruce Dover, who spent most of the 1990s working for the mogul in China trying to wrench open its market, argues in his book *Rupert's Adventures in China* that Murdoch never really understood the country and although he achieved some of his goals, including the entry of his social networking site MySpace into the Chinese market in 2007, the regime also used him to rehabilitate its image in the West after the 1989 Tiananmen Square massacre.[135]

The founder of Yahoo's Chinese partner Alibaba has said that he is content to run websites that are censored because good money is coming in.[136] The company ran images on its Chinese home page of wanted Tibetans in the aftermath of the uprising in Lhasa in early 2008. A police phone number was included for citizens to report any information about the 'fugitives'.[137] An executive for the large Chinese site Sina. com said in 2001 that his company was all too willing to work with the regime. Hurst Lin said that, 'the first rule we take is that we only work with state-sponsored media … We actually do not have any, how shall I say, censorship issues because the content has already been cleared'.[138] In the same year Chinese internet portal Sohu.com, whose major investors included Goldman Sachs, Intel Corporation and Dow Jones, told visitors to its chat room that 'topics which damage the reputation of the state' are forbidden. Furthermore, 'if you are a Chinese national and willingly choose to break these laws, Sohu.com is legally obliged to report you to the Public Security Bureau'.[139]

Along with state censoring of the net, the regime has cleverly co-opted private businesses into the process, forcing them to censor touchy material or face expulsion from the country. *Shanghai Daily* reported in September 2007 that authorities had blocked access to over 18 401 'illegal' sites since April, while a senior executive from a large Chinese internet company told McClatchy Newspapers in October 2007 that her company employed many net monitors and received directions from authorities 'nearly every hour'.[140] *The South China Morning Post* revealed in March 2007 that Sohu.com deleted around 100 000 comments made to its site every day.

I was surprised to find that many web users in China were willing to overlook Western internet companies colluding with the regime. Blogger Mica said it was 'simply the price of doing business'. Jeremy Goldkorn, founder of Danwei.org, told me that he thought Yahoo had overstepped the mark by so actively assisting the regime, but others such as Microsoft and Google were 'infusing skills ... [and] bringing more people into the economy of the internet. It's bringing more people into shared discussions than would be if they weren't here.'

Progress one Chinese step at a time

I met Gin (an alias), a book editor, in a beautiful, lush Shanghai park.[141] A softly spoken man with a wispy beard, he was fairly proficient in English and, while critical of the regime at times, overall he believed it was doing 'OK'. Gin repeatedly said that he hoped I would not simply write about an oppressed Chinese people longing for Western freedoms, something he regretted seeing in the *New York Times* on a regular basis. Gin, like most Chinese I met, was happy to talk about most subjects, but he didn't want politics to be a focus. I sensed that this was not because he was afraid but simply that it wasn't a major focus in his life.

Gin painted a Chinese society that had far bigger issues to worry about than internet censorship. He said that life was much freer than ten years ago and the situation was not as black and white as Westerners often portrayed. Books were routinely banned but, if someone really wanted a title, the active black market in books could usually oblige. An average print run was between 5000 and 10 000, he said, but many Western titles, with the exception of Harry Potter and Dan Brown, sold poorly. China's book market is one of the biggest in the world, fourth behind the US,

Germany and Japan, and online literature has exploded the popularity of new writers.[142] Political writing remains rare, however. Literature on mobile phones is a rapidly rising trend and publisher Penguin has struck a deal with a local mobile company to place Penguin Classics on phones.[143] John Makinson, world head of the Penguin Group, said in early 2008 that the service had been so popular in China that his company was now looking towards India. 'There used to be a cultural hauteur among publishers: an idea had to prove itself in New York or London first—then we'd export it to India and China,' Makinson said. 'Now we'll take something that works first in Beijing or Delhi and try it elsewhere.'[144]

'Chinese people are still not used to the law protecting them,' Gin argued. Although a number of citizens were starting to challenge this passive relationship with establishment power, it was still rare. Not unlike the unwritten and constantly changing banned 'keywords' on the internet, Gin said that book publishers faced a similarly evolving but erratic situation. 'It changes from governor to governor,' he sighed.

Gin's attitude towards the country's media was mixed. He suspected that many of the young censors employed by the regime 'don't believe in what they're doing, because there isn't much pressure from the media, but they feel they have no choice, receiving the government salary'. But without the internet, he said, the Chinese wouldn't know anything about dissenters, even though '99 per cent' of blogs talked about food and daily life. Gin read websites that discussed democracy but was circumspect about the sincerity of leaders who talked about 'democracy with Chinese characteristics': 'Is the country ready for free elections?'

In perhaps his most perceptive comment, Gin said that censorship worried Western human rights campaigners more than the Chinese themselves. 'If you're clever enough [online], you can find a way around government rules,' he said. The fact that most Chinese appear unruffled about these restrictions—nationalism and consumerism are the rising ideologies in the country—indicates that the state has fairly successfully neutered any serious challenge to its rule.

I heard similar sentiments from Shanghai-based advertising guru Richard Hsu about Western misconceptions over China.[145] His office, situated in a nondescript building near the centre of the city, was designed like a luxurious apartment, with leather couches, brightly lit modern Chinese art, a friendly white husky and a fully fitted kitchen.

The place was spotless but overlooked a smog-filled horizon. Over a delicious lunch with some of his staff—many of whom were young students from New York University, a connection he had made during his years working in the city—he said that the advertising market in China was massive and growing. Money is the new God in the industry, he said, as long as political content was generally avoided. As the economy grows, Hsu said, the Chinese appetite for products will only increase. 'Somebody has to sell it to them,' he argued confidently. Hsu, with a baby face and short floppy hair, told me he had returned to China from America because he could not have creative 'freedom' there.

Not unlike Gin, Hsu said that locals couldn't understand why Westerners seemed obsessed with the 1989 Tiananmen Square massacre[146] led by democracy activists from the elite. It was never talked about, he said. 'People just want to get on with their lives. It's in the past.' Internet censorship was equally something that didn't bother most netizens. It was merely a fact of life. 'You make a problem for us,' said the head of China's internet surveillance system in 1996, 'and we'll make a law for you.'[147]

Despite the restrictions, it is true that online activists in China have found creative ways to push their message.[148] Pro-Tibet campaigners caught the world's attention in 2007 by unfurling a banner on the Great Wall of China that read, 'One World, One Dream, Free Tibet 2008', a photo of which they sent to New York using Skype and YouTube.[149] Users regularly utilise internet proxies specifically designed to circumnavigate the regime's censorship. A number of bloggers have started to challenge hosting companies for censoring their posts[150] and online censorship has forced users to design imaginative ways to explain it. If a website or blog post is pulled, bloggers often say 'I've been harmonised', but many hosting companies discovered this phrase and added the term to the banned keywords list. A more recent example is 'river crab'. If a blogger appears to talk randomly about 'river crab', they're referring to censorship.

Australian Sinologist Geremie Barme argues that the 'hype' surrounding the internet is reminiscent of the explosion of literary expression in the 1980s, a time when popular writing of all kinds seemed to challenge the country's established mores. The reach of the web is clearly far greater, but Barme cautions against exaggerating the changes (though he notes the often salacious nature of internet fiction and its ability to further cannibalise the market). The online posting of raunchy diaries and photos excited a generation that were used to reading such material surreptitiously.[151]

The Google-owned site YouTube is often blocked, but a range of alternatives has surfaced. Tudou ('potato' in Chinese) is one of the largest online video sites: the company claimed in early 2008 to have overtaken YouTube with more than one billion megabytes of data transfers daily.[152] Its 34-year-old founder, Gary Wang, is an unassuming, slightly built man who works in the company's cavernous warehouse office in Shanghai. After only two and a half years in existence, the site had become hugely popular. Wang told me the company was experiencing 10 to 15 per cent growth every week, 60 million clips were watched daily and 40 million users visited monthly. It was a phenomenon on an unprecedented scale.[153] The Tudou office didn't necessarily look like it belonged to an internet company. Colourful toys dotted the expansive rooms and a few IT geeks sat glued to their computers. Wang said some employees never went home—they slept at work. He joked that some didn't even have anywhere else to sleep. I think he was being half-serious.

Wang, who is French- and American-educated, used to work for various global media companies before he realised the need for an online video site, not least because he found Chinese state television so boring and wanted to access foreign content. He said he was frustrated by the necessity of filtering, but the company had been forced to design sophisticated ways to detect keywords and delete 'suspect' videos. The authorities usually called at least once a week to alert Tudou to one video or another and Wang and his team either automatically removed the video or argued for its validity. Wang remained optimistic that Chinese society would continue to open up, but nobody knew how far the regime would push its censorship policies. Technically speaking, the government has to approve every moving image, but sites like Tudou make that impossible.[154] Wang said that his site, like many others, could be closed down at any time. The company received a light slap on the wrist and a fine in early 2008 and was forced to institute tighter content filtering. Tudou was accused by authorities of being 'slightly unhealthy'.[155]

Wang told me that many users had uploaded videos of a popular Japanese manga series, *Death Note*, and authorities told them that the films were causing high suicide rates among school students and had to be removed. Wang and his team opened negotiations and suggested that they could block certain words on their search engine, making it difficult to find the videos. Eventually they were directed to remove the offending films. Working in an internet company in China wasn't simply about turning a profit and market share; it was equally about tough negotiations with communist drones. The entry of Facebook into the Chinese market was also filled with potential traps. What if individuals try to set up a group that the Communist Party deems inconsistent with its vision?[156] (though this didn't stop Prime Minister Wen Jiabao creating a Facebook page of his own in May 2008). Murdoch's MySpace faced similar challenges and the launch of the social networking site in 2007 resulted in human rights campaigners expressing concern that the regime could monitor the text, pictures, music and videos posted by users.[157]

During our conversations, Wang struck me as somebody who was philosophical about why companies such as Yahoo and Google filtered their material and didn't express any anger towards them. Although most of the keywords involved political issues—Falun Gong, Taiwan and political reform—Wang didn't 'see any revolution coming and personally I don't want to see any revolution. I think it's nice to move gradually.' Although acknowledging that he would love to see democracy in China in the long run, he was also of the view that most Western journalists he met only wanted to ask how he coped with 'oppressive censorship', the clear implication being that life in the West was superior and the reporter only wanted information that confirmed this view. 'They seem to pity us,' Wang said.[158] For my own part, I didn't pity his plight but did want to know how the dynamics of Chinese censorship worked.

Wang was media savvy and often surprisingly frank; he clearly didn't fear expressing displeasure with the regime. He said he felt more American than Chinese—and I understood why. He could have decided to live in America but couldn't resist the lure of China's internet explosion, something far more challenging in many ways than the West's relative openness. It was a sentiment I sensed throughout my visit: the tenacity of many web gurus to navigate the censors while producing a useful product. Many Chinese emigrants have returned home to work in a previously untapped market, at a time in history when China's products and knowledge are in great demand. Unquestioning and apolitical capitalism is an intoxicating mix.

I recalled with Wang that I'd seen promos on CNN for the YouTube presidential debates. Viewers filmed questions on video and emailed them to CNN, who then chose a small selection to be answered by Democratic and Republican presidential candidates a year before the 2008 election. The idea was that citizens would feel more empowered in the political process and didn't simply have to rely on hackneyed questions from journalists. I asked Wang whether he could imagine a similar experiment in China. He joked that it was hard to imagine a regional mayor using Tudou to promote his message, but he could dream (though a number of officials in a town in eastern China established blogs in 2006 to better communicate with citizens[159]). I wondered if YouTube's ever-increasing association with the establishment, including its purchase by Google, would kill the 'cool' factor with its army of users. Wang said he was having a similar conversation earlier in the day and concluded that the popularity of YouTube didn't seem to be decreasing. If anything, it was growing by the day, but competitors would inevitably challenge its dominance.

We dined together a few nights later in Beijing with Wang's girlfriend and blogger friends who were mostly IT gurus. We met at a large new development near the centre of the city, a maze of high-rise buildings, manicured grass, 7-Eleven outlets and gyms. It was immaculate and a little anodyne. Wang said that such sites were springing up across the country, though he wondered if the thousands of empty office spaces would be filled. Over countless courses of rich Chinese food, I conversed with Bo Yang, the founder of Douban.com, a site launched in 2005 that compiled user-generated reviews and recommendations of movies, books and music. He had studied in America and worked for IBM before returning to China and entering the internet boom. Bo said that the government sometimes called and requested 'suspect' postings to be removed. Unlike Tudou, where the site automatically removed videos related to certain keywords when activated, only users could report problematic postings. Softly spoken, Bo said he was frustrated that it was rarely clear what subjects were beyond the pale, apart from the obvious ones such as Falun Gong.

Douban's massive popularity, according to Bo, was due to young Chinese, especially those born in the 1980s, who wanted to read and rate other people's opinions on local and international works. In a country where expressing individual views was not encouraged, sites like Douban were almost revolutionary, even if, Bo told me, the site was often filled with passionate pros and cons of the *Transformers* movie.

Wang featured in *New York Times* columnist Thomas Friedman's 2005 book, *The World is Flat*, as an example of the ways in which the internet represented the 'newest anti-homogenising force'. Tudou was praised in Friedman's overly optimistic and exaggerated tome as representing 'China's newest Cultural Revolution ... driven this time from the bottom-up'. The author went on: 'That's why I am confident that this flattening phase of globalisation is not going to mean more Americanisation, but more globalisation of local cultures, art forms, styles, recipes, literature, videos and opinions—more and more local content made global.'[160]

Friedman's thesis was almost compelling—and the internet in China has undoubtedly democratised information for the masses—but he conveniently ignored the role of Western companies and governments in continuing the repressive nature of non-democratic regimes. Furthermore, his quasi-religious belief in the power of the market to equally distribute resources to everybody across the globe was a refusal to see the millions of Chinese peasants still struggling and unlikely to find much consolation in an internet connection.

Nevertheless, it is undeniable that the internet has pressured authorities that are deemed incompetent or unresponsive. In 2007 the city of Xiamen saw residents stage mass protests against a proposed chemical plant, and postings on websites helped organise the dissent. As a result, officials pledged to tighten controls on the net and force users to post their real names when commenting.[161] Protestors launched what local media claimed was the world's biggest text message campaign, sending one million messages to authorities. The project was shelved.[162]

When hundreds of men and boys were discovered working as slave labourers in brick kilns in central China in 2007, shocking a nation and the world, the internet allowed outrage and despair to be aired. Four hundred fathers of other missing children joined together and posted a petition accusing local officials of ignoring their plight.

It soon ricocheted around the web. There were limits to what the net censors allowed to be posted, but the fact that provincial governments were temporarily in the spotlight was an encouraging step towards greater accountability.[163]

Other cities have seen bloggers expose police physically attacking street sellers after local television journalists refused to cover the incidents. Officials regularly deny or downplay these incidents, but the ability to post mobile phone footage on Tudou or other online video sites makes their positions untenable.[164] Bloggers are slowly undermining the authority of state-run media and both parties know it. I noticed in China's English-language papers during my visit that bloggers' posts were published on a variety of non-political topics. Some officials recognised that they could no longer play by the old rules of obfuscation. The sheer number of bloggers had forced the regime to incorporate new media into its strategy, but it's impossible to prevent ever-increasing leaks and web-led embarrassment of corrupt or incompetent authorities.

Nevertheless, Fons Tuinstra, a former foreign correspondent and Shanghai-based internet entrepreneur, urges Westerners not to rush to judgement on the potentially liberating possibilities of the new technology. He writes that the internet has in fact 'strengthened the power of the central government, not undermined it'.[165] Tuinstra argues that 'for the first time in China's history the central government has a popular and relatively easy means of eavesdropping on what is happening and being said in the country'. While a small number of Chinese want to overthrow the government and ditch the Communist Party, the vast majority 'engage with the internet … not in fear of what the government might learn, but knowing that what they are doing offers them a powerful new way to reach the government'. Unlike in the West, the media is not generally seen as independent and therefore the Chinese internet 'fits well into the long-standing tradition of other media by acting as a negotiation tool between the state and its citizens'. Like all previous forms of communication, most Chinese are not surprised that the regime wants to regulate and control the message and 'tend to see the control as an inherent part of their reality—and most of them would rather look for ways to deal with it than have their energy consumed by opposing it'.[166] The regime has cleverly harnessed an invaluable safety valve that releases society's frustrations and desires. 'Most of what people do on the internet is complain,' said blogger Wang Xiaofeng. 'At least we now have a place to blow off some steam.'[167]

This is one argument. However, as a 2003 study by the University of California found, nearly 80 per cent of Chinese thought that the internet would teach them more about politics; this compares with 43 per cent in America, 31 per cent in Japan and 48 per cent in South Korea.[168] The internet in China may be restricted, censored and filtered, but the potential of the technology is there for citizens to participate in a system that until recently was little more than a spectator sport.

Taking 'our' values elsewhere

One evening I met an Australian journalist working for Dow Jones news wire in Shanghai. Although he primarily wrote financial stories, he said he had never been warned by his employer or the Chinese authorities to censor himself. He acknowledged he was in China at the 'pleasure of the Chinese government' and recalled only one occasion, when invited to speak on CNBC TV, that he let slip that a number of representatives in Shanghai attending an economic conference were from 'non-democratic governments'. He was initially anxious that his bosses would worry the Chinese could read this statement as an attack on China itself, but he heard nothing more about it. The journalist alluded to the fact that self-censorship was a key factor in maintaining order. Many of his Chinese colleagues regularly avoided political discussions, but he said he wondered if they used the internet to engage privately.

China has changed radically since my first visit in 2000. By 2007 the country felt far more confident, proudly Chinese yet keen to appropriate certain Western motifs. Restaurant entrepreneur Cho Chong Gee, a 50-year-old Malaysian who moved to China in 2000 to ride the economic boom and with whom I spent time in Beijing, personified this transformation.[169] Ad man Richard Hsu had asked me to bring an iPod to Cho and it gave me the opportunity to savour some of the finest food I'd eaten in months. Cho had just opened an Asian-style restaurant, Sambal Urban, housed in an ultra-modern apartment complex, adjacent to a large gym and other high-class restaurants. He owned three other enterprises across the city, all beautifully decked out in Bang & Olufsen chic. Clean lines and a modern Chinese design paid homage to the country's artistic history but equally embraced a hybrid style unafraid to liberally borrow from whatever took Cho's fancy. He was intending to build a boutique hotel in time for the 2008 Olympic Games.

Cho had invited me to share a meal with him in the restaurant. A handful of Westerners were eating around us, seated on white chairs at white tables decorated with yellow flowers and vases, with large windows and an oddly Gothic style setting the mood. Cho said his usual clientele was a combination of expatriates and moneyed Chinese. After a few strongly mixed mojitos and Vietnamese rolls with mango, followed by beef, vegetables and fish, I asked Cho about the rise of his primary customers, the wealthy elite. He told me that none of his friends—in the arts, film-making, fashion or fine dining—ever talked about the perilous position of the country's vast peasant class. He was intrigued that I was investigating internet censorship in China and the crackdown on dissent. It wasn't something he encountered or thought about. He said he didn't like the fact that the regime was filtering websites, but his position in a tight circle meant it wasn't an issue that needed to bother him. He wasn't indifferent to human rights issues, but economic empowerment, a key plank of contemporary Communist Party thinking, had rendered such thoughts largely irrelevant.

Cho spoke with a warmth that was common in many Chinese that I met, though he was disconnected from the social cost of the country's rapid growth. He worked hard—we drank together on a few nights in one stylishly appointed bar and he skilfully moved around the smoky dance floor mingling with virtually every client, including cashed-up locals and brash Americans—and saw himself as the kind of entrepreneur who could far more easily succeed in China than anywhere else. He was willing to sacrifice political freedom; it didn't seem to be an onerous decision.

Cho's story was just like that of millions of others in China and highlighted how censorship is an issue to which many remain oblivious. But political and social activists were starting to be heard. Not unlike every other country discussed in this book, the internet will not on its own simply transform China into a pro-Western nation, nor did anybody I met want this to happen. While new technology has certainly empowered millions of netizens to communicate with each other, the world and officials in ways that have the potential to spark thoughts of political change, it has thus far primarily led to an explosion of China's entertainment economy. Although I heard many people express dissatisfaction with elements of one-party rule, it was very rare to hear anybody take what would seem to be the next logical step. What else could exist? The transformative effect of the internet has been the introduction of choice. 'I only watch TV if it's playing on the bus or in the background,' a Beijing web user said. 'You find a more interesting perspective on the internet.'[170]

Early twenty-first century China, almost shamelessly showy in the face of massive economic development, is becoming even more paranoid in maintaining the kind of social control over its one billion people. For the vast majority of Chinese, the world outside still barely exists. Blogger Mica told me she was interested in visiting a country in the Middle East with her American friend but was immediately told that the US State Department's website said it was dangerous for tourists. Her friend was amazed that Mica had never read about the troubles but Mica protested. Local media had reported nothing about it and the State Department website was blocked. 'I don't know what the truth is,' she said.

The media manipulation of the Beijing Olympic Games within China reinforced this reality. In early 2008 when Australian Prime Minister Kevin Rudd, speaking in Mandarin to students at Peking University, gently chastised the Chinese over its human rights abuses in Tibet, the local media completely airbrushed his criticisms. The regime's insecurity dictated shielding its citizens from the truth. Nine men, the unelected figures in the politburo, are determined to maintain control at any cost.

This determination will never succeed.

Afterword

ONE YEAR AFTER I returned from my travels, in April 2008, Democratic presidential hopeful Hillary Clinton said that as president of the United States she would 'obliterate' Iran if the Islamic Republic launched a nuclear attack on Israel.[1] It was a typically bellicose statement eerily reminiscent of US president George W Bush's bluster. Clinton's hawkish position was both irresponsible and depressingly reminiscent of similar outbursts by fundamentalist mullahs in Iran.

While Clinton happily talked about the destruction of an ancient nation—and most of the mainstream media elicited little outrage since similar statements had become commonplace during the Bush years—this merely reinforced my belief that alternative sources of information and communication were essential to foster greater understanding between the West and the rest. The ease with which Clinton tossed out a comment that would mean the death of millions of Iranians, including friends there, reminded me of an evening in Tehran in 2007.

One night, journalist and editor Bozorgmehr Sharafedin invited some colleagues to his apartment to discuss life and love in Iran. We ate ham (illegal, but sourced at Armenian shops), smoked cheese and potato salad and downed countless shots of Smirnoff vodka. In the privacy of Bozorg's home, the group felt comfortable speaking frankly about politics. A mullah had died in the city of Qom the day before and Bozorg and a few others threw their arms up to celebrate. 'That's one less of the old bastards.' For these progressive, worldly souls who craved an Iran that could readily engage with the global community, Clinton's outburst diminished these possibilities and defined them solely through the perceived position of President Mahmoud Ahmadinejad.

Bozorg emailed me in early 2008 to say he'd received a job with BBC Persia in London and would be leaving his homeland for the first time. He wrote: 'The good news is that I am leaving in April, the cursed place. I love my country but I really hate it. That's Iranian life. Always dealing with dilemmas.'

It was a sentiment that perfectly captured the view of many people I met across the globe. 'I adore my country but loathe the government.' 'I admire the regime but detest its rules and regulations.' 'Why can't life be easier?' 'Why does Washington insist on meddling in our affairs?' 'How can we forge an identity that encompasses various political, social and religious perspectives?' 'I want my country to be better so I have to go online to find like-minded individuals.' Unsurprisingly, bloggers in Saudi Arabia, China and Egypt all share similar dreams and desires to those of us in the West, including a right to self-determination and hope for personal and political freedoms. Our role should be to engage individuals from across the political spectrum who believe in open debate and listen to their wants and desires.

Yet many in the Western media are still failing to achieve these simple aims. An intriguing experiment devised by the British-based Online Journalism blog in 2008 featured a series of cartograms that showed how the world was seen through global media outlets.[2] British-based dailies such as Rupert Murdoch's *Sun* and *Daily Mail* favour news about countries closer to home, predominantly with white, British immigrants who speak English. *The Economist* covers the world more equally and *The Guardian* is the foremost daily publication to attempt a semblance of global reach. Murdoch's *Australian* is embarrassingly parochial in its obsession with the West.

Web-based outlets (such as Slate and France's Rue 89) are able to expand their scope because of the decreasing amount of resources for journalists. Freelance correspondents in various countries simply send regular dispatches. The greatest coverage of world affairs is featured by the blogosphere, which, according to the report, 'seems unbeatable at providing niche news'. This will never replace the invaluable infrastructure of a major news organisation to make and break stories, but online media have already filled the gaping holes left by falling advertising revenue[3] and shrinking imagination in the West.[4]

Personal stories that resonated across the world during my travels offered telling examples of courage. I was particularly moved and angered by the late 2007 arrest of Saudi blogger Fouad Al-Farhan (he was released without charge in April 2008). His generosity of spirit and rejection of the unyielding Islam practised in the country should be embraced in the West as an example of a moderate Muslim fighting for a more inclusive religious atmosphere. As our friend Ahmed Al-Omran of the Saudi Jeans blog wrote in April 2008, after the regime filtered a number of Saudi websites campaigning for Farhan's release: 'They [the authorities] are wrong if they think the blockage will stop us from raising Fouad's issue over and over again until he is free and back to his family and friends.'[5] This was the kind of solidarity that the blogging community was generating.

I remain in regular contact with many of the individuals featured in this book, informing them of my work and hearing their tales of activism and even personal lives. I feel privileged to have entered worlds that remain nearly impossible to penetrate without an appreciation of their blogging bravery. I never viewed my interview subjects as merely a journalistic project; rather, they represented an opportunity to develop ongoing relationships with people who could continually broaden my knowledge of the Middle East, China and Cuba.

Central to the thinking behind this book is challenging the Western-centric perspectives of the mainstream media and its elite. *New York Times* foreign affairs columnist Thomas Friedman, in his book *The World is Flat*, argues that, 'several technological and political forces have converged, and that has produced a global, web-enabled playing field that allows for multiple forms of collaboration without regard to geography or distance—or soon, even language'.[6] Friedman believes that every citizen of the world aspires to Western opulence because they enjoy using Google and eBay to buy products online. The 'global supply chain' of products and ideas is supposedly too intoxicating for most people to resist.

He optimistically concludes that Indian IT workers or Chinese manufacturers are helping to reduce the world's poverty by servicing the needs of increasingly demanding Western markets. It's an appealing image but fundamentally flawed. In my experience, this is an overly simplistic understanding of the information technology revolution. Not every Cuban wishes to purchase Nike trainers online (though they should have the option of doing so, of course). Rampant consumerism hardly solves many of the world's problems; it merely exacerbates them.[7]

Friedman's ideas are widely traded in the mainstream media, but the internet and blogosphere challenge his notion of a truly connected world. While students in Saudi Arabia are chatting online to friends in Egypt or Syria, their values, goals and dreams are radically different to the equivalent scene in Australia or America. Political goals—Islamism, secular democracy, socialism or dictatorship—are not something to be imported from the West to 'save' the non-developed world. Western hypocrisy is ably assisted by loudly objecting to rigged elections in Zimbabwe but remaining silent when US allies such as Jordan and Egypt engage in equally egregious behaviour.[8] An enduring colonial mindset predominantly challenges regimes that are useless to 'us'. Friedman aggressively supported the disastrous 2003 Iraq War, thus he's clearly in favour of violently importing his 'flat world'. The editor of *Newsweek International*, Fareed Zakaria, who also supported the Iraq invasion, similarly argues in his book *The Rise of the Rest* that the world is becoming nothing more than 'consumers, producers, inventors, thinkers, dreamers and doers … because of American ideas and actions'.[9]

Inherent in Friedman's (and Zakaria's) musings is the declining ability of America to influence global affairs. This is something Friedman fears, whereas I welcome it more cautiously. Most people in this book would agree with me. The blogosphere allows conversations about the shifting centres of power in ways that the state media in repressive regimes refuse to do. The underlying presumptions of those who believe in the combination of capitalism, free trade and rising prosperity leading inevitably to liberal democracies ignore the fact that autocratic regimes, such as China, are increasingly showing citizens around the world how the benefits of remarkable growth can neuter a desire for political freedom. My experience in China bears this theory out.

Writer Mark Leonard, in his book *What Does China Think?*[10], argues that the years of the Bush administration have heightened these attitudes: 'Whereas American diplomats talk about regime change, their Chinese counterparts talk about respect for sovereignty and the diversity of civilisations.'[11] It may be a hopelessly naive position, but much of the world finds it compelling. Tragically, argues author Ian Buruma, 'democracy would be a far more persuasive model than Chinese or Russian autocracy if some of its proponents were less eager to believe that the open society comes out of a barrel of a gun'.[12] This book hopes to show how incomplete and inadequate are our stereo-typical images of a world that has become at once smaller thanks to the internet but seemingly more threatening due to misunderstand-ings between people and cultures. A global poll released on the 2008 anniversary of International Press Freedom Day found that the vast majority of citizens supported the idea of media freedom and opposed government control over the internet.[13] It was an encouraging indica-tion that people understood the importance of gaining diverse and unbi-ased information.

I have argued that coverage of the vast majority of the globe is almost inevitably viewed through the lens of a Western filter and its usefulness to 'us'. It's unsurprising that bloggers, with all their faults, prejudices and blind spots, would enter the fray and offer alternative perspectives. This is not about dispensing with the well-resourced mainstream but recognising the inherent worth of other players. Arianna Huffington, founder of the hugely successful news site the Huffington Post, has said that 'traditional media just need to realise that the online world isn't the enemy. In fact, it's the thing that will save them, if they fully embrace it.'[14] Collaboration between writers, readers and editors should be welcomed as a possible way to re-energise accountable journalism. The web's inventor, Sir Tim Berners-Lee, said in 2008 that a future internet would place 'all the data in the world' at the fingertips of every user, inevitably making journalism and life itself more inclusive.[15]

Improving our media's reach and accountability is an important task. Greater involvement between the Western media and the rest of the world would be a start.[16] I remember talking in Havana to independ-ent journalist Ana Leonor Diaz, who told me about her years living in the United States and consuming various media outlets. It was a plethora compared to Cuban state media and Fidel Castro's dirge-like pronouncements. She missed the ability to access various perspectives easily—and this was before the internet age—but relished the challenge of reforming her own nation from within. She wanted the world to hear her and listen to her dreams about a post-Castro country. But most Western reporters aren't interested. Providing a critical platform for people such as Diaz is surely the role of journalists, not merely reporting the utterances of the rich and powerful. Untrained monkeys can regurgitate press releases.

Propagandists on all sides are the enemy of open enquiry. This book wouldn't have been written without the terror attacks of September 11, 2001; they forced me to understand how it's now more important than ever to hear the voices of the non-Western world, the majority of the planet. From Saudi Arabia to Cuba, Egypt to Iran and Syria to China, alternative media and the blogosphere are providing an outlet to hear the hopes and fears of a generation that wants to be heard.

Are we listening?

Acknowledgements

This book covers multiple continents and time zones. The sensitivity of the material makes the work necessarily collaborative. Without trust between contacts and myself, I could not have completed the research. My safety wasn't unimportant, but I was able to pack my bags and leave. From Cuba to Egypt, Iran to Syria and Saudi Arabia to China, I was privileged to observe lives that remain largely hidden in the West.

The book is the culmination of two years of research and travel, though I have been thinking about the issues for far longer. The following individuals offered time, insight and guidance: Wael Abbas, Ammar Abdulhamid, Mohammad Ali Abtahi, Azadeh Akbari, Nima Akbarpour, Shahram Akbarzadeh, Faiza Ambah, Issandr El Amrani, Andre De Angelis, Anthony Arnove, Iason Athanasiadis, Amar C. Bakshi, Geremie Barme, Zhila Bavafa, Barry Carr, Oscar Chepe, Avi Chomsky, Noam Chomsky, John Dagge, Ana Leonor Diaz, Gamal Eid, Samuel Farber, Fouad Al-Farhan, Carol Fleming, Jamie Florcruz, Marc Frank, Sami Ben Gharbia, Cho Chong Gee, Jeremy Goldkorn, Jordan Halevi, Ayman Haykal, Yacob Berezniak Hernandez, Ibrahim Hamidi, Hossam el-Hamalawy, Abdul Salam Haykal, Georgina Henry, David Hoorizadeh, Curt Hopkins, Ibrahim El Houdaiby, Richard Hsu, Matt Jasper, Arash Kamangir, Tony Karon, Arash Khoshkhou, Phillip Knightley, Saul Landau, Joshua Landis, Miriam Leiva, Marcelo Lopez, Jonathan Lundqvist, Rebecca MacKinnon, Dinny McMahon, Hany Massoud, Alex Mitchell, Ali Moazzami, Dr Sami Moubayed, Mousavi, Imad Moustapha, Ahmed Al-Omran, Stephen McDonell, Carlos Menendez, Hassan Nazer, Caroline Nellemann, Ayman Abdel Nour, Benython Oldfield, Julien Pain, Hector Palacios, Salam Pax, Sophie Peer, John Pilger,

Farid Pouya, Mohammed Qass, Chip Rolley, Richard Rosello, Lily Sadeghi, Amin Saikal, Shahinaz Abdel Salam, Elizardo Sanchez, Mohammed Sharqawi, Bozorgmehr Sharafedin, Deb Shaw, Rob Shilkin, Margaret Simons, Tammam Sulaiman, Salma Abu Taleb, Golnar Tabibzadeh, Fons Tuinstra, the late Andrew Vincent, Gary Wang, Philip Weiss, Andrew West, Bo Yang, Mica Yu, Dalia Ziada and Elijah Zarwan.

To the many bloggers, dissidents and writers who are unable to be identified due to personal threats and professional restrictions, I salute their desire to be heard.

Robert Fisk's lucid writings are a beacon in dark times. His ongoing support of my work—despite not using the internet—is the kind of intergenerational encouragement that I hope to pass on to others.

James Bodero-Smith and Jon Seltin were invaluable transcribers and researchers. Their insights gave the book much-needed depth. Vince Scappatura was a transcriber extraordinaire and relentlessly pursued the internet multinationals to answer questions about their activities in repressive countries. Rodrigo Acuña translated and transcribed the material from Cuba and offered never-ending information about the legacy of the 1959 Revolution and Latin America in general.

Mike Otterman, a New Yorker with Australian characteristics, was an invaluable sounding board and a source of wonderful web-links.

University of New South Wales academic Peter Slezak provided hours of intellectual stimulation, provocation, a roof over my head and friendship.

Countless friends have given advice, criticism, insights and comfort, without which this book would never have happened. I dearly thank them all: Tanveer Ahmed, Vivien Altman, Eran Asoulin, Leah Bolton, Jose Borghino, Rory Buck, Scott Burchill, Eliza Butt, Marni Cordell, Amy Corderoy, Alexandra Craig, Peter Cronau, Clare Doube, Nicky Drake, James Eyers, Clinton Fernandes, Jon Fox, Iain Giblin, Edwina Hanlon, Alina Hughes, Emily Howie, Linda Jaivin, Mark Jeanes, Sonja Karkar, Will King, Kellie King, Margo Kingston, Caitlin Kwan, Ollie Kwan, Lisa Lee-Horn, James Levy, Peter Manning, David Marr, Rory Mee, Karen Middleton, Mariesa Nicholas, Rachel Nicolson, Sybil Nolan, Cameron Olsen, Selena Papps, Alex Papps, Jack Robertson, Kath Rowley, Emma Schneider, Michael Shaik, Sharon De Silva, Luke Skinner, Michael Slezak, Jamie Slezak, Margaret Slezak, John Stace, Helga Svendsen, Sally Totman, Jason Webb and Liz Wise.

Thanks to the many readers who looked over the manuscript and provided essential thoughts and insights.

It's hard to imagine my professional life without agent Lyn Tranter. She's a force of nature that constantly offers honest truths about the industry; long may it continue.

Thanks to the indefatigable Melbourne University Press team who shepherded this project from start to finish.

The head of MUP, Louise Adler, is that rare figure in the publishing game; she takes political risks. I thank her for tackling issues that many others avoid and for offering me the time and space to deliver this work. Thank you, comrade.

My publisher, Elisa Berg, has shaped and moulded the manuscript and shared insights and sources that have greatly strengthened the text. Copyeditor Sally Moss provided essential advice.

My parents, Violet and Jeffrey Loewenstein, are the kind of people that anybody would be privileged to know, let alone an only child. They instilled in me a belief that questions should always be asked. They have shown boundless love, support, determination, appropriate concern and insight. I love them both.

Thanks to the thousands of bloggers, writers, dissidents and citizens from across the world who continue to inspire me, send invaluable information and challenge my presumptions.

This book is dedicated to the countless imprisoned journalists, dissidents, bloggers and democracy activists in every corner of the globe. They are not forgotten and their voices are being heard. Their struggle for a better tomorrow should inspire us all.

Bibliography

The following works provided valuable information about the issues raised in this book and are helpful in gaining further knowledge about the internet, the featured countries and human rights.

Ahmed, Nafeez Masaddeq, *The War on Truth: 9/11, Disinformation and the Anatomy of Terrorism*, Olive Branch Press, Northampton, 2005

Alavi, Nasrin, *We are Iran: The Persian Blogs*, Soft Skull Press, New York, 2005

Alterman, Eric, *What Liberal Media? The Truth about Bias in the News*, Basic Books, New York, 2003

Armstrong, Jerome and Markos Moulitsas Zuniga, *Crashing the Gate: How American Politics is About to Change*, Pluto Press Australia, Melbourne, 2006

Auletta, Ken, *Backstory: Inside the Business of New*, Penguin Books, London, 2003

Barme, Geremie and Linda Jaivin (eds), *New Ghosts, Old Dreams*, Times Books, New York, 1992

Blum, William, *Rogue State*, Zed Books, London, 2002

Boehlert, Eric, *Lapdogs: How the Press Rolled Over for Bush*, Free Press, New York, 2006

Borjeson, Kristina (ed.), *Into the Buzzsaw: Leading Journalists Expose the Myth of a Free Press*, Prometheus Books, New York, 2002

Burton, Bob, *Inside Spin: The Dark Underbelly of the PR Industry*, Allen and Unwin, Sydney, 2007

Buzzell, Colby, *My War: Killing Time in Iraq*, Berkley Caliber, New York, 2005

Chandrasekaran, Rajiv, *Imperial Life in the Emerald City: Inside Baghdad's Green Zone*, Bloomsbury, London, 2006

Chavez, Lydia (ed.), *Capitalism, God and a Good Cigar: Cuba Enters the Twenty-First Century*, Duke University Press, Durham, 2005

Chen, Guidi and Chuntao Wu, *Will the Boat Sink the Water? The Life of China's Peasants*, Public Affairs, New York, 2006

Chomsky, Noam, *Hegemony or Survival*, Allen and Unwin, Sydney, 2003

Chomsky, Noam, *Failed States*, Allen and Unwin, Sydney, 2006

Chomsky, Noam and David Barsamian, *What We Say Goes*, Allen and Unwin,
    Sydney, 2007
Coll, Steve, *The Bin Ladens: The Story of a Family and its Fortune*, Allen Lane,
    London, 2008
Curtis, Mark, *Web of Deceit: Britain's Real Role in the World*, Vintage, London, 2003
Dabashi, Hamid, *Iran: A People Interrupted*, The New Press, New York, 2007
Deibert, Ronald, John Palfrey, Rafal Rohozinksi and Jonathan Zittrain (eds), *Access
    Denied: The Practice and Policy of Global Internet Filtering*, MIT Press,
    Cambridge, 2008
Dover, Bruce, *Rupert's Adventures in China: How Murdoch Lost a Fortune and Found a
    Wife*, Viking, London, 2008
Edwards, Jorge, *Persona Non Grata*, Pomerica Press, New York, 1976
Ehteshami, Anoushiravan and Mahjoob Zweiri, *Iran and the Rise of the
    Neoconservatives: The Politics of Tehran's Silent Revolution*, I.B. Tauris, New York,
    2007
Estrada, Alfredo Jose, *Havana: Autobiography of a City*, Palgrave Macmillan,
    New York, 2007
Fisk, Robert, *The Age of the Warrior*, Fourth Estate, London, 2008
Franken, Al, *Lies and the Lying Liars Who Tell Them*, Penguin Books, London, 2003
Garcia, Luis M., *Child of the Revolution: Growing Up in Castro's Cuba*, Allen and
    Unwin, Sydney, 2006
Grey, Stephen, *Ghost Plane: The Untold Story of the CIA's Torture Programme*, Scribe,
    Melbourne, 2007
Herman, Edward and Noam Chomsky, *Manufacturing Consent: The Political Economy
    of the Mass Media*, Vintage, London, 1994
Hersh, Seymour, *Chain of Command: The Road from 9/11 to Abu Ghraib*, Harpercollins,
    New York, 2004
Hiro, Dilip, *The Iranian Labyrinth: Journeys through Theocratic Iran and its Furies*,
    Nation Books, New York, 2005
Hughes, Solomon, *War on Terror Inc.: Corporate Profiteering from the Politics of Fear*,
    Verso, New York, 2007
Jafarzadeh, Alireza, *The Iran Threat: President Ahmadinejad and the Coming Nuclear
    Crisis*, Palgrave Macmillan, New York, 2007
Jamail, Dahr, *Beyond the Green Zone: Dispatches from an Unembedded Journalist in
    Occupied Iraq*, Haymarket Books, Chicago, 2007
Keen, Andrew, *The Cult of the Amateur*, Nicholas Brealey Publishing, London, 2007
Kinzer, Stephen, *All the Shah's Men: An American Coup and the Roots of Middle East
    Terror*, John Wiley and Sons, New Jersey, 2003
Klein, Noami, *The Shock Doctrine: The Rise of Disaster Capitalism*, Allen Lane,
    London, 2007
Latham, Mark, *The Latham Diaries*, Melbourne University Press, Melbourne, 2005
Leith, Denise, *Bearing Witness: The Lives of War Correspondents and Photojournalists*,
    Random House Australia, Sydney, 2004
Miles, Hugh, *Al-Jazeera: How Arab TV News Challenged the World*, Abacus,
    London, 2005

Moaveni, Azadeh, *Lipstick Jihad*, Public Affairs, New York, 2005

Naji, Kasra, *Ahmadinejad: The Secret History of Iran's Radical Leader*, I.B. Tauris, New York, 2008

Okrent, Daniel, *Public Editor #1: The Collected Columns (with Reflections, Reconsiderations, and Even a Few Retractions) of the First Ombudsman of The New York Times*, Public Affairs, New York, 2006

Otterman, Michael, *American Torture: From the Cold War to Abu Ghraib and Beyond*, Melbourne University Press, Melbourne, 2007

Palast, Greg, *Armed Madhouse*, Dutton, New York, 2006

Pax, Salam, *The Baghdad Blog*, Text Publishing, Melbourne, 2003

Phillips, Peter and Andrew Roth (ed.), *Censored 2008: The Top 25 Censored Stories of 2006–07*, Seven Stories Press, New York, 2007

Pilger, John, *The New Rulers of the World*, Verso, London, 2002

Politkovskaya, Anna, *A Dirty War: A Russian Reporter in Chechnya*, The Harvill Press, London, 1999

Rampton, Sheldon and John Stauber, *Weapons of Mass Deception: The Use of Propaganda in Bush's War in Iraq*, Hodder, Sydney, 2003

Rejali, Darius, *Torture and Democracy*, Princeton University Press, Princeton, 2007

Remnick, David, *Reporting: Writings from the New Yorker*, Vintage Books, New York, 2006

Riverbend, *Baghdad Burning: Girl Blog From Iraq*, The Feminist Press at the City University of New York, New York, 2005

Riverbend, *Baghdad Burning II: More Girl Blog From Iraq*, The Feminist Press at the City University of New York, New York, 2006

Roy, Arundhati, *War Talk*, South End Press, Cambridge, 2003

Rubin, Barry, *The Truth about Syria*, Palgrave Macmillan, New York, 2007

Shadid, Anthony, *Legacy of the Prophet*, Westview Press, Colorado, 2002

Schultz, Julianne, *Reviving the Fourth Estate*, Cambridge University Press, Melbourne, 1998

Simons, Margaret, *The Content Makers: Understanding the Media in Australia*, Penguin Books, Melbourne, 2007

Sites, Kevin, *In the Hot Zone: One Man, One Year, Twenty Wars*, Harper Perennial, New York, 2007

Takeyh, Ray, *Hidden Iran: Paradox and Power in the Islamic Republic*, Times Books, New York, 2006

Unger, Craig, *House of Bush House of Saud*, Scribner, New York, 2004

Wilpert, Gregory, *Changing Venezuela by Taking Power: The History and Politics of the Chavez Government*, Verso, London, 2007

Websites

The following websites and blogs offer insightful information about current affairs, human rights and media across the world.

http://bloggingrevolution.com/
The website of this book, with sources and further information.

http://antonyloewenstein.com/
The website of Antony Loewenstein, with information about his work, articles and blog.

http://afamilyinbaghdad.blogspot.com/
   An Iraqi blog detailing the reality of life in the occupied country.
http://www.a-mother-from-gaza.blogspot.com/
   A female blogger in the Gaza Strip discusses life in a war zone.
http://andrewbartlett.com/blog/
   A political blog written by a former Australian Democrats senator.
http://andrewsullivan.theatlantic.com/
   A leading conservative American blogger on war and peace.
http://www.andyworthington.co.uk/
   A British author blogs about torture and the 'War on Terror'.
http://www.antiwar.com/blog/
   An American blog on the 'War on Terror'.
http://www.back-to-iraq.com/
   Freelance journalist Christopher Allbritton's blog on the Middle East.
http://blogs.news.com.au/news/blogocracy/
   Australian blogger Tim Dunlop on local news and views.
http://www.buzzmachine.com/
   Leading US blog by Jeff Jarvis on media and its future.
http://www.committeetoprotectbloggers.org/
   A site to highlight global repression of bloggers.
http://dailykos.com/
   One of America's most popular, Democrat-aligned blogs.

http://firedoglake.com/
   A popular US blog on politics and the media.
http://blog.foreignpolicy.com/
   The blog of the establishment journal.
http://www.salon.com/opinion/greenwald/
   Glenn Greenwald's razor-sharp blog on US media and politics.
http://icga.blogspot.com/
   A group blog by academics on global affairs.
http://washingtonbureau.typepad.com/iraq/
   McClatchy Newspapers' Iraqi journalists blog about life in their country.
http://ejectiraqikkk.blogspot.com/
   An Iraqi blogger, now living in Jordan, on the politics of his home country.
http://jewssansfrontieres.blogspot.com/
   A dissenting Jewish blogger in Britain.
http://johnquiggin.com/
   An Australian academic blog on politics and media.
http://jonathanturley.org/
   An American legal scholar's blog on politics and the internet.
http://jotman.blogspot.com/
   A Burmese blogger, living in Thailand, on politics in Asia.
http://www.antiwar.com/justin/
   Libertarian blogger Justin Raimondo on US politics.
http://www.leftwrites.net/
   An Australian group blog on politics and media.
http://www.ethanzuckerman.com/blog/
   A blog about Africa, development and 'hacking the media'.
http://leninology.blogspot.com/
   Left-wing analysis of politics and the media.
http://www.livefromoccupiedpalestine.blogspot.com/
   An Australian living in the West Bank describes life in the occupied territory.
http://maxblumenthal.com/
   Leading American political commentator with a satirical edge.
http://www.mefaith.org/
   Voices from across the Middle East.
http://www.mideastyouth.com/
   Young Middle Eastern voices on politics.
http://www.philipweiss.org/
   Dissenting American Jew on Zionism and Israel.
http://reasonsyouwillhateme.com/
   Australian satirist pulls apart the political news of the day.
http://www.muzzlewatch.org/
   Examines the role of the Zionist lobby in America.
http://postsecret.blogspot.com/
   The darkest, deepest secrets emerge online.
http://www.prospectsforpeace.com/
   Former Israeli peace negotiator on the Middle East.
http://riverbendblog.blogspot.com/
   A female Iraqi blogger, now in Syria, on life in her home country since 2003.
http://www.roadtosurfdom.com/
   An Australian group blog on issues of the day.
http://www.roryoconnor.org/blog/
   A critical look at the American media.

http://www.talkingpointsmemo.com/
   Agenda-setting American blog on domestic politics and media.
http://angryarab.blogspot.com/
   Critical look at the Middle East and Western meddling.
http://nafeez.blogspot.com/
   A British academic blogs about the 'War on Terror'.
http://robertdreyfuss.com/blog/
   A veteran Middle East watcher.
http://themagneszionist.blogspot.com/
   An Orthodox Jewish dissident blogs about the Middle East.
http://theonlinecitizen.com/
   Singapore blogger on life in a one-party state.
http://www.richardsilverstein.com/tikun_olam/
   Dissident American Jew on the Middle East.
http://tonykaron.com/
   Time.com's senior editor on the 'War on Terror' and the Middle East.
http://www.warandpiece.com/
   The 'War on Terror' from a critical perspective.
http://harpers.org/subjects/WashingtonBabylon
http://harpers.org/subjects/NoComment
   Harper's magazine on American politics and media.
http://newsweek.washingtonpost.com/postglobal/
   The Washington Post online debates global issues.
http://www.adbusters.org/home/
   Culture jamming the mainstream media.
http://www.africanpath.com/p_home.cfm
   Latest news about Africa.
http://english.aljazeera.net/English
   News from a non-Western perspective.
http://www.americantorture.com/
   News and views about torture and the 'War on Terror'.
http://www.arabmediawatch.com/amw/
   Examining the Western media from an Arab perspective.
http://www.aldaily.com/
   A daily collection of the world's best writings.
http://atimes.com/
   News and views about Asia.
http://cyber.law.harvard.edu/
   Harvard University's Berkman Centre for Internet and Society.
http://anoniblog.pbwiki.com/
   Resources to blog in repressive regimes.
http://www.business-humanrights.org/Home
   Tracking the activities of multinationals around the world.
http://www.prwatch.org/
   Debunking media spin.
http://www.citizenlab.org/
   Examining the world of internet censorship.
http://www.cjr.org/
   Columbia Journalism Review's look at the media.
http://www.guardian.com.uk/commentisfree
   The *Guardian*'s daily coverage of global news and views.

http://www.cpj.org/index.html
   Committee to Protect Journalists.
http://conflictsforum.org/
   A dialogue between the West and the Muslim world.
http://consortiumnews.com/
   Independent investigative journalism since 1995.
http://www.corpwatch.org/
   Exposing corporate violations of human rights.
http://www.counterpunch.com/
   Leading US source of alternative information.
http://www.craigmurray.org.uk/
   Former British ambassador in Uzbekistan on human rights and the 'War on Terror'.
http://www.crikey.com.au/
   Australian news magazine on politics, media and business.
http://www.crooksandliars.com/
   Daily compilation of American news, views and politics.
http://www.cyberjournalist.net/
   News about online media.
http://dahrjamailiraq.com/index.php
   An American journalist on the Middle East.
http://www.democracynow.org/
   Daily American news program on politics and the media.
http://www.editorandpublisher.com/eandp/index.jsp
   Covering the American media industry.
http://electroniciraq.net/
   Alternative news about Iraq.
http://www.fair.org/index.php
   Fairness and Accuracy in Reporting is a leading American media watchdog.
http://www.fpif.org/
   Foreign Policy in Focus is a progressive American think-tank.
http://www.globalvoicesonline.org/
   Daily roundup of the global blogosphere.
http://advocacy.globalvoicesonline.org/
   Fighting censorship in the blogosphere.
http://www.gregpalast.com/
   Leading muckraker journalist on global politics.
http://www.harpers.org/
   American magazine on politics and the media.
http://www.hrw.org/
   Leading human rights organisation.
http://www.amnesty.org/
   Global human rights organisation.
http://www.informationclearinghouse.info/
   Daily update of global news.
http://accuracy.org/
   Institute for Public Accuracy analyses the American media.
http://www.ifj.org/
   International Federation of Journalists campaign for repressed journalists.
http://www.internationalpen.org.uk/internationalpen/
   Global group that defends imprisoned and silenced writers and journalists.
http://journalism.nyu.edu/pubzone/weblogs/pressthink/
   New York University lecturer Jay Rosen on media criticism.

http://www.juancole.com/
  Leading American blogger on the Middle East.
http://mediamatters.org/
  American website monitoring media bias.
http://www.markcurtis.info/
  Dissenting British historian and journalist on global politics.
http://www.medialens.org/
  British group debunking the corporate media.
http://www.nartv.org/
  Nart Villeneuve is a Canadian researcher on global web censorship.
http://newmatilda.com/
  Australian website of alternative news and views.
http://www.naomiklein.org/main
  Canadian writer and journalist.
http://opennet.net/
  Global project monitoring internet censorship.
http://www.poynter.org/column.asp?id=45
  Leading American column on media issues.
http://www.projectcensored.org/
  Issues ignored by the mainstream media.
http://rawstory.com/
  Alternative American news site.
http://www.reliefweb.int/rw/dbc.nsf/doc100?OpenForm
  News about the global humanitarian community.
http://www.rsf.org/
  Reporters Without Borders is a human rights group focused on censorship and repression.
http://www.salon.com/
  American news site.
http://news.sbs.com.au/dateline/
  Australian television current affairs program on global events.
http://www.sourcewatch.org/index.php?title=SourceWatch
  Getting behind the spin of daily news.
http://www.huffingtonpost.com/
  American news site.
http://www.thememoryhole.org/index.htm
  Sourcing rare and lost documents.
http://www.tomdispatch.com/
  Alternative American source of news and analysis.
http://wikileaks.org/wiki/Wikileaks
  Revealing secrets and hidden documents ignored by the mainstream media.
http://youtube.com/
  The source for online video.
http://www.zcommunications.org/znet
  Alternative American source of news and views.

Iran

http://academic.reed.edu/poli_sci/faculty/rejali/rejali/academic.html
  American-based Iranian academic Darius Rejali on torture and the 'War on Terror'.
http://www.globalvoicesonline.org/-/world/middle-east-north-africa/iran/
  A regular compilation of Iranian-related blogs.

http://persianimpediment.org/
  Information about web censorship in Iran.
http://www.40cheragh.org/
  Website of youth magazine *Chelcheragh*.
http://iraniantestament.blogspot.com/
  Blog of writer and editor Bozorgmehr Sharafedin.
http://hoder.com/weblog/
  Blog of Hossein Derakhshan (aka Hoder).
http://www.presstv.ir/
  State-run media outlet.
http://www.ahmadinejad.ir/
  Blog of Iranian President Mahmoud Ahmadinejad.
http://soundsiranian.wordpress.com/
  Group blog on Iranian issues.
http://en.wikipedia.org/wiki/Nikah_Mut%E2%80%98ah
  Explanation of temporary marriage.
http://photoblogs.ir/
  Iranian photoblogs.
http://www.omidmemarian.blogspot.com/
  American-based Iranian writer Omid Memarian.
http://kamangir.net/
  Canadian based Iranian blogger.
http://www.kosoof.com/
  Iranian photoblogger.
http://www.webneveshteha.com/en/
  Website of Iran's former vice-president.
http://mrbehi.blogs.com/
  Iranian blogger.
http://www.iranjewish.com/English.htm
  Tehran's Jewish community.
http://www.meydaan.org/english/default.aspx
  Campaign against Iran's program of stoning.
http://tehranwalls.blogspot.com/
  Iranian graffiti artist A1one.
http://www.femirani.com/english/
  London-based, female Iranian activist.
http://www.parsarts.com/
  Information for Iranian expatriates.

Egypt

http://arabist.net/arabawy/
  Political blog by activist and journalist Hossam el-Hamalawy.
http://arabist.net/
  Blog founded by Issandr El-Amrani.
http://www.bigpharaoh.com/
  Prominent local blogger.
http://elijahzarwan.net/blog/
  Cairo-based American journalist and human rights activist.
http://www.ikhwanweb.com/
  Muslim Brotherhood website.

http://www.hrinfo.org/en/
   The Arabic Network for Human Rights Information.
http://weekly.ahram.org.eg/index.htm
   Cairo-based weekly newspaper on the Middle East.
http://www.freekareem.org/
   Site dedicated to imprisoned blogger Kareem Amer.
http://www.globalvoicesonline.org/-/world/middle-east-north-africa/egypt/
   A regular compilation of Egyptian-related blogs.
http://www.sandmonkey.org/
   Conservative, pro-US Egyptian blogger.
http://wa7damasrya.blogspot.com/
   Blog of female activist Shahinaz Abdel Salam.
http://daliaziada.blogspot.com/
   Blog of female activist Dalia Ziada.
http://misrdigital.blogspirit.com/
   Blog of leading activist and journalist Wael Abbas.
http://www.bibalex.org/English/index.aspx
   Site of the Bibliotheca Alexandrina.
http://ihoudaiby.blogspot.com/
   Site of Muslim Brotherhood member Ibrahim Houdaiby.
http://www.monaeltahawy.com/
   New York–based Egyptian commentator on Middle East issues.

Syria

http://imad_moustapha.blogs.com/
   Blog of the Syrian Ambassador in Washington.
http://pentra.blogspot.com/
   Iraqi blogger Caesar, who spent time in Syria.
http://www.joshualandis.com/blog/
   Blog of leading American-based Syria expert.
http://www.syplanet.com/
   Compilation of Syrian bloggers from around the world.
http://www.globalvoicesonline.org/-/world/middle-east-north-africa/syria/
   A regular compilation of Syrian-related blogs.
http://www.syria-today.com/pkg05/
   Independent Syrian magazine.
http://www.damasceneblog.com/
   American-based Syrian blogger.
http://levantdream.blogspot.com/
   American-based Syrian blogger.
http://www.mideastviews.com/
   Website of Damascus-based commentator Sami Moubayed.
http://www.tharwacommunity.org/amarji/
   Blog of Syrian dissident Ammar Abdulhamid

Saudi Arabia

http://saudijeans.org/
   Saudi blogger Ahmed Al-Omran.

http://rasheedsworld.blogspot.com/
    Saudi-American blogger based in Abu Dhabi.
http://projects.washingtonpost.com/staff/articles/faiza+saleh+ambah/
    Articles by Jeddah-based *Washington Post* journalist Faiza Saleh Ambah.
http://www.globalvoicesonline.org/-/world/middle-east-north-africa/saudi-arabia/
    A regular compilation of Saudi-related blogs.
http://www.arabnews.com/
    Saudi-based English newspaper.
http://www.saudigazette.com.sa/
    Saudi-based English newspaper.
http://delhi4cats.wordpress.com/
    American woman American Bedu, blogging in Riyadh.
http://www.alfarhan.org/
    Blog of leading activist Fouad Al-Farhan.

Cuba

http://www.globalvoicesonline.org/-/world/americas/cuba/
    A regular compilation of Cuban-related blogs.
http://www.desdecuba.com/generationy/
    Cuba's most famous blogger, Yoani Sánchez.
http://www.granma.cu/ingles/index.html
    English-language version of the Cuban Communist Party site.
http://www.cubanow.net/
    Online magazine about Cuban arts and culture.
http://www.cubanet.org/cubanews.html
    Regular updates about life on the island.
http://en.wikipedia.org/wiki/Cuban_hip_hop
    Information about Cuban hip-hop.

China

http://www.chinaherald.net/
    Internet news from a foreign entrepreneur.
http://washingtonbureau.typepad.com/china/
    McClatchy Newspapers' Beijing-based journalist blogs about life in the country.
http://www.danwei.org/
    Beijing-based website about Chinese media and politics.
http://www.zonaeuropa.com/weblog.htm
    Translations of the Chinese blogosphere and related issues by Roland Soong.
http://rconversation.blogs.com/
    Hong Kong–based American academic Rebecca MacKinnon on Chinese media and the
        blogosphere.
http://www.chinadialogue.net/
    China and the world discuss the environment.
http://chinadigitaltimes.net/
    Website covering the Chinese online community, politics and media.
http://www.globalvoicesonline.org/-/world/east-asia/china/
    A regular compilation of China-related blogs.

http://www.xinhuanet.com/english/
    Official state-run media.
http://www.rsf.org/article.php3?id_article=25234
    Reporters Without Borders report on human rights in China.
http://china.hrw.org/
    Human Rights Watch on China.
http://www.isaacmao.com/meta/
    Blog by Isaac Mao.
http://www.tudou.com/
    Leading Chinese video-sharing site.

Notes

Introduction

1 Firas Al-Atraqchi, Interview with Iraqi blogger 'Riverbend', Al-Jazeera, 9 April 2006.
2 President Bush visits Prague, Czech Republic, discusses freedom, 5 June 2007.
3 A week after the conference, Sharansky praised Bush for his dedication to 'democracy' and inspiration for dissidents the world over who 'were ultimately waging the same struggle, one that fits democrats versus dictators, freedom versus fear'. Natan Sharansky, 'Dissidents of the world unite', *International Herald Tribune*, 11 June 2007. In late 2007, Sharansky continued the rhetoric and falsely argued that thanks to the Iraq invasion, a war he supported, 'the terrorists are in retreat'. Not unlike many fellow supporters of Bush, Sharansky, a former leading politician in Israel, expresses support for democracy but appears unwilling to allow the Palestinians the opportunity to be free of Israeli occupation. Dinah A Spritzer, 'Q&A: Natan Sharansky', JTA, 29 November 2007.
4 To counter America's image problem in the Arab world, the State Department utilised a handful of its Arabic speakers to engage in online forums and challenge perceived misconceptions about Washington's goals. Neil MacFarquhar, 'At state dept., blog team joins Muslim debate', *New York Times*, 22 September 2007.
5 *The Atlantic* magazine asked a group of foreign policy 'authorities' in early 2008 to determine the prospects for democracy around the world. A majority said that the US was 'capable of meaningfully affecting the prospects for democracy in most non-democratic states'. 'The end of history', *Atlantic*, March 2008.

6   Internet television is likely to herald a new era of interactive enter-
      tainment and information. 'Bobbie Johnson, Vint Cerf, aka the
      godfather of the net, predicts the end of TV as we know it', *Guardian*,
      27 August 2007.

7   Stephen Brook, 'News reporting faces web challenge, warns *New York
      Times* editor', *Guardian*, 29 November 2007.

8   One of the ways the *New York Times* has attempted to regain trust with its
      readership is the establishment of a 'public editor', a person able to cri-
      tique, question and challenge the newspaper's stories and perspectives:
      http://topics.nytimes.com/top/opinion/thepubliceditor/index.html

9   Eric Boehlert, *Lapdogs*, p. 210.

10   The *Guardian* published Salam Pax's dispatches before, during and after
      the war. His moving descriptions of a country bombed to smithereens
      captured the imagination of many readers around the world, highlight-
      ing the advantages of unfiltered, raw blogging. Salam Pax, 'Return of
      the Baghdad blogger', *Guardian*, 8 May 2003.

11   Julia Day, 'Middle East suffers from bad press', *Guardian*, 6 June 2006.

12   'AP explores media's role in popular belief in Iraq WMD', Associated
      Press, 6 August 2006.

13   Faiza al-Arji, 'The Iraq War and truth—between blog and corporate
      media', Bitterlemons International, 25 May 2006.

14   'Tom Friedman's flexible deadlines', Fairness and Accuracy in Reporting,
      16 May 2006.

15   The myth of the liberal media, particularly in Britain, is examined by
      the media watchdog Medialens (http://www.medialens.org/).

16   Thomas Friedman on the *Charlie Rose* show, PBS, 30 May 2003.

17   Matthew Klam, 'Fear and laptops on the campaign trial', *New York
      Times* magazine, 26 September 2004.

18   An Australian study found that Australians had an average of ten vir-
      tual identities, including profiles on MySpace, Facebook, YouTube,
      email and game avatars. Asher Moses, 'Australians unleash true selves
      online', *Sydney Morning Herald*, 30 November 2007.

19   'Stop the presses', *Mother Jones*, 1 March 2007.

20   News Corporation, General Electric, Disney, Time Warner, Viacom and
      CBS Corporation are America's leading media companies.

21   'Zogby poll: 67% view traditional journalism as "out of touch"',
      27 February 2008.

22   Joe Strupp, 'Study: more than 60% don't trust campaign coverage',
      Editor & Publisher, 28 November 2007.

23   Dan Froomkin, 'On calling bullshit', Nieman Watchdog, 1 December 2006.

24   Walter Pincus, 'Fighting back against the PR presidency', Nieman
      Watchdog, 13 July 2006.

25 *Breaking the Shackles: The Continuing Fight against Censorship and Spin*, 2008 report into the state of press freedom in Australia, The Media, Entertainment and Arts Alliance.

26 Christopher Allbritton, 'Blogging from Iraq', Nieman Reports, Volume 57, Issue 3, Fall 2003.

27 'Large majority of Australians think the media is "often biased"', Roy Morgan, 13 August 2007.

28 EJ Dionne, 'New media and old can work together', *Age*, 24 August 2006.

29 Bree Nordenson, 'Who's least sincere—politicians, journalists or readers?', CJR Daily, 9 April 2006.

30 Stephen Moss, 'I wanted to report on where the silence was', *Guardian*, 8 May 2008.

31 Jay Rosen, 'Chris Nolan: the stand alone journalist is here", PressThink, 21 April 2005.

32 Associated Press is a notable exception and has expanded its foreign services. There are now 243 bureaus in 97 countries, with the potential to reach one billion people every day. Sherry Ricchiardi, 'Covering the world', *American Journalism Review*, December/January 2008.

33 Media commentator and lecturer Jeff Jarvis wants to replace the term *citizen journalism* with another he thinks is more appropriate. '"Networked journalism" takes into account the collaborative nature of journalism now: professionals and amateurs working together to get the real story, linking to each other across brands and old boundaries to share facts, questions, answers, ideas, perspectives. It recognizes the complex relationships that will make news. And it focuses on the process more than the product.' Jeff Jarvis, 'Networked journalism', Buzz Machine, 5 July 2006. CNN launched iReport in early 2008, a site built entirely on user-produced content, allowing users to upload video, audio and photos. Some of the material is used by CNN on its TV channel. Mike Shields, 'CNN launches web site for citizen journalists', Reuters, 11 February 2008. Despite the rise in networked journalism, a survey by legal firm DLA Piper found that a majority polled would support a voluntary code of conduct for online commentators and bloggers, designed to reflect concerns over defamation, incitement and intellectual property. There was clearly limits to people's online tolerance. Jemima Kiss, 'Web users back code for bloggers', *Guardian*, 13 May 2008.

34 The Burmese regime soon recognised how damaging the internet was to its survival and essentially shutdown communications to the outside world. OpenNet Initiative conducted a study after the uprising and reviewed the 'internet shutdown': http://opennet.net/research/bulletins/013/ (November 2007).

35 Ronit Roccas, 'Peace minded residents of Gaza, Sderot meet online, write blog', Haaretz, 19 February 2008. The blog address is: http://gaza -sderot.blogspot.com/
36 Alive in Baghdad address: http://www.aliveinbaghdad.org/
37 Riverbend address: http://riverbendblog.blogspot.com/
38 Delphine Schrank, 'Blogging under the radar', *Washington Post*, 28 August 2006.
39 Gal Beckerman, 'The new Arab conversation', *Columbia Journalism Review*, January/February 2007.
40 An Islamic website claimed in 2001 that 65 per cent of the total number of Arabic websites were concerned with Islam. This figure has decreased since this time, but it indicates that Islam remains a key concern of many in the Arab world. Gamal Eid, 'The internet in the Arab world: a new space of repression?', The Arabic Network for Human Rights Information, June 2004.
41 Special report 2007, Committee to Protect Journalists, 5 December 2007.
42 Western human rights have devised handbooks for bloggers and dissidents in repressive regimes in an attempt for them to avoid internet censorship. *Handbook for bloggers and cyber-dissidents*, Reporters Without Borders, 2008. 'Everyone's guide to by-passing internet censorship: for citizen's worldwide', A Civisec Project, September 2007. Global Voices' advocacy has designed a mapping of worldwide censorship: http://advocacy.globalvoicesonline.org/maps/
43 OpenNet Initiative reported in March 2008: 'YouTomb, a project of the MIT Free Culture group that studies takedown notices by the video-sharing website YouTube, has identified a mechanism used by Google to restrict video content in specific countries. This appears to be the method YouTube is using to filter videos on behalf of governments and private actors that request it.' 'YouTube and the rise of geolocational filtering', OpenNet Initiative blog, 13 March 2008. Google has denied, though allegations persist, that it provided email records to the US–based National Security Agency's recent surveillance of web content. Chris Soghoian, 'Google: we didn't help the NSA (or did we?)', News.com, 17 March 2008.
44 A Microsoft executive told British MPs in early 2008 that forcing software companies to install web-filtering technology would send the country back to the 'dark ages'. Mark Sweeney, 'MPs get filter "dark ages" warning', *Guardian*, 26 February 2008. Google announced in early 2008 a joint project with a Cleveland medical clinic to manage customers' medical records. It was a worrying sign that internet companies were gathering too much information. Cade Metz, 'Google eyes Cleveland medical records', *Register*, 21 February 2008.

45   Earth OutReach from Google allows high-definition images of humanitarian crisis zones to assist human rights groups in their work with refugees. 'Google maps give close-up view of UN refugee camps', Reuters, 9 April 2008.

46   Google has started to campaign against some elements of global web censorship in an attempt to salvage its advertising-driven business model. Principles were not the main issue. Christopher S Rugaber, 'Google fights global internet censorship', Associated Press, 25 June 2007.

47   Alexi Mostrous and Rob Evans, 'Google "will be able to keep tabs on us all"', *Guardian*, 3 November 2006. After concern over how much information Google was keeping, the company agreed to delete search records after 18 to 24 months. Bobbie Johnson, 'Google to erase information on billions of internet searches', *Guardian*, 15 March 2007.

48   John Lanchester, 'Big Google is watching you', *Sunday Times*, 29 January 2006. Google announced in early 2008 that its philanthropic arm would give more than US$26 million in investments and grants to companies interested in solving global warming. 'Google.org to disburse more than $26M', Associated Press, 18 January 2008.

49   The Bush administration has colluded with communications companies to monitor phone and internet traffic. The European Union has called for bomb-making instructions to be blocked from internet web searches. From America to Australia, Israel to India, Japan to France and Germany to Britain, a growing number of Western nations are now talking about placing restrictions on web access, whether for 'terrorism' material or 'pornography'. It remains to be seen whether this is simply the beginning of serious censorship or merely the occasional blocking of certain sites. Google, for its part, has claimed that it refuses to censor material on its site, though there are examples where the global giant has removed material. US Democratic senator Joseph Lieberman tried to pressure Google's YouTube in May 2008 to pull videos he didn't like, allegedly because they incited terrorism. The company complied with some of his requests but ignored the rest. 'Joe Lieberman, would-be censor', *New York Times*, 25 May 2008. The British government announced in May 2008 that it was considering holding details of every phone call, email and time spent on the internet by the public in its attempt to fight 'crime and terror.'

50   David Leigh and Jonathan Franklin, 'Whistle while you work', *Guardian*, 23 February 2008. The role of the US National Security Agency (NSA) during the Bush administration years remains unclear though the organization have undoubtedly expanded its spying role, being granted powers to monitor vast numbers of individuals and corporations. The

American Civil Liberties Union (ACLU) provides a good overview here: http://www.aclu.org/safefree/nsaspying/23989res20060131.html

51 Adam Cohen, 'The already big thing on the internet: spying on users', *New York Times*, 5 April 2008. We will soon be experiencing internet speeds up to 10 000 times faster than a current broadband connection, making information even easier to access. Jonathan Leake, 'Coming soon: superfast internet', *Sunday Times*, 6 April 2008. A survey of Australian web users in 2008 found that people with broadband connections spent more time online than watching television, proving that traditional television is dying. Michael Janda, 'Net starts to overtake TV', ABC News, 21 May 2008. In the US, however, TV remains the major source of political news, across all age groups. John Eggerton, 'Study: TV still top campaign news source', Broadcasting & Cable, 19 May 2008.

52 There is a growing realisation that American internet providers have the power and legal right to snoop on personal email. Peter Svensson, 'Your internet provider is watching you', Associated Press, 4 April 2008.

53 'Public knowledge of current affairs little changed by news and information revolutions', Pew Research Centre, 15 April 2007.

54 Asher Moses, 'Net dumbs us down: Nobel prize winner', *Sydney Morning Herald*, 10 December 2007.

55 Johann Hari, 'Beware the internet's looming class divide', *Independent*, 28 January 2008.

56 Tunku Varadarajan, 'Happy blogiversary', *Wall Street Journal*, 14 July 2007.

57 Keen, *The Cult of the Amateur*, p. 3.

58 Blogging transparency is essential. Bloggers being paid for pushing products in the West is becoming a growing ethical issue because some people involved aren't disclosing their relationship with a corporate entity. 'Polluting the blogosphere', *Business Week*, 10 July 2006.

59 Australian Democrat Senator Andrew Bartlett has published one of the most insightful blogs about the political process since 2004: http://andrewbartlett.com/blog/

60 'Voces Bolivians: leaping forward to the next round', Global Voices, 11 January 2008. In early 2008 Global Voices Online released a citizen media guide providing step-by-step instructions to help bloggers in developing countries establish websites.

61 'Small town leads Chilean wifi revolution', Reuters, 8 January 2007.

62 Ismet Hajdari, 'Using the net for ethnic harmony', AFP, 24 June 2005.

63 Barney Jopson, 'Kenya lays ground for cable broadband links', *Financial Times*, 9 July 2007. After the disputed Kenyan elections in late 2007, bloggers across the country rallied to gather information about the

violence. 'Kenya: cyberactivism in the aftermath of political violence', Global Voices, 15 January 2008. Bloggers published emotional and raw accounts that challenged mainstream media narratives. Blogger Ethan Zuckerman explained: 'Immediately after the election, many newspapers offered a narrative of the Kenyan violence in terms of "long-simmering ethnic tensions"—bloggers reminded us that these tensions had been consciously stoked by political parties, and that the nation had been largely free of serious ethnic tension for most of its history.' Ethan Zuckerman, 'The Kenyan middle class … or is it the digital activist class?', My Heart's in Accra, 13 February 2008. Bloggers in Zimbabwe and in the Diaspora expressed their disgust after the rigged election of Robert Mugabe in early 2008. 'Zimbabwe cannot move on with Mugabe at the helm,' one wrote. 'Mugabe must go, and he must go before he plunges our beloved country into chaos and bloodshed.' 'Zimbabwe blogs: "Mugabe must go. He must go now"', *Independent*, 2 April 2008.

64   Ron Nixon, 'Africa, offline: waiting for the web', *New York Times*, 22 July 2007.

65   'Who owns the African blogosphere?', Global Voices Online, 22 September 2007. A Nigerian born blogger living in Spain has given African women a voice and discussed a taboo subject such as gay and lesbian issues. Clark Boyd, 'Nigerian blogger tackles taboo', BBC News, 5 July 2005. The blogosphere is growing. For example, in 2004 there were only 10 blogs in Kenya and today there are more than 450. Steve Bloomfield, 'Boom in blogs gives Africans a voice on the web', *Independent*, 2 August 2007.

66   During the Paris riots in 2005, a Swiss magazine utilised new technology to deeply investigate the issues, placing journalists and bloggers on rotations of seven to ten days in the area experiencing difficulties. They lived among the people, hearing their stories. Bruno Giussani, 'A first blog of the first draft of history', *International Herald Tribune*, 30 January 2006.

67   Rebecca MacKinnon and Ethan Zuckerman, 'Gathering voices to share with a worldwide online audience', Nieman Reports, Winter 2006.

68   'Myanmar's "Dictator's Dilemma"?, The internet and democracy project', Berkman Center for Internet & Society at Harvard Law School, 9 October 2007.

Iran: Welcome to the Axis of Evil

1   Alavi, *We are Iran*.

2   Iranian blogger Arash Abadpour, living in Canada, wrote on his blog that the Iranian regime glorifies the Ayatollahs as holy figures.

He joked that at the residence of the former leader of the Islamic Republic Ayatollah Khomeini, rooms and couches were effectively regarded as 'blessed' because he had lived here. 'Now, the question is,' he wrote, 'how many of these worshippers do you think will not slap you on the face if you tell them that someone has farted on this holy couch?' Many comments on his blog slammed him for being an 'infidel'. Arash Abadpour, 'Do Ayatollahs fart?', *The Manitoban*, 30 January 2008.

3   Amir Hassan Cheheltan, 'Hell up close, heaven from afar', *Sydney Morning Herald*, 7 September 2007.

4   A collection of the documents can be found at the Memory Hole website (http://www.thememoryhole.org/espionage_den/index.htm).

5   Princeton University Press, 2007.

6   'Torture and democracy: scholar Darius Rejali details the history and scope of modern torture', Democracy Now!, 12 March 2008

7   Bill Berkeley and Nahid Siamdoust, 'The hostage-takers' second act', *Columbia Journalism Review*, November/December 2004.

8   One of the loudest supporters in the West of the 1979 revolution was French philosopher Michel Foucault. He admired the Islamist take-over and whereas other Western intellectuals admired the socialist and feminist forces that initially sprung up in 1979 and were soon crushed, Foucault was suspicious of these and saw the revolution as a legitimate response to the disease of modernity. It was an intriguing and blind position for a gay French radical to take. 'What's the Persian for "liberal"', *Philosopher's Zone*, ABC Radio National, 10 February 2007.

9   Michelle Goldberg, 'Any attack on Iran will be good for the government', Salon, 15 May 2006.

10   'Iran's new President', *New York Times*, 30 June 2005.

11   Executions and amputations have increased under Ahmadinejad's rule. According to a count by *Agence France-Presse*, Iran hanged 298 people in 2007, compared with 177 hangings in 2006. Nazila Fathi, 'Spate of executions and amputations in Iran', *New York Times*, 11 January 2008.

12   Borzou Daragahi, 'Iran tightens screws on internal dissent', *Los Angeles Times*, 10 June 2007.

13   The extent of the ever-increasing crackdown was clear when the Iranian authorities arrested partygoers at a 'satanic' concert organised over the internet in August 2007. Drugs, alcohol and CDs were confiscated at an event in the town of Karaj, near Tehran. Rock, rap and female performers featured, all illegal in Iran. Most of the detainees were Iranians from rich families who had travelled from Sweden and Britain. Tehran's provincial police chief told the semi-official ISNA news agency that it was 'the first time that tens of male and female participants have been

invited to such an event through an internet call'. Robert Tait, 'Iranian morals police arrest 230 in raid on "satanist" rave', *Guardian*, 6 August 2007. The morals patrols had even been told to arrest young men with 'Western' haircuts. The country's police chief boasted in 2007 that 150 000 people, an unprecedented number, were arrested in the annual assault against unIslamic clothing. Neil MacFarquhar, 'Iran cracks down on dissent, parading examples in streets', 24 June 2007. Ahmadinejad, according to a source close to the *New York Times*, believes that enforcing a strict dress code 'will only stir up dissent among other apolitical kids'. There is an obvious split in the regime's attitude towards social mores. Dan Ephron and Maziar Bahari, 'Iran's hard-liners lash out at women, youth', *Newsweek*, 21 May 2007.

14 Ahmadinejad pledged to offer home loans but many poor residents have never seen the money. He also talked of maintaining low interest rates but unofficial estimates place the figure at at least double the official 12 percent. A poll by the conservative think-tank Terror Free Tomorrow—Republican presidential hopeful John McCain is on its board—released a study in early 2008 that found the Iranian public's satisfaction with the economy had doubled since June 2007. Hoder, 'Poll: satisfaction with Iranian economy doubled since June 2007', 23 March 2008.

15 Naji, *Ahmadinejad*, p. xi.

16 Bill Spindle, 'Iranian President's setbacks embolden his domestic critics', *Wall Street Journal*, 30 January 2007.

17 'Frozen!', Global Voices, 10 January 2008.

18 Borzou Daragahi and Ramin Mostaghim, 'Iran sanctions ripple past those in power', *Los Angeles Times*, 20 January 2008.

19 Neil MacFarquhar, 'Iran cracks down on dissent, parading examples in streets', *New York Times*, 24 June 2007.

20 Ehteshami and Zweiri, *Iran and the rise of its neo-conservatives*, p. 71.

21 Robert Tait, 'As the regime cracks down, life goes on behind closed curtains', *Guardian*, 7 January 2008.

22 'Iranian favour direct talks with US, mutual access for journalists, more trade', WorldPublicOpinion.org, 7 April 2008.

23 Anne Penketh, 'Iron poll delivers challenger to President', *Independent*, 17 March 2008.

24 'Iran: Elections under threat', Democracy Now!, 5 May 2008.

25 Nazila Fathi, 'In this election, Ahmadinejad ally is now a critic', *New York Times*, 14 March 2008.

26 Kamangir, 'What's next for Ahmadinejad? More populism or more fundamentalism?', 19 December 2006, http://kamangir.net/2006/12/19/whats-next-for-ahmadinejad-more-populism-or-more-fundamentalism/

27 I was in Iran in June 2007.

28 The *Washington Post* columnist Charles Krauthammer, one of the strongest advocates of the Iraq War, has been talking about military strikes against Iran for years. In one column in September 2006, he wrote: 'An aerial attack on Iran's nuclear facilities lies just beyond the horizon of diplomacy. With the crisis advancing and the moment of truth approaching, it is important to begin looking now with unflinching honesty at the military option.' Nowhere in his column did he mention the price that would be paid by the Iranian people. Charles Krauthammer, 'The Tehran Calculus', *Washington Post*, 15 September 2006. Neo-conservatives claimed in May 2008 that the Iranian people would 'welcome' airstrikes, so desperate were they to destroy the Islamic leadership. Even *New York Times* 'liberal' foreign affairs columnist Thomas Friedman labelled the struggle between Tehran and Washington as the 'new cold war', not recognising that the Iraq War, something he supported, was one of the key reasons for the Islamic Republic's current strength. Former US President Jimmy Carter, in contrast to the bellicose pronouncements of pundits and the Bush administration, called in May 2008 for his country to be 'friends' with Tehran.

29 The regime released dozens of photographs in April 2008 of the Natanz nuclear site, perhaps as a way to show off their achievements in enrichment. William J Broad, 'A Tantalising Look at Iran's Nuclear Program', *New York Times*, 29 April 2008.

30 David Wurmser, former Middle East adviser to Vice President Dick Cheney, told Britain's *Daily Telegraph* in September 2007 that the goal of Washington should be regime change in Tehran. Arguing that a military strike against nuclear targets would be useless, he said: 'Only if what we do is placed in the framework of a fundamental assault on the survival of the regime will it have a pick-up among ordinary Iranians.' Toby Harnden, 'US "must break Iran and Syria regimes"', *Daily Telegraph*, 5 October 2007. Sadly, many in the mainstream media continued to publish alarmist charges against Iran fanned by the Bush administration. Eric Umansky, 'Lost Over Iran', *Columbia Journalism Review*, March/April 2008.

31 Trita Parsi, 'Long division', *American Conservative*, 10 September 2007.

32 Hamid Tehrani, 'Virtual writers, real victims', 15 December 2006, http://persianimpediment.org/sustainers/?p=4

33 Email interview with the author, 27 December 2006.

34 'Blogger jailed over presidential dogs', Global Voices Online, 4 December 2007.

35 Saeed Kamali, 'Iran's big brother for bloggers', *Guardian*, 7 June 2007.

36 'Iran's population tops 70mn', *Middle East Times*, 15 May 2007.

37   Babak Rahimi, 'Cyberdissident: The internet in revolutionary Iran', *Middle East Review of International Affairs*, Volume 7, Number 3, September 2003.

38   Jordan Halevi (pseudonym). Iranian Weblog Research Project: Survey Results, Persian Impediment Blog – Article 19, http://www.persianim pediment.org/research/iwrpresults.pdf, 2006

39   Halevi, ibid.

40   Interview with the author, Tehran, 5 June 2007.

41   Iranian police often cracked down harshly on internet cafes during Ahmadinejad's regime. In late 2007, twenty-four web cafes and other coffee shops were closed down. A provincial police commander said: 'Using immoral computer games, storing obscene photos ... and the presence of women wearing improper hijab were among the reasons why they have to be closed down.' Iran shuts down 24 cafes in internet crackdown, Reuters, 17 December 2007.

42   Iran blocks access to Google, AFP, 17 September 2007.

43   Iran is also often invisible on the web. When users use a pull-down menu on a website to select their country, Iran is not on the list. Google Earth has often been inaccessible—it has been difficult to determine whether Google was to blame or simply the Iranian authorities—and it was generally impossible to register websites on popular US-based hosting sites like GoDaddy.com. Many US hosting services refused to deal with potential Iranian customers altogether. There is little e-business in the country because it is very difficult to obtain international credit cards like Visa and Mastercard (and even if you do, very few places actually accept them). One of the major frustrations is that blogging-service Blogger doesn't support the Persian calendar, despite Persian being one of the most popular languages online. Microsoft only recently adapted Word for Persian users and Western mobile phones were also only recently modified. 'Hebrew has always been supported by all companies,' one person bitterly complained.

44   Azar Nafisi, 'Don't ban Dan Brown', *Guardian*, 25 November 2006.

45   Global Voices interview with Omid Memarian, 24 December 2006, http://www.globalvoicesonline.org/2006/12/24/iran-interview-with-omid-memarian-blogger-and-human-rights-activist/

46   Bill Berkley, 'Bloggers vs. Mullahs: How the internet roils Iran', *World Policy Journal*, Spring 2006.

47   'Hillary or Obama—America is the winner', Voices Without Votes, 3 April 2008.

48   Scot MacLeod, 'Blogging in Iran', *Time* Middle East Blog, 24 April 2008

49   Interview with the author, Tehran, 10 June 2007.

50   Shirin Hakimzadeh, 'Iran: A Vast Diaspora Abroad and Millions of Refugees at Home', *Migration Immigration Service*, September 2006.

51 Over the last few years, I have received many emails detailing the alleged 'crimes' of Derakhshan claiming that he is able to criticise the regime freely because his family maintains excellent relations with the leadership and that his frequent revealing of private information is also troublesome. I have been unable to independently verify such claims, but the accumulation of dirt, from Iranian blogging sources that I trust, suggests that there is some truth to them.

52 Hoder's Florida-based hosting provider terminated his account in 2007 after a defamation allegation by Mehdi Khalaji, an Iranian fellow at a Washington based neo-conservative think-tank. Hoder had written that Khalaji supported the Iran Freedom Initiative, a regime change-style operation. It was a worrying sign that wealthy litigants could intimidate hosting companies to remove material deemed inappropriate. 'Shutting down Hoder', Iranian.com, 13 August 2007.

53 Meron Rapoport, 'King of the Iranian bloggers', *Haaretz*, 12 January 2007.

54 Hossein Derakhshan, 'Reviving the Iranian revolt', *Guardian* Comment is Free, 16 February 2008.

55 Hossein Derakhshan, 'Stop bullying Iran', *Guardian*, 23 February 2007.

56 'Iran: Government celebrates Journalist Day', Global Voices, 18 August 2007, http://www.globalvoicesonline.org/2007/08/18/iran-government-celebrates-journalist-day/

57 Statistics of the Persian blogosphere, a report, Kamangir, 12 February 2008.

58 Ibid.

59 'Iran: Jailed teachers, nuclear ceremony and UK sailors', Global Voices, 13 April 2007, http://www.globalvoicesonline.org/2007/04/13/iran-jailed-teachers-nuclear-ceremony-and-uk-sailors/

60 Borzou Daragahi, 'Ordeal leaves Iranian dissident with doubts', *Los Angeles Times*, 23 December 2007.

61 On page 2 of the English-language newspaper *Tehran Times*, an article was headlined: 'Chomsky: Iran has right to nuclear energy'. Press TV, 10 June 2007.

62 'Iran: Second Cultural Revolution coming?', Global Voices, 7 June 2007, http://www.globalvoicesonline.org/2007/06/07/iran-second-cultural-revolution-coming/

63 Ahmadinejad's website, despite attempts to maintain a civil and adulatory tone, featured many critical comments about the President, including about the economic crisis and petrol rationing. Robert Tait, 'Iran leader's blog attracts critics', *Guardian*, 26 November 2007.

64 Kamangir, 'Freedom, Ahmadinejad's new post', 13 December 2006, http://kamangir.net/2006/12/13/freedom-ahmadinejads-new-post/

65 Many on the international left, who praised Venezuela's president Hugo Chavez, remained silent over his relationship with Ahmadinejad and Iran's human rights abuses. A number of Iranians urged the left

not to ignore Ahmadinejad's excesses. An open letter from Iranian labour and student activists in early 2008 urged Chavez to pressure the Iranian regime to release student prisoners, 'people who merely protested for better rights for workers, students, women, journalists and other sections of society.' Open letter to President Chavez from Iranian labour and student activists, 13 January 2008. Iran and Venezuela aimed, through oil wealth, to build an alliance against Washington.

66　'Islamist bloggers hail Imad Mughniyeh', Global Voices, 27 February 2008.

67　Hamid Tehrani, 'A comparative study of Iranian Islamist bloggers', Global Voices, October 2007.

68　Hamid Tehrani, 'Iranian anti-Semitic bloggers: from Mickey Mouse to Gaddafi's Jewishness', History News Network, 9 June 2008.

69　Kim Murphy, 'In Iran, web-savvy clerics reach out to Shiite faithful', *Los Angeles Times*, 7 April 2007.

70　'The verdict of Qom', *Economist*, 21–27 July 2007.

71　Nima Akbarpour, 'Mullahs are not martians', *Chelcheragh*, Volume 239, 8 April 2007, translated by Hooman Askary.

72　*The Guardian* reported in December 2006 that YouTube and Wikipedia were blocked (around the time that photo sharing site Flickr was also filtered) but little reason was given for the action. Robert Tait, 'Censorship fears rise as Iran blocks access to top websites', *Guardian*, 4 December 2006. Blogger Hossein Derakhshan claimed that his sources in Iran proved that the *Guardian* story was misleading—the sites were blocked but not for the reasons stated—and indicated a growing tendency in the Western media to 'show a policy shift in line with Ahmadinejad's presumed policy of rejecting anything Western'. He claimed that the vast majority of sites in English were available 'and the reason obviously is that the number of people who can read [them] is so small that the government can easily afford letting them accessible[sic]. Because their impact on the public debate is next to zero.' Hossein Derakhshan, Editor: Myself, 6 December 2006.

73　Interview with FarsiTube co-founder Sherwin Noorian, Global Voices, 1 March 2007, http://www.globalvoicesonline.org/2007/03/01/inter view-with-farsi-tube-co-founder-sherwin-noorian/

74　Rahimi, ibid.

75　Rahimi, ibid.

76　'Student gets nearly four years for criticising regime online', Reporters Without Borders, 18 August 2004.

77　*Iran's internet censorship among strictest in the world documents OpenNet Initiative report*, OpenNet Initiative press release, 21 June 2005.

78　'Secure Computing backs away from Iran censors', *IT News*, 27 June 2005.

79   Email interview with Sarah Tolle, Director of Global Public Relations, Secure Computing, 7 September 2007.

80   The SmartFilter categories can be found at http://www.securecompu ting.com/index.cfm?skey=86#categories

81   Akbar Ganji, 'Why Iran's democrats shun aid', *Washington Post*, 26 October 2007.

82   Email interview with Caroline Nelleman, 12 September 2007.

83   Chris Williams, 'Yahoo! Mail and Hotmail strike out Iran', *The Register*, 7 November 2007.

84   A Google spokesperson responded to my answers via email on 21 February 2008.

85   James F Smith and Anne Barnard, 'Iran bloggers thrive despite repression', *Boston Globe*, 18 December 2006.

86   Boghrati, ibid.

87   Smith, ibid.

88   The regime announced in December 2007 that it would allow singer Chris de Burgh to perform in Iran, the first Western act to be granted permission since 1979. Stephen Foley, 'Iranians wait nearly 30 years to see a Western pop star—and then they get Chris de Burgh', *Independent*, 17 December 2007.

89   Farouz Farzami, 'Iranian moolah', *Wall Street Journal*, 29 October 2006.

90   Farnaz Seifi, 'And the prize for Best Actress? We're not entirely sure ...', *The Observers*, 14 February 2008.

91   Leading women's magazine forced to close, Adnkronos, 28 January 2008. From 1991 until *Zanan*'s closure, the magazine's founder, Shahla Sherkat, campaigned on issues that rarely received coverage in Iran, such as violence against women, discrimination in society, the sex trade, honour killings and marital abuse. Wendy Kristiansen, 'Stop the presses', *Le Monde diplomatique*, April 2008. A growing number of cyber-feminists were jailed in 2008 for the crime of 'harming national security' and many of their websites were blocked. 'Authorities urged to halt threats to "cyber feminists"', Reporters Without Borders, 6 May 2008. Iranian authorities blocked even more websites and women's advocates' blogs in May 2008 and seemed to target the 'One Million Signatures' campaign that seeks to amend the country's marriage, divorce and inheritance laws. "Iran launches fresh crackdown on websites: report", AFP, 20 May 2008.

92   'Protests over ban of women's magazine', Global Voices, 14 February 2008.

93   'Students protest against "gender apartheid"', Global Voices, 6 March 2008.

94   Ziauddin Sardar, 'Will you marry me?—temporarily?', *New Statesman*, 7 February 2008.

95 Mansour Zabetian, 'Talk with Hamid Tavakoli: The founder of Temporary Marriage website', *Chelcheragh*, Volume 206, 15 July 2006, translated by Hooman Askary.

96 Meeting with the author, Tehran, 8 June 2007.

97 Iason Athanasiadis, 'Iran's unseen art', *Toronto Star*, 8 August 2006.

98 During a peaceful protest for women's rights in March 2007, a number of women were beaten and arrested. One blogger launched a petition that was subsequently sent to the judicial authorities: 'Your Excellency, we, undersigned, are writing to you to express our great concern about the recent persecutions and prosecutions of the women's rights defenders in Iran. We are especially dismayed at the news of the arrest of 38 women's rights defenders on March 4, 2007, in Tehran while gathering in a peaceful protest in front of the Islamic Revolutionary Court.' 'Iran: Women activist's jailed, teachers on the street and war whispers', Global Voices, 5 March 2007, http://www.globalvoicesonline.org/2007/03/05/iran-women-activists-jailed-teachers-on-the-street-and-war-whispers/

99 Azadeh Akbari, 'How I became a journalist', A journalist from Iran, 19 February 2007, http://iranianjournalist.blogfa.com/post-13.aspx

100 Since 1979, the Iranian regime has battled Afghan drug dealers who have used Iran as a transit point for their goods on the way to Europe. When Afghan President Hamid Karzai told CNN in 2007 that Iran was 'a helper and a solution' to his country, President George W Bush suggested that he be 'very cautious about whether or not the Iranian influence there in Afghanistan is a positive force'. After September 11, however, the Iranians helped the Americans overthrow the Taliban and provided aid for the struggling government. Dilip Hiro, 'Tehranophobia', *Guardian*, 10 August 2007.

101 Hussain Dojakam, a former drug addict who runs the Human Regeneration Society, says that the regime is learning how to manage addiction. 'The government has belatedly realised that using force and throwing people in jail won't solve the drug epidemic or the problem of AIDS and hepatitis. Eighty per cent of AIDS patients are addicts who picked it up by using dirty syringes in prison. The laws haven't changed, but attitudes have.' Jeffrey Fleishman, 'Iran shifts slightly in treatment of drug addicts', *Los Angeles Times*, 20 April 2008.

102 Brian Whitaker, 'No homosexuality here', *Guardian* Comment is Free, 25 September 2007. Arsham Parsi, director of the Toronto-based Iranian Queer Organisation, told Global Voices that many gay, lesbian and trans-gender Iranians used the internet to communicate with each other, though the exact number in Iran itself was impossible to determine. He said the last years had seen an explosion of websites dedicated to these issues, though far less for lesbians 'because of Iran's general lack of women's rights.' The full interview is here: http://www.

globalvoicesonline.org/2008/05/16/iran-the-internet-is-a-gift-to-us/. 'The internet is a gift to us', Global Voices, 16 May 2008.

103 David Shariatmadari, 'No gay people in Iran, Mr President? News to me … ', *Guardian*, 26 September 2007.

104 Robert Tait, 'Sex change funding undermines no gays claim', *Guardian*, 26 September 2007.

105 Tait, ibid.

106 Meeting with the author, Tehran, 8 June 2007.

107 Lisa Goldman, 'Notes from the underground: Iranians and Israelis connect online', On the Face, 13 February 2008.

108 Members of the country's Jewish community gathered at a holy shrine in the southwest part of the country in February 2008 to celebrate their Persian roots. 'The gathering in Susa is to highlight our presence in Iran since ancient times,' said Farhad Aframian, the editor of a monthly Jewish magazine. 'Iran Jews celebrate Persian roots, seek to maintain shrinking community', Associated Press, 15 February 2008.

109 'Iranian President: If Holocaust happened, why must Palestinians pay?', *Haaretz*, 25 September 2007.

110 Stephen Zunes, Middle East editor of *Foreign Policy in Focus*, joined an audience of mainly Christian clergy to engage with Ahmadinejad during his New York visit. He was unimpressed. 'Indeed, with his ramblings and the superficiality of his analysis, he came across as more pathetic than evil.' Stephen Zunes, 'My meeting with Ahmadinejad', *Foreign Policy in Focus*, 29 September 2007.

111 Seven chancellors and presidents of Iranian universities issued a letter in response to Bollinger's denunciation of Ahmadinejad, asking him a number of questions related to US policy in Iraq, Washington's role in overthrowing the 1953 Iranian Government and the failure to find Osama Bin-Laden. Bollinger was invited to Tehran to 'speak directly with Iranians'. 'Iranian university chancellors ask Bollinger ten questions', *Fars News Agency*, 26 September 2007.

112 Dudi Cohen, 'Jewish community in Iran slams US protest against Ahmadinejad's visit', Ynetnews, 26 September 2007.

113 'Iran's Jews won't mark Yom Ha'atzmaut', *Jerusalem Post*, 7 May 2008.

114 'Ahmadinejad: Israel a "stinking corpse"', *Jerusalem Post*, 8 May 2008.

115 Marc Perelman, 'Iranian Jews reject outside calls to leave', *Forward*, 12 January 2007.

116 The statement can be read at: http://www.iranjewish.com/News_e/Iranian.htm (12 July 2007).

117 Anshel Pfeffer, 'Israel welcomes largest group of Iran olim since Islamic revolution', *Haaretz*, 25 December 2007.

118 Iranian writer Azadeh Moaveni explained: 'There are two types of Holocaust sceptics in Iran. There's the Ahmadinejad type, and then

there's the ordinary Iranian, who lives in denial about everything, not just one of the great tragedies of the twentieth century. Iranians think all governments lie.' Azadeh Moaveni, 'A nation of Holocaust deniers?', *Time*, 2 October 2006.

119 Jonathan Cook, 'Israel's Jewish problem in Tehran', Counterpunch, 3 August 2007.

120 The *Guardian*'s Jonathan Steele examined Ahmadinejad's statement when in 2006 he allegedly called for Israel to be 'wiped off the map'. Although this has become supposed fact in news reports, Steele, along with Middle East expert Juan Cole, discovered that there were many different translations of the offending statement and the most likely was 'eliminated from the page of history'. In other words, he is opposed to the Zionist regime but the false 'wiped off the map' comment was used to justify a pre-emptive strike against Iran. Jonathan Steele, 'Lost in translation', *Guardian*, 14 June 2006. Former Israeli Prime Minister Benjamin Netanyahu subsequently urged the international community to try Ahmadinejad in The Hague for inciting genocide. Before the Iranian leader's visit to New York in September 2006, Harvard Law Professor Alan Dershowitz took the hyperbole even further: 'He is an international war criminal. He has repeatedly violated the anti-genocide convention. He is as guilty as the Rwandans who are convicted and sentenced to years in prison for inciting genocide.'

121 Interview with the author, Tehran, 16 June 2007.

122 A 2000–2006 report detailed the various works engaged by the institute. It 'endeavours to promote respect and mutual understanding among all faiths and cultures through partnership with other religious and inter-religious organizations and also by holding cultural meetings and conferences that allow interested students and faculties to learn more about religions in a respectful atmosphere.' *A brief report on the Institute for Inter-Religious Dialogue's Activities 2000–2006*, Winter 2007.

123 Hamid Tehrani, 'A comparative study of Iranian Islamist blogger's, Global Voices, October 2007.

124 Gareth Smyth, 'Breaking eggs in Iran', *British Journalism Review*, Vol. 18, No. 4, 2007.

125 Mohammed Ali Abtahi, 'Iranian look to Saddam Hossein's execution', 1 January 2007, http://www.webneveshteha.com/en/weblog/?id=2146308455

126 'Reformist Iranian opposition slams Ahmadinejad's Holocaust denial', DPA, 14 December 2007.

127 Hojjatoleslam Hasan Yousefi Eshkevari, PEN American Center.

128 Anthony Shadid, *Legacy of the Prophet*, Westview, 2002, p. 189.

129 Bill Berkeley, 'Bloggers vs mullahs: how the internet roils Iran', *World Policy Journal*, Spring 2006.

Egypt: Challenging a 'Moderate' American Dictatorship

1   Anthony Shadid, 'Egypt shuts door on dissent as US officials back away', *Washington Post*, 19 March 2007.

2   Interview with the author, Cairo, 26 May 2007.

3   Egypt received US$71.7 million in aid in 1974 but this skyrocketed to US$5.9 billion in 1979. 'US willingness to reward Egypt and Jordan in this way,' write American academics John Mearsheimer and Stephen Walt, 'is yet another manifestation of Washington's generosity towards the Jewish state.' John Mearsheimer and Stephen Walt, *The Israel lobby and US foreign policy*, Allen Lane, 2007, p. 31. The US House of Representatives voted in June 2007 to withhold US$200 million in military aid until the country's human rights improved and Cairo could prove that weapons were not being smuggled from Egypt into Gaza. 'House okays Egypt aid cut over Gaza smuggling, human rights', Reuters, 22 June 2007. Egypt's foreign minister told a visiting US Senator in early 2008 that the regime rejected any pre-conditions on receiving US aid. Pro-Israel forces in Washington were allegedly pressuring the Bush administration to withhold aid but the foreign minister threatened to use his country's influence to harm US interests in the region. 'Egyptian minister sceptical of US aid', UPI, 5 January 2008.

4   Shadid, ibid.

5   Shadid, ibid. US Vice President Dick Cheney visited Egypt during my visit and spoke to Mubarak. A report in *Al-Ahram Weekly* stated that both countries discussed Iran, Iraq and the Israel/Palestine conflict. A Presidential spokesman said: 'Mubarak made it very clear that all attempts to address the present regional crisis are unlikely to bear fruit if stagnation continues on the peace process, especially on the Palestinian front.' Dina Ezzat, 'Agendas to reconcile', *Al-Ahram Weekly*, 17–23 May 2007.

6   Chris Hedges, 'Outsourcing torture', Truthdig, 15 October 2007.

7   The chaos in Iraq, the rise of Iran and the moribund Israel/Palestine conflict forced the Bush administration to maintain the status quo with Egypt. Michael Slackman, 'Rice speaks softly in Egypt, avoiding democracy push', *New York Times*, 16 January 2007. When the Egyptian opposition complained in early 2007 about proposed constitutional changes that would grant Mubarak even greater powers, the State Department downplayed the moves. 'You have to put this in the wider context of political and economic reform in Egypt,' said spokesman Sean McCormack. Only around 5 per cent of Egyptians bothered to turn out for the vote. Sylvie Lanteaume, 'US tones down Egypt democratic requirements', Middle East Online, 21 March 2007.

Amnesty International called the proposed changes 'the greatest erosion of the people's rights in 26 years' and warned that Mubarak would be allowed to increase the powers of the security services and bypass ordinary courts to try terrorism suspects. Almost a quarter of Egypt's parliament walked out in protest at the proposed changes in March 2007. 'Egyptian MPs stage walkout', al-Jazeera, 18 March 2007.

8   Shadid, ibid.

9   A number of US-funded NGOs in Egypt have been closed since 2005, despite protestations from the US Congress. Although some of these groups, such as the Association for Human Rights Legal Aid (AHRLA), had received funding from the US-based National Endowment for Democracy (NED), a source known to meddle in country's affairs, the Mubarak regime was opposed to their role in exposing the use of torture throughout the country. William Fisher, US ally thumbs nose at its biggest donor, Truthout, 25 September 2007. Despite the Bush administration's stated opposition to the Muslim Brotherhood, members of the US Congress met an Egyptian parliamentary delegation in Cairo in May 2007 that included the official spokesman of the group. Mubarak's regime was highly displeased. Gamal Essam El-Din, 'A separate meeting', *Al-Ahram Weekly*, 31 May – 6 June 2007

10   'Denial and democracy in Egypt', *New York Times*, 6 May 2007.

11   'Government shuts down protest following Bush visit', Human Rights Watch, 21 January 2008.

12   William Fisher, 'Governments ever more draconian, groups says', Inter Press Service, 28 March 2008.

13   'Number of Islamist Detainees "Exaggerated"', Elijah Zarwan blog The Skeptic, 29 January 2008.

14   Email responses from former Human Rights Watch researcher Elijah Zarwan and lecturer in political science at the British University in Egypt Joshua Stacher, 26 February 2008.

15   A publisher of a leading Egyptian progressive publication, Hisham Kassem, told the *New York Times* that he worried the Brotherhood was offering lip-service to issues such as democracy and women's rights. 'I have no doubt that they would implement Sharia if ever they came to power. I see them as a menace.' James Traub, 'Islamic Democrats?' *New York Times Magazine*, 29 April 2007.

16   'Charting the rise of the Muslim Brotherhood', *Der Spiegel*, 3 July 2007.

17   The Brotherhood's cause was harmed in December 2006 when students at Cairo's Al-Azhar University, sympathetic to the group, paraded in Hizbollah-style uniforms. The regime used the demonstration to further repress the group and highlight its supposed extremism. Simon Tisdall, 'Mubarak's spring chill', *Guardian*, 20 February 2007.

18   Ibrahim El Houdaiby, 'Behind closed doors', *Guardian*, 14 November 2007.
19   Dan Murphy, 'Egypt keeps Muslim Brotherhood boxed in', *Christian Science Monitor*, 7 June 2005.
20   The *New York Times* reported in February 2008: 'More young people are observing strict separation between boys and girls, sociologists say, fuelling sexual frustrations. The focus on Islam is also further alienating young people from the West and aggravating political grievances already stoked by Western foreign policies.' Michael Slackman, 'Dreams stifled, Egypt's young turn to Islamic fervour', *New York Times*, 17 February 2008.
21   Egyptians without an ID card are non-existent citizens and only Muslims, Christians or Jews can obtain one. One Baha'i blogger lamented in 2007 that religious persecution was codified in the Egyptian system. 'Baha'i faith in Egypt', 22 August 2007, http://bahai-egypt.blogspot.com/2007/08/egypt-id-cards-vs-ancient-civilization.html
22   I visited Egypt in May and June 2007.
23   Michael Slackman,' A city where you can't hear yourself scream', *New York Times*, 14 April 2008.
24   The Egyptian government is the country's largest employer but the regime has fundamentally failed to deliver decent services for many of its citizens. Decades of repression have allowed a tiny elite to remain in power and not be seriously challenged (bloggers notwithstanding.) 'People [in Cairo] see the government as something quite foreign or removed from their lives,' says Diane Singerman, a professor in government at the American University in Washington. 'Commuters to the city, or poor peddlers and working people, do not see the government as particularly interested in their lives, and they also see politics as quite elite and risky and something to stay away from.' Michael Slackman, 'In Arab hub, the poor are left to their fate', *New York Times*, 1 March 2007.
25   Ehab El-Kelaky, 'Implacable adversaries: Arab governments and the internet', The Arabic Network for Human Rights Information, December 2006.
26   'Egypt bans German mag edition', AFP, 2 April 2008.
27   During a sentencing in September 2007, a judge praised the President and son during his verdict. Many of the editors had reported Mubarak's supposed sickness (and possible death) and the regime reacted with fury. Ian Black, 'Egyptian editors jailed for defaming Mubarak', *Guardian*, 14 September 2007. In mid-2007, many independent publications protested a bill that made it illegal to accuse state officials of corruption. Aziz El-Kaissouni, 'Egypt newspapers don't print to protest press law', Reuters, 9 July 2007. In October 2007, a number of opposition newspapers refused to publish on one day in protest at the crackdown

against the media. Another outspoken editor, Ibrahim Eissa, was given a six-month sentence in March 2008 for spreading 'false information' about Mubarak's health. 'Egypt editor given six-month sentence for Mubarak rumours', AFP, 27 March 2008. A television boss was charged by a Cairo court in May 2008 for broadcasting images of protestors tearing down posters of Mubarak during civil unrest in April. 'Egypt TV boss to be tried after attacks on Mubarak posters', AFP, 5 May 2008.

28 Gamal Nkrumah, 'Asylum-seekers abused', *Al-Ahram Weekly*, 17–23 May 2007.

29 Dina Ezzatm, 'Human rights, of sorts', *Al-Ahram Weekly*, 24–30 May 2007.

30 Interview with the author, Cairo, 23 May 2007.

31 Human Rights Watch reported in December 2007 that the Mubarak regime had used torture and false confessions in a well-known anti-terrorism case. HRW accused the regime of fabricating the name of a supposed terrorist organisation to justify ongoing emergency laws. 'Similar claims are regularly made by Western human rights groups. Egypt "fabricated terror group"', BBC News, 11 December 2007.

32 'Flawed Military Trials for Brotherhood Leaders', Human Rights Watch, 5 June 2007.

33 Elijah Zarwan, 'The tale of the weeping state security officer', The Skeptic, 5 March 2008.

34 Saad Eddin Ibrahim, 'The "New Middle East" Bush is resisting', *Washington Post*, 23 August 2006.

35 Saad Eddin Ibrahim, 'Democracy Now!', 10 October 2007.

36 Intel Corporation signed a deal with the regime in August 2007 to distribute a multimedia tool that helped the spread of e-content in schools across the country. Sherine El Madany, 'Intel bring localised e-content and multimedia technology to the classroom', *Daily Star Egypt*, 15 August 2007.

37 Like most Arab dictatorships, Mubarak's regime has had a tempestuous relationship with al-Jazeera, though authorities recognised the channel's influence by giving its staid state-run news channel an al-Jazeera makeover (with the old propaganda simply dressed up). Hugh Miles, 'Al-Jazeera: How Arab TV news challenged the world', Abacus, 2005, pp. 331–2.

38 Alexandra Sandels, 'Online campaign supports detained blogger', *Daily News Egypt*, 21 December 2007.

39 'Social responsibility and the safety of individuals', Global Voices, 14 January 2008.

40 Internet World Stats, August 2007, http://www.internetworldstats.com/africa.htm#eg

41 Shadid, ibid.

42 Numerous cases of torture in police stations have emerged online, including the case in 2007 of a twelve year old whose dead body was discovered with burns, fractures and electric shock injuries to his buttocks and testicles. He was alleged to have stolen two packets of tea from a local shop. Bloggers, including Wael Abbas, have led the charge. A full report on the case can be read here: http://politikia.blogspot. com/2007/08/12-year-old-boy-die-from-torturing-in.html

43 Ellen Knickmeyer, 'Egyptian police sentenced in landmark torture case', *Washington Post*, 6 November 2007.

44 Conditions in detention have been described as inhumane and desperate. Blogger Ramy Siyam, aka Ayoub, who spent 108 hours in prison in late 2006, has written how 'money is the law in a detention centre' and detailed the various charges for using a mobile phone, a bed or a sheet and getting food and cigarettes. More at: http://www.globalvoic esonline.org/2006/11/30/arabisc-arrested-blogger-released-and-the- civilisation-of-terrorism/. Photos of detention conditions are at: http:// www.muslimbrotherhood.co.uk/Home.asp?zPage=Systems&System=P ressR&Press=Show&Lang=E&ID=6670

45 Interview with the author, Cairo, 25 May 2007.

46 Kifaya ('Enough' in Arabic), formed in 2004, is a relatively small but vocal opposition group and campaigns for a transition to democracy. Egyptian blogger Baheyya wrote in April 2005: 'If the state cracks down, if Kifaya's tactics cease to capture the public's imagination, if international attention is averted, then the movement will wither. It might fade from the scene, devolve into contending factions, or morph into one of the familiar slots in the current political mould.' 30 April 2005, http://baheyya.blogspot.com/2005/04/kifaya-asking- right-questions.html. Kifaya's website was blocked in May 2008, undoubtedly because the organisation was at the forefront of anti- Mubarak protests.

47 'Egypt: Investigate Torture, Rape of Activist Blogger', Human Rights Watch, 19 March 2007.

48 The Arabic Network for Human Rights Information, 16 April 2008.

49 Ibid, 'Egypt: Investigate Torture, Rape of Activist Blogger'.

50 Coptic human rights blogger Hala El-Masry was arrested in October 2007 for unknown reasons, though she claimed it was due to her calls for religious freedom. She said that the state security forces had been watching, raided her house and stolen her mobile phone. Coptic blogger arrested, harassed by state security, *Daily News Egypt*, 28 October 2007. High-profile Brotherhood blogger Abdul Monem Mahmoud was arrested at Cairo airport in April 2007 for belonging to the banned Islamic movement, though human rights activists claimed it was due to his blog linking to reports and photos of state-sanctioned torture.

He was released after being held for nearly 50 days in inhumane conditions. He was tortured in 2003 during a previous imprisonment. Importantly, activists from across the political spectrum, including those who opposed the Brotherhood, campaigned for his release. Egyptian blogger Monem to be freed, Global Voices, 31 May 2007, http://www.globalvoicesonline.org/2007/05/31/egyptian-blogger-monem-to-be-freed/. There are around 15 million Coptic Christians around the world and 11 million in Egypt. The foundations of the church are based in Egypt and it belongs to the Orthodox tradition. There are growing signs of the Coptic Christians engaging in dialogue with the Muslim Brotherhood. Although the Copts remain suspicious of the group's intolerance of other faiths, their growing political power means ignoring them is no longer an option.

51 Interview with the author, Cairo, 24 May 2007.
52 Issandr El Amrani, 'Heroes or martyrs?', *Guardian* Comment is Free, 3 May 2007.
53 Interview with the author, Cairo, 24 May 2007.
54 Hamalawy has campaigned for the union rights of striking workers across Egypt, especially textile workers, and their demands for better pay and conditions. The Mubarak regime has campaigned against the workers and their highly political rhetoric. A number of opposition groups have joined the workers in their campaign. Joel Beinin and Hossam el-Hamalawy, Strikes in Egypt spread from centre of gravity, Middle East Report Online, 9 May 2007. Joel Beinin, 'The militancy of Mahalla al-Kubra', Middle East Report Online, 29 September 2007.
55 The next step, Sand Monkey, 2 May 2007.
56 Not welcome, Sand Monkey, 13 January 2008.
57 Hamza Hendawi, 'Egyptian activists turn against Israel', Associated Press, 14 September 2006.
58 Interview with the author, Cairo, 23 May 2007.
59 A moderate form of Islam is spreading among some young Egyptians. A television preacher, Moez Masoud, has emerged as a huge influence in the Arab world. At an event in Alexandria in 2007, the mostly teens and twenty-somethings, who had heard about the event through Masoud's website or Facebook page, came to hear him preach about rejecting extremism. A gay Egyptian man told the *Washington Post* that he felt more confident to be himself after hearing Masoud. Kevin Sullivan, 'Younger Muslims tune in to upbeat religious message', *Washington Post*, 2 December 2007.
60 'Egyptian bloggers test the limits', Reuters, 7 March 2007.
61 The Arabic Network for Human Rights Information released a statement in November 2007 that detailed the allegations against the regime and included torture, physical abuse and other human rights

violations. The group demanded that the prosecutor-general investigate the issue. The Arabic Network for Human Rights Information, 12 November 2007.

62 Raja M Kamal and Tom G Palmer, 'The "crime" of blogging in Egypt', *Washington Post*, 21 February 2007.

63 Interview with the author, Cairo, 25 May 2007.

64 Interview with the author, Cairo, 26 May 2007.

65 Michael Slackman, 'Voices rise in Egypt to shield girls from an old tradition', *New York Times*, 20 September 2007.

66 Abbas's Yahoo email account and YouTube account were temporarily suspended in late 2007. He blogged that YouTube claimed complaints had been received from users about the graphic nature of the torture videos and therefore the account had been suspended. He wondered if Google, owner of YouTube, had conspired with the American and/or Egyptian authorities to remove the material. After an international outcry, YouTube restored the account and said Abbas could upload the videos again. A YouTube statement read: 'Our general policy against graphic violence led to the removal of videos documenting alleged human rights abuses because the context was not apparent...If he chooses to upload the video again with sufficient context so that users can understand his important message we will of course leave it on the site.' Sara Bonisteel, 'YouTube restores account of award-winning Egyptian blogger', FoxNews.com, 1 December 2007. His YouTube channel is here: http://www.youtube.com/user/waelabbas

67 Abdel Monem Said Aly, director of the Al Ahram Centre for Political and Strategic Studies in Cairo, has cautioned against presumptions regarding the rise of Gamal Mubarak: 'This [political manoeuvres by Mubarak] will not guarantee the post for Gamal Mubarak, as often rumored, not only because of the denials of the Mubaraks, but because Egypt is more institutionalised as a republic than to allow for a Syrian-style succession from father to son, and less democratic than to grant legitimacy to an Indian Rajiv Gandhi family-style change in power.' Abdel Monem Said Aly, 'Lessons of continuity', Bitterlemons International, 25 October 2007.

68 Wael Abbas, 'Help our fight for real democracy', *Washington Post*, 27 May 2007.

69 Interview with the author, Cairo, 26 May 2007.

70 The co-editor in chief of Ikhwanweb.com, Khaled Hamza Salam, was arrested in Cairo in February 2008. Brotherhood blogger Ibrahim Houdaiby said it was because he had strongly campaigned for the rights of Brotherhood members.

71 John Walsh, 'Egypt's Muslim Brotherhood', *Harvard International Review*, Vol. 24 (4)—Winter 2003.

72   Ibrahim El Houdaiby, 'The Brotherhood opens up', *Guardian* Comment is Free, 2 January 2008.

73   Traub, ibid.

74   Ibrahim El Houdaiby, 'Your best friend hates you', Conflicts Forum, 30 September 2007.

75   Marc Lynch, 'Young brothers in cyberspace', Middle East Report Online, Winter 2007.

76   Lynch, ibid.

77   Ibrahim El Houdaiby, 'Engagement behind bars', 14 April 2008.

78   Dr Shirin Abul Naga, 'Islamic weblogs', IkhwanWeb, 26 February 2008.

79   Mariam Fam, '"Brotherhood" blogs in Egypt offer view of young Islamists', *Wall Street Journal*, 20 April 2007.

80   Abdel al-Monem Mahmoud, al-Jazeera Talk, 8 December 2007.

81   Mona Eltahawy, 'I will stand up for the Muslim Brotherhood', *Forward*, 19 September 2007.

82   Ibrahim El Houdaiby, 'The Muslim Brotherhood will stand up for all Egyptians', *Forward*, 26 September 2007.

83   Houdaiby wrote in an opinion article in November 2007: 'I find it very difficult to understand what makes Western governments, unlike civil society organisations, sceptical about engaging in healthy dialogue with moderate Islamists. I find it very difficult to understand their awkward silence in the face of ongoing violations of such activists' human rights by their authoritarian regimes—banning them from political participation, and sending them to prisons by the hundreds. I find it even more difficult to comprehend the clear bias and lack of even-handedness illustrated by the Western silence regarding the ongoing military tribunals for moderate Islamists acquitted by civilian courts in Egypt.' Ibrahim El Houdaiby, 'What today's Islamists want', Common Ground News Service, 6 November 2007.

84   Essam El Erian, 'Egypt's Muslim Brotherhood belongs on the ballot, not behind bars', *Forward*, 3 April 2008.

85   Hossam el-Hamalawy, 'Strike shake US ally', Socialist worker, April 2008. An American activist was arrested during the protests and alerted colleagues to his plight by using the micro-blogging site Twitter. By typing the word *arrested* into his mobile phone he was able to message friends. Mallory Simon, 'Student "Twitters" his way out of Egyptian jail', CNN.com, 28 April 2008.

86   'Bloggers on the frontline', Global Voices, 9 April 2008. Many of the bloggers and activists involved in the protests were arrested and tortured. Bloggers such as Wael Abbas published photographs of individuals with signs of physical trauma on his blog. YouTube, Twitter, Flickr, Facebook and other online tools were all used to spread the word to

the world about the abuses. 'Torture for bloggers and activists', Global Voices, 16 May 2008.

87 Mariam Fam, 'Egyptian political dissent unites through Facebook', *Wall Street Journal*, 5 May 2008.

88 An Egyptian female blogger, Wahda Maseyya, has written about her fears that the Brotherhood's Islamic hue is too radical for Egypt. She urged the 'reformers' within the party to pressure the 'radicals' for change. 'But at the end of the day,' she wrote, 'I do not want to see Egypt turning out to become another Iran. On the contrary, I wish to see it like Britain or even Mauritania where there is a democratic and civil government without any intervention of the military and the Islamists.' 'Muslim Brotherhood', Global Voices, 29 October 2007, http://www.globalvoicesonline.org/2007/10/29/egypt-muslim-broth erhood/

89 Ibrahim Houdaiby, 'Egypt's uncertain future', *Daily News Egypt*, 25 February 2008.

90 El-Kelaky, ibid.

Syria: Dissent behind the Assad Curtain

1   Guy Taylor, 'After the Damascus spring', *Reason*, February 2007.

2   'A black week for freedom, back to our Golan and censorship', Global Voices, 13 May 2007, http://www.globalvoicesonline.org/2007/05/13/ syria-a-black-week-for-freedom-back-to-our-golan-and-censorship/

3   *Syria—Annual Report 2007*, Reporters Without Borders, 1 February 2007.

4   I visited Syria in June 2007.

5   Joshua Landis, SyriaComment.com, 20 May 2004.

6   Taylor, ibid.

7   Khaled Yacoub Oweis, 'Syria expands "iron censorship" over internet', Reuters, 14 March 2008.

8   Taylor, ibid.

9   'Syrian PM lashes out against electronic media', Menassat, 15 April 2008.

10 2006 Middle East and North African Programs, National Endowment for Democracy

11 Human Rights Watch, ibid.

12 http://www.shril.info/english.php

13 *Syria*, Amnesty International Report 2007.

14 'US slams Syria for jailing young democrats', *Agence France-Presse*, 22 June 2007.

15 'Syria jails human rights activist', BBC News Online, 24 April 2007.

16 Bloggers across the Arab world, especially in Syria, have campaigned for the release of fellow blogger Tariq Baiasi, Global Voices, 8 February 2008.

Baiasi was sentenced to three years in prison in May 2008 for 'dwindling the national feeling' and 'weakening the national ethos'.

17 One Syrian-Kurdish female student at the Institute of Business Management in Damascus said that, 'one of the things he [Assad] did was to make changes in the higher education and IT system. Today we have many types of higher education, like private universities and open learning colleges. These were all created thanks to Assad's directives.' Others expressed similar sentiments. 'The people's say on the referendum', *Syria Today*, June 2007.

18 Joshua Landis, 'The blogging association of Syria', 19 May 2005, http://faculty-staff.ou.edu/L/Joshua.M.Landis-1/syriablog/2005/05/blogging-association-of-syria.htm

19 Jihad Yazigi, editor of the online business newsletter *The Syrian Report*, gave me this figure. Email interview with the author, 3 July 2007.

20 'Ababeyes: no to "offensive" blogs', Global Voices, 14 February 2008.

21 'Free Kareem, towards a democratic Syria, Arabism and more', Global Voices, 26 February 2007, http://www.globalvoicesonline.org/2007/02/26/syrian-blogsphere-free-kareem-towards-a-democratic-syria-arabism-and-more/

22 'Free Kareem echoes, expats living in Syria and certifying your documents', Global Voices, 4 March 2007, http://www.globalvoicesonline.org/2007/03/04/syrian-blogsphere-free-kareem-echoes-expats-living-in-syria-and-certifying-your-documents/

23 'Syria: Stop arrests for online comments', Human Rights Watch, 8 October 2007.

24 Dagge wrote a story in late 2007 that debunked the Western media's acceptance of White House spin over the Israeli bombing of a suspected Syrian nuclear site in September 2007. 'Regardless of whatever we eventually find out about what Israel bombed in the Syria desert, the Western media's treatment of the event again highlights how the burden of evidence is decisively lower for countries it deems as being 'bad'—Syria Iran, Cuba and North Korea to name a few. Until journalists and editors apply the same journalistic norms throughout all the work, regardless of whether the story is covering Washington or Damascus, their credibility will remain severely compromised.' John Dagge, '"Bad" countries and bad reporting', *New Matilda*, 5 December 2007.

25 Stack, ibid.

26 'A black week for freedom, back to our Golan and censorship', Global Voices, 13 May 2007, http://www.globalvoicesonline.org/2007/05/13/syria-a-black-week-for-freedom-back-to-our-golan-and-censorship/

27 Interview with the author, Damascus, Syria, 23 June 2007.

28 Sami Moubayed, 'The S-word: Syrianism', *Washington Post*, Post Global, 14 January 2008.

29 'US expands "Axis of Evil"', BBC News online, 6 May 2002.

30 'Bush says patience with Syria's Assad ran out long ago', Reuters, 20 December 2007.

31 After Israeli warplanes struck, in September 2007, what sanctioned media leaks said was a North Korean-built nuclear facility in Syria, Assad remained remarkably silent over the matter, despite minor complaints to the UN. Investigative journalist Seymour Hersh reported in early 2008 that he could find no evidence that the destroyed site housed a nuclear weapons program. Seymour Hersh, 'A strike in the dark?', *New Yorker*, 11 February 2008.

32 Joe Conason, 'Seven countries in five years', Salon, 12 October 2007.

33 By 2007, according to Israel's intelligence services, Damascus was keen to end its international isolation, enter the global and Arab mainstream and withdraw from its troublesome relationship with Iran. It was difficult to determine if this was merely wishful thinking. 'How Israel thinks', *Forward*, 19 October 2007.

34 'Israel plays down prospects of starting Syrian track', Reuters, 28 November 2007.

35 Ned Parker, 'Saudis' role in Iraq insurgency outlined', *Los Angeles Times*, 15 July 2007.

36 *The Financial Times* reported in October 2005, citing 'sources close to the Bush administration', that Washington was 'actively seeking an alternative who would take over from President Bashar al-Assad … and is also said to be considering military strikes on the Syrian border in response to its alleged support for Iraqi insurgents.' Guy Dinmore, 'US "seeks now Syrian leader" as pressure mounts', *Financial Times*, 9 October 2005. An Israeli or American strike against a suspected North Korean-built nuclear facility in Syria in September 2007 only heightened international suspicion against Assad. Leonard Doyle, 'US claims photos show Syrian nuclear reactor', *Independent*, 25 October 2007.

37 Interview with the author, Damascus, Syria, 23 June 2007.

38 Ibrahim Hamidi, *Al-Hayat*, 4 January 2006.

39 Joshua Landis and Joe Pace, 'The Syrian opposition', *The Washington Quarterly*, Winter 2006/07.

40 Taylor, ibid.

41 Robert Fisk, 'Silenced by the men in white socks', *Independent*, 15 March 2008.

42 Ammar Abdulhamid, 'Assad's olive branch can bear no fruit', *Forward*, 29 December 2006.

43 Robert Fisk, 'Silenced by the men in white socks', *Independent*, 15 March 2008.

44 Yitzhak Benhorin, 'Towards a democratic Syria', Ynetnews, 24 February 2007.

45 Ammar Abdulhamid, 'Few Necessary Clarifications!', 17 June 2007, http://tharwacommunity.typepad.com/amarji/2007/06/few_necessary_c.html

46 'Syria: change in Syria', Global Voices, 8 August 2007, http://www.globalvoicesonline.org/2007/08/08/syria-change-in-syria/

47 'Suu Kyi spends birthday under house arrest', *USA Today*, 19 June 2006.

48 'A black week for freedom, back to our Golan and censorship', Global Voices, 13 May 2007, http://www.globalvoicesonline.org/2007/05/13/syria-a-black-week-for-freedom-back-to-our-golan-and-censorship/

49 'UN warns of Iraq refugee disaster', BBC News Online, 7 February 2007.

50 Scott Wilson, 'Iraqi refugees overwhelm Syria', *Washington Post*, 3 February 2005.

51 Riverbend, 'Bloggers without borders', 22 October 2007.

52 Omar Sinan, 'Iraqi refugees turn to prostitution', Associated Press, 24 October 2007.

53 Interview with the author, Damascus, Syria, 24 June 2007.

54 Pentra, 'Hi … I'm here', 19 December 2007.

55 Pentra, 'From Caesar to Kitten … "Don't panic, dear!"', 29 April 2007

56 Tony Karon, 'Maliki's fate and America's, Rootless Cosmopolitan', 24 August 2007.

57 'Syria: The bloggers', Global Voices, 13 August 2007, http://www.globalvoicesonline.org/2007/08/13/syria-the-bloggers/

58 Borzou Daragahi, 'Syria tunes in the West on Madina FM', *Los Angeles Times*, 22 April 2008.

59 Joshua Landis and Joe Pace, 'The Syrian opposition', *The Washington Quarterly*, Winter 2006/07.

60 'Syria: Facebook banned', Global Voices Advocacy, 20 November 2007.

Saudi Arabia: Blooming Online in a Fundamentalist Desert

1 Comment to the author, Riyadh, 2 July 2007.

2 Colin Brown, 'Minister says UK and Saudi Arabia have "shared values"', *Independent*, 30 October 2007.

3 'Awkward guests', *Guardian*, 30 October 2007.

4 The Thatcher Government in the 1980s sold over 20 billion dollars worth of Tornado jets to Saudi Arabia, built by arms manufacturer BAE Systems. When investigations later revealed possible fraud claims against all parties, Tony Blair said that Britain's national security was at risk if the fraud inquiry continued. It was promptly dropped. Richard

Norton-Taylor, 'Huge arms deals and terror intelligence links', *Guardian*, 30 October 2007. The key allegation was that BAE Systems had a 'slush fund' of millions of pounds to entertain Saudi officials and paid Saudi diplomat Prince Bandar £30m every quarter for at least 10 years. David Leigh and Rob Evans, 'BAE accused of secretly paying £1bn to Saudi prince', *Guardian*, 7 June 2007.

5   The Saudi Kingdom has instituted a 'reintegration program' for Saudis released from Guantanamo Bay, an idea to re-train terror suspects into modern society and Islam. Josh White and Robin Wright, ' After Guantanamo Bay, "reintegration" for Saudis', *Washington Post*, 10 December 2007.

6   Martin Bright, 'What did the Saudis know about 7/7?', *New Statesman*, 1 November 2007.

7   Robert Fisk, 'King Abdullah flies in to lecturer us on terrorism', *Independent*, 30 October 2007.

8   Soon after the September 11, 2001, attacks, the Kingdom started to recognise that the terrorism issue wasn't simply a foreign problem; it was often home-grown. The 2005 elections were a small way to prove that political inclusion might mitigate some internal angst. Reformer and author Turki al-Hamad told the *New York Times* that many conservatives argued that even discussing change was undermining the Islamic nature of the Kingdom. 'The will is there,' he said, 'but there is hesitation because Saudi Arabia's Islam is based on a certain kind of Islam. If you meddle with that culture, you are meddling with the legitimacy of the system.' Neil MacFarquhar, 'Reformers in Saudi Arabia: seeking rights, paying a price', *New York Times*, 9 June 2005. By mid 2007, the reformers who held out some hope that the 2005 elections heralded a shift in government thinking were disappointed. Little had changed. 'The curse of the oil is that it has stopped all reforms,' said Sulaiman al-Hattlan, editor in chief of *Forbes Arabia*, based in Dubai. 'The more money you have, the more arrogant you become, because you think you can implement anything your way.' Hassan M. Fattah and Rasheed Abou Alsamh, 'After first steps, Saudi reformers see efforts stall', *New York Times*, 26 April 2007.

9   Western media outlets are increasingly trying to cover life in Saudi Arabia. The *New York Times* has launched a blog in Arabic for Saudi readers to comment on stories about their homeland. 'NY Times on Saudi youth', Saudi Jeans, 10 May 2008.

10   I visited Saudi Arabia in June and July 2007.

11   Faiza Saleh Ambah, 'Frustrations drive Saudi youth to the graffiti wall', *Washington Post*, 23 September 2007.

12   Every Muslim has the right to enter Saudi Arabia and visit Mecca to perform the Hajj pilgrimage. For women, however, the experience is

likely to be frustrating. A female *Guardian* journalist writes that she was regularly sexually harassed and ignored by officials. Riazat Butt, 'Our dirty little secret', *Guardian* Comment is free, 21 April 2008.

13 'Saudi Arabia eases rules for women in hotels', Reuters, 21 January 2008. The first female-only hotel opened in Riyadh in March 2008 and featured luxurious design and health and beauty facilities. The facility is women-owned, women-managed and women-run. Andrew Hammond, 'Saudi Arabia opens its first women-only hotel', *Independent*, 20 March 2008.

14 Faiza Saleh Ambah, 'For cloaked Saudi women, colour is the new black', *Washington Post*, 28 May 2007.

15 Karen Elliot House, 'A declaration of independence', *Wall Street Journal*, 7/8 April 2007.

16 Daniel Howden and Rachel Shields, 'Saudi women appeal for legal freedoms', *Independent*, 21 April 2008. Human Rights Watch demanded that the Kingdom address these gender inequalities and allow women full access to legal, health and social benefits.

17 Human Rights Watch expressed outrage in May 2008 after a Saudi court dropped charges against a couple who severely abused their Indonesian maid. The woman, 25, was allegedly tied up for a month, left without food and contracted gangrene. She was forced to have some fingers and toes amputated. Saudi maid verdict 'outrageous', BBC Online, 22 May 2008.

18 Fifty young men were accused in early 2008 of wearing indecent clothes, dancing and playing loud music to attract the attention of women in Mecca. Authorities also banned the sale of red roses and other symbols of Valentine's Day. 'Saudi men arrested for "flirting"', BBC News, 23 February 2008.

19 Howden, ibid.

20 Saudi blogger Hayfa encouraged the establishment of cinemas in the Kingdom: 'Why can't we find a way to separate the women's and children's cinemas from the men's cinema? We don't want a cinema to showcase the culture of others, as much as we need it produce our own culture.' 'Why are there no cinemas?', Global Voices, 12 May 2008.

21 'Electronic games—the good, the bad and the overlooked', Global Voices, 1 April 2008.

22 Ibtihal Hassan, 'Frustrated Saudi youth take shine to YouTube', Reuters, 17 December 2007.

23 Faiza Saleh Ambah, 'A young Saudi's online gambit', *Washington Post*, 19 July 2007.

24 Ambah, ibid.

25 Records discovered by the Americans in Iraq in 2006 found that Saudis accounted for the majority of foreign fighters. Richard A Oppel Jr,

'Foreign fighters in Iraq are tired to allies of US', *New York Times*, 22 November 2007.

26 The gender division in the country appears largely accepted by most women. Some details—such as whether it's permissible to allow men as Facebook friends or the rules around showing first male cousins an uncovered face—are mainly on the edges. One woman told the *New York Times* that even the act of speaking on the phone to her fiancé risked severe punishment. Katherine Zoepf, 'The gulf that separates the sexes in Saudi Arabia', *New York Times*, 13 May 2008. For men, although given more social freedoms, connecting with the opposite sex is equally fraught. A number of young men told the *New York Times* that they believed they were more 'rational' than women and it was their job to protect them. The sight of a single woman in a restaurant in Riyadh, before being joined by her husband, caused them to show contempt for the woman and her male relatives. Michael Slackman, 'Young Saudis, vexed and entranced by love's rules', *New York Times*, 12 May 2008.

27 Rasheed Abou-Alsamh, 'Ruling Jolts Even Saudis: 200 Lashes for Rape Victim', *New York Times*, 16 November 2007.

28 'Saudi tutor gets lashes for meeting student', *London Daily Telegraph*, 27 February 2008.

29 Rasheed Abou-Alsamh, 'Saudi women unveil opinions online', *Christian Science Monitor*, 19 June 2006.

30 Ruthven, ibid.

31 Faiza Saleh Ambah, 'An unprecedented uproar over Saudi religious police', *Washington Post*, 22 June 2007.

32 Faiza Saleh Ambah, 'Second case brought against Saudi religious police in death of a suspect', *Washington Post*, 28 June 2007.

33 Ali Al-Zahrani, 'Young men not allowed', *Arab News*, 29 June 2007.

34 A Jeddah-based businesswoman was arrested and physically assaulted in detention in early 2008 after having coffee with an unrelated man at a Starbucks in Riyadh. Raid Qusti, 'Saudi human rights official slams vice cops in Yara case', *Arab News*, 10 February 2008.

35 Najah Alosaimi, 'Restaurant partitions—part of culinary experience', *Arab News*, 4 July 2007.

36 One female Saudi blogger has written eloquently of the frustration felt by her gender at the lack of rights in the Kingdom. Lubna Hussain, also a journalist at *Arab News*, says that it's a struggle even convincing many Saudi men that women crave and deserve equal rights. The post is at http://saudijeans.org/2008/05/05/to-choose-or-not-to-choose-that-is-the-question/

37 Ebtihal Mubarak, 'Riyadh literary club hosts women bloggers', *Arab News*, 2 July 2007.

38   Interview with the author, Riyadh, 2 July 2007.
39   Karen Elliot House, 'For Saudi women, a whiff of change', *Wall Street Journal*, 7/8 April 2007.
40   House, ibid.
41   Suzan Zawawi, 'Be patient, we'll deliver, King tells Saudi women', *Saudi Gazette*, 27 April 2008.
42   Many American women are moving to Saudi Arabia to marry Saudi men. Although they forgo many personal freedoms, their children are relatively safe and free from drugs and violence and the country's sense of family is paramount. One woman told *The Los Angeles Times* that September 11 had made life more difficult for Westerners in the Kingdom because 'many Saudis didn't want to be friendly with the infidel'. Jeffrey Fleishman, 'Pursuing happiness behind the veil', *Los Angeles Times*, 14 January 2008.
43   'Don't walk in blind', American Baidu, 26 January 2008.
44   Interview with the author, Jeddah, 28 June 2007.
45   Fahad Al-Qurashi, 'How we've changed', *Saudi Gazette*, 28 June 2007.
46   Daniel Howden, 'Saudi press told to stop printing pictures of women', *Independent*, 18 May 2006.
47   Donna Abu-Nasr, 'Saudi women can sell—not drive—cars', *Associated Press*, 3 December 2006.
48   Megan K. Stack, 'In Saudi Arabia, a view from behind the veil', *Los Angeles Times*, 6 June 2007.
49   Terri Judd, 'Saudi women to put their foot down on driving ban', *Independent*, 14 September 2007.
50   Faiza Saleh Ambah, 'Saudi women petition for right to drive', *Washington Post*, 24 September 2007.
51   Octavia Nasr, 'Saudi woman seeks driving acceptance on YouTube', CNN.com, 11 March 2008.
52   Abu-Nasr, ibid.
53   According to a columnist in the *Saudi Gazette*, 'most boys now go out in blue jeans and T-shirt, which was not the norm only 15 years ago. Their haircuts and caps indicate that they belong to a different culture from that of their parents.' Fahad Al-Qurashi, 'How we've changed', *Saudi Gazette*, 28 June 2007.
54   Interview with the author, Jeddah, 29 June 2007.
55   Faiza Saleh Ambah, 'New clicks in the Arab world', *Washington Post*, 12 November 2006.
56   Fouad was detained, according to authorities, 'for violating rules not related to state security'. Very little information was issued about the reasons for his detention. His wife said he was arrested because of his blog. Officials informed him shortly before his arrest that he could be released if he issued an apology for his activism. He wrote on his blog:

'I'm not sure I'm ready to do that. An apology for what? Apologising because I said the government lied when they accused those guys [democracy activists] of supporting terrorism?' Ahmed al-Omran, of Saudi Jeans blog, said Fouad's arrest would possibly intimidate other bloggers and could make others fearful of using their real names when blogging, 'but it could also cause a backlash in the blogosphere, and spur bloggers to write even harsher criticisms'. Faiza Saleh Ambah, 'Dissident Saudi blogger is arrested', *Washington Post*, 1 January 2008. The Saudi authorities blocked both Fouad's website and another site dedicated to his cause in April 2008.

57 Many bloggers around the world expressed solidarity with Fouad after his arrest, including within Saudi Arabia. The UK *Independent* newspaper editorialised about the case, praising the rise of internet activism in Saudi Arabia and the futility of the Kingdom in trying to censor the 'online insurrection'. 'Blogging for freedom', *Independent*, 14 January 2008. Saudi Jeans campaigned regularly for his friend's release, including the publication of Fouad's 25 reasons why he returned to blogging after a short hiatus (http://saudijeans.org/2008/01/03/fouad-says/). It was a strong statement of defiance and included the following comment: '[We blog] because blogging is our only option. We do not have a free media and freedom to assemble is not allowed.' Saudi Jeans, Fouad says ..., 3 January 2008. Saudi Jeans wrote: 'I have no doubt that King Abdullah is pushing for a reformist agenda. However, it is very unfortunate that some elements in the government are not happy with this agenda because it could curb their powers and change their status.' 'You got the wrong guy', Saudi Jeans, 1 January 2008.

58 Faiza Saleh Ambah, 'New clicks in the Arab world', *Washington Post*, 12 November 2006.

59 King Abdulaziz City for Science and Technology (KACST) is based in Riyadh and much of the country's web traffic goes through this central hub. The organisation has admitted that it sometimes inadvertently filters websites and web users regularly lobby authorities to unblock them. 'The blacklist we use is a combination of an international commercial blacklist and a local blacklist,' said Mishaal Al-Kadhi, head of KACST's Internet Service Unit, to the *Christian Science Monitor* in 2006. 'Ninety-five percent of blocked sites are pornographic. But we do make mistakes sometimes and urge people to email us with their unblock requests.' Rasheed Abou-Alsamh, 'Saudi women unveil opinions online', *Christian Science Monitor*, 19 June 2006.

60 Joshua Teitelbaum, 'Duelling for Da'wa: state vs society on the Saudi internet', *Middle East Journal*, Vol. 56, No. 2, Spring 2002.

61 Faiza Saleh Ambah, 'Detained Saudis described as democracy activists', *Washington Post*, 7 February 2007.

62 Whitaker, ibid.

63 Ambah, ibid.

64 Raid Qusti, 'Treat us like human beings, Saudi reporters tells US ambassador', *Arab News*, 8 December 2005.

65 Donna Abu-Nasr, 'Saudi public leery of Bush', *Anchorage Daily News*, 14 January 2008.

66 Jim Lobe, 'Attitudes towards US worsen in Arab world', Inter Press Service, 14 April 2008.

67 Thanassis Cambanis, 'Saudi King tries to grow modern ideas in desert', *New York Times*, 26 October 2007.

68 'Bush visits his odious Saudi friend', *The Progressive*, 10 January 2008.

69 The Saudi information minister announced a nationwide ban on all live broadcasts on Saudi public television channels in early 2008 after viewers expressed anger about senior officials on a popular news channel. 'Information minister bans live programmes on state television', Reporters Without Borders, 1 February 2008.

70 Al-Jazeera's management and financial backers in Qatar have reportedly toned down their criticisms of Arab dictatorships as the fear of Iran's nuclear program grows. Robert F Worth, 'Al-Jazeera no longer nips at Saudis', *New York Times*, 4 January 2008. Arab countries started to fight back against al-Jazeera by agreeing in early 2008 to punish satellite channels perceived to offend Arab leaders and religious or national symbols. Qatar was the only country that refused to sign the charter. 'Arab TV broadcasters face curbs', BBC News, 12 February 2008.

71 'Saudi blogger misses chance to meet Karen Hughes', Global Voices, 1 October 2005.

72 Roger Hardy, 'Saudi Arabia's bold young bloggers', BBC News, 17 October 2006.

73 Interview with the author, Riyadh, 1 July 2007.

74 Hassan M Fattah, 'Talk in Saudi Arabia turns to "Iranian threat"', *International Herald Tribune*, 21 December 2006.

75 Saudi Jeans, 'Riyadh vs. Me', 5 May 2006, http://saudijeans. org/2006/05/05/riyadh-vs-me/

76 'Saudi blogger posts internet video on Christian extremism', Associated Press, 11 April 2008.

77 Suzan Zawawi, 'Exploring new ground', *Saudi Gazette*, 24 July 2007.

78 Rasheed Abou-Alsamh, 'Saudi women unveil opinions online', *Christian Science Monitor*, 19 June 2006.

79 Rasheed Abou-Alsamh, 'Finding freedom in blogosphere', *Arab News*, 30 June 2006.

80 Saudi Jeans, 'Love/Hate', 24 October 2007, http://saudijeans. org/2007/10/24/lovehate/

81   Saudi Jeans, 'Mixing Banned at Saudi Banks', 27 June 2007, http://
     saudijeans.org/2007/06/27/mixing-banned-at-saudi-banks/
82   Lawrence Wright, 'The Kingdom of silence', *New Yorker*, 5 January 2004.
83   Cambanis, ibid.

Cuba: Blogging away the Castro Blues

1   Wayne Ellwood, 'Keeping the lid on dissent', *New Internationalist*,
     May 1998.
2   Miriam Leiva, 'Whose country is it, anyway?', Salon, 24 May 2004.
3   Gabriel Garcia Marquez, 'The Fidel I think I know', *Guardian*,
     12 August 2006.
4   Johann Hari, 'Chavez must avoid the trap of dictatorship', *Independent*,
     19 November 2007.
5   Frances Robles and Pablo Bachelet, 'Bush calls Cuba a "tropical gulag"',
     Miami Herald, 25 October 2007.
6   John   Lyons,   'Diggers   in   Iraq   symbolic: Blix',   *Australian*,
     7 November 2007.
7   I visited Cuba in April 2007.
8   The myth of Che Guevara continues to this day. On the fortieth anni-
     versary of his execution by CIA-backed thugs in Bolivia in 1967, a
     former CIA operative, who was present in the moments before his
     death, said that he was killed against the wishes of the US government
     (a highly unlikely claim). David Usborne, '"We should have saved Che
     from execution", says ex-CIA operative', *Independent*, 9 October 2007.
     In Venezuela, on the anniversary, Che was hailed as a hero in the
     wake of Hugo Chavez's '21st century socialism'. Of course, critics
     of Castro and Che are also ubiquitous, labelling them both blood-
     thirsty despots.
9   Estrada, *Havana*, p. 5.
10   Patrick Symmes, 'Che is dead', *Wired*, February 1998.
11   Despite the illegality of private property, Havana has experienced a
     boom in the buying and selling of property in the last years. Prices
     are on the rise, according to the *New York Times*, 'as people try to get
     their hands on historic homes in anticipation of a time when private
     property may return to Cuba. Exiles in Cuba are also getting in on the
     act, Cubans say, sending money to relatives on the island to help them
     upgrade their homes.' Marc Lacey, 'With a whisper, Cuba's housing
     market booms', *New York Times*, 28 January 2008.
12   Carol J Williams, 'Change may be brewing in Cuba', *Los Angeles Times*,
     20 January 2008.
13   Wilpert, p. 162.

14 'Passions fuelled tyrant's 50 years in power', AFP, 19 February 2008.

15 An American director of Project Censored visited Cuba in 2008 and found Havana's two main radio stations had access to the web and journalists told him that they were free to report any stories they wanted. It was an unlikely tale.

16 A journalist for the *Guardian* reported from the island in 1960: 'For the moment, they [the Cuban people] believe literally everything that Fidel Castro tells them ... For a long time to come, I think, he and his advisors will be able to manipulate these country Cubans as he wishes. This vision is limited to black and white, and they scarcely know what red looks like.' James Morris Dayaniguas, 'Castro still a demi-God', *Guardian*, 23 July 1960.

17 Tariq Ali, 'Notoriety and popularity', *Guardian*, 20 September 2007.

18 Edwards, *Persona non grata*.

19 US President George W Bush issued a warning to Cuba in October 2007 that Washington would never accept a political transition in Cuba from Fidel to Raul. The Cuban people, he claimed, should be able to choose between 'freedom and the force used by a dying regime'. Ginger Thompson, 'Bush warns Cuba on plan for transition', *New York Times*, 24 October 2007. Raul started to initiate minor changes to the country's economy, encouraging private enterprise within the state-run economy. Carol J Williams, 'Hold the reforms—Castro is back', *Los Angeles Times*, 28 April 2007. Raul has also attempted to improve the food shortages that sometimes bedevil the island, by raising payments to milk and meat producers, helping to pay off debts to farmers and eliminating the restrictions on the importation of parts for vintage cars. Anita Snow, 'Cuba perks show a post-Fidel touch', Associated Press, 13 September 2007.

20 Cuban officials nominated Fidel Castro in December 2007 for a seat as president in the country's parliament in the early 2008 election, continuing his virtually unbroken rule of the island. 'Fidel Castro nominated for election', AFP, 3 December 2007. The sham of Cuban democracy was revealed after the January 2008 National Assembly elections. Raul Castro won 99.3 per cent of the ballots in his race while Fidel won 98.2 per cent. 'Raul Castro won more votes than Fidel for assembly: Cuba', AFP, 30 January 2008.

21 Saul Landau, '47 years later in Havana', Counterpunch, 1 June 2007.

22 Cuba is the number one organic country in the world and can boast a lower infant mortality rate than the US.

23 Chomsky, *Failed States*, p. 114.

24 Chomsky, *Hegemony or Survival*, p.95

25 Chomsky, *Failed States*, pp. 32–3.

26 Chomsky, *Failed States*, p. 113.

27   Marc Frank, 'Castro gives farmers more control over food production', Reuters, 25 March 2008.

28   Patricia Grogg, 'Dissidents, preachers welcome decision', Inside Costa Rica, 30 April 2008.

29   'Cubans free to buy gadgets, PCs from now', *Economic Times*, 27 March 2008. After Cubans were able to purchase desktop computers in May 2008, many Cubans were excited at the opportunity, despite the clunky machines that were on offer. The price of US$780 for a PC and monitor was prohibitive for the vast bulk of citizens. 'Cubans get first glimpse of computers', Associated Press, 4 May 2008.

30   Haroon Siddique,' Cuba lifts mobile phone restrictions', *Guardian*, 28 March 2008. Cubans lined up for blocks in April 2008 after being allowed to purchase mobile phones, even though the cost of the device and calls were prohibitive for most citizens. The communist press said the changes were initiated by Fidel. Many wanted the phones to keep in touch with relatives overseas. Will Weissert, 'Cubans line up for cell phone service', Associated Press, 14 April 2008. George W Bush, in a small concession, finally allowed Americans in 2008 to send mobile phones to relatives in Cuba.

31   Anthony Boadle, 'UN food envoy praises Cuba, sees need for reform', Reuters, 6 November 2007.

32   Ignacio Ramonet, 'Politics' last superstar', *Guardian*, 10 October 2007.

33   John Pateman and John Vincent, 'Information for social change', October 2000.

34   'Righting past wrongs—defending the right to sexual diversity in Cuba: Interview with Mariela Castro', Inside Costa Rica, 14 December 2007.

35   Andrea Rodriguez, Cuban government backs calls to combat homophobia, Associated Press, 18 May 2008.

36   Interview with the author, Havana, 20 April 2007.

37   Vaclav Havel, 'Europe needs solidarity over Cuba', *Guardian* Comment is Free, 16 March 2008.

38   Ellwood, ibid.

39   Farber, ibid.

40   Sanchez said in 1998: 'The [Cuban] government says I and my companeros are paid by Washington and the CIA. And the radical exiles in Miami say we're paid by Fidel. In the end nobody pays us. We're completely independent.' Wayne Ellwood, 'Keeping the lid on dissent', *New Internationalist*, May 1998.

41   Ellwood, ibid.

42   Ellwood, ibid.

43   The Bush administration's attempts to praise Cuban dissidents have only harmed the cause. When President Bush awarded the Presidential Medal of Freedom to Cuban dissident Oscar Elias Biscet in November

2007, he could be classed as a Washington stooge. Likewise, when US Secretary of State Condoleezza Rice said in June 2007 that she was 'particularly concerned that the dissidents in Cuba get the right message' and that 'people who are struggling for a democratic future need to know that they are supported by those of us who are lucky enough to be free', the words were empty rhetoric. All Cuban dissidents I met consistently said that American help was counter-productive to their cause. Victoria Burnett, 'From Rice, blunt talk for Spain over Cuba', *International Herald Tribune*, 2–3 June 2007. During the 2008 US Presidential campaign, the leading candidates on the Democratic and Republican sides argued for maintaining a hard line against Cuba. Only Democratic hopeful Barack Obama openly talked about engaging with the island's leaders and loosening the embargo. Fareed Zakaria, 'The wrong experience', *Newsweek*, 2 February 2008.

44 After Hugo Chavez lost a bid in early December 2007 to amend Venezuela's constitution and increase his powers, Cuban-born writer Carlos Alberto Montaner wrote in the *Washington Post* that Castro had expected Chavez to win the vote and continue the socialist revolution. 'That means that the top-rank leaders, deep in their hearts, celebrated Chavez's defeat. Now, the reformers, wielding good arguments, can discourage a union between the two countries and explain that it is very dangerous for Cuba to gamble away its future by placing it in the hands of a precarious leader with his own uncertain future. It is true that Fidel Castro, even on his deathbed, keeps control over the reins of the regime, but he can no longer seriously say that Latin America is marching toward 21st-century socialism.' Carlos Alberto Montaner, 'Cuba reels at Chavez's defeat', *Washington Post* Post Global, 7 December 2007.

45 'Cuba's long black spring', Committee to protect journalists, 18 March 2008.

46 Very few Cubans have access to the internet at home, except foreigners, some state officials and company executives. A number of academics and government workers also have internet accounts.

47 James C McKinley Jr, 'Cyber-rebels in Cuba defer state's limits', *New York Times*, 6 March 2008.

48 Willy Wright, 'Cuban artists open internet forum on their upcoming congress', Cubanow.net, 28 March 2008.

49 Alfonso Chardy, 'Over internet, Cuban youths offer rare insights', *McClatchy Newspapers*, 26 March 2008.

50 Press release from the Cuban Mission to the United Nations, 17 October 2007.

51 A fibre-optic ring around the Caribbean was laid in late 2001 but Cuba was bypassed. The ring passes within 12 miles of Havana. The

international consortium has claimed that no negotiations have taken place with the Cubans to install the cable. John Cote, 'Cubans log on behind Castro's back', in Chevez (ed.), *Capitalism, God, and a Good Cigar*, pp. 168–9. Venezuela has pledged to install an underwater fibre-optic cable between the two countries by 2009. Brian Ellsworth, 'Cuba, Venezuela extend ties despite Castro's illness', *New Scotsman*, 25 January 2007.

52   A number of Western journalists have been expelled from the island over the last years. A reporter from the *Chicago Tribune* was told in early 2007 that he had been in Cuba for a long time and 'they felt my work was negative'. Frances Robles, 'Tribune reporter is ousted in Cuba crackdown', *Miami Herald*, 22 February 2007. The journalist, Gary Marx, told *The Nation* that he was informed by the authorities that, 'this is nothing personal, this is business. Our overseas image is very important to us. We weighed your positive stories against your negative stories. There are too many negative stories. We think we can do better with someone else.' John Dinges, 'Watching the reporters', *The Nation*, 14 May 2007.

53   'Cuba internal dissidents seek unity', Al-Jazeera English, 6 September 2007.

54   'Top dissident calls Cuban elections a "farce"', AFP, 21 January 2008.

55   Ed Vulliamy, 'In the last act of Castro's Cuba, a search is on for a new beginning', *Observer*, 20 January 2008.

56   'Cuba inches into the internet age', *Los Angeles Times*, 19 November 2006.

57   'Dominican republic: technology leader in free trade bloc', Dominican Today, 13 December 2007.

58   Cote, ibid. Cote explains that even in the middle years of the early twenty-first century, many Cuban state employees were only allowed to access an intranet, rather than the internet. For many Cubans, who simply cannot afford computers on the black market, they can visit a local library and ask a staff member to research information for them online.

59   'Seven questions: Castro's daughter speaks out', Foreign Policy, March 2008.

60   Castro has promoted computer literacy in the education system and advocates a strong software development industry but internet access is a telling omission in this program. Ian Katz, 'Cubans are tangled in Castro's web revolution', *South Florida Sun-Sentinel*, 18 June 2006.

61   'Cuban official calls for controlling "wild colt of new technologies"', Associated Press, 12 February 2007.

62   'Cuba inches into the internet age', *Los Angeles Times*, 19 November 2006.

63   Geri Smith, 'Yahoo, stay home', *Business Week*, 29 November 1999.

64 Despite the restrictions on internet access, the last years have seen an explosion of 'virtual capitalism' online, with a number of sites selling everything from a 1956 Chevrolet to an internet access account and rooms for rent. 'Virtual capitalism arrives in Cuba', EFE News Service, 28 August 2007.

65 Taylor C Boas, 'The director's dilemma? The internet and US policy toward Cuba', *Washington Quarterly*, Summer 2000.

66 The Paris-based Reporters Without Borders (RSF) is routinely criticised for being too close to the US government's foreign policies objectives, receiving US funds and working with Miami-based Cuban exile groups. Salim Lamrani, a leading writer on US–Cuba relations, has accused RSF of having a 'limitless obsession' with Cuba and fabricating 'evidence' against Castro's regime. Lamrani wrote in 2005 that, due to taking money from the Reagan-initiated program National Endowment for Democracy (NED), RSF was simply doing the bidding of the US administration in Latin America, namely the goal 'to weaken governments that would oppose the foreign hegemonic power of Washington … The two targets are Cuba and Venezuela.' There seems to be validity in some of these views, but Lamrani, among others, appears to find no problems with freedom of speech in places like Cuba. Salim Lamrani, 'The reporters without borders fraud', Znet, 13 May 2005.

67 'Cuba inches into the internet age', *Los Angeles Times*, 19 November 2006.

68 Amaury del Valle and Juventud Rebelde, www.thecubannation.com, 1 October 2007.

69 Although irrefutable evidence of Google's behaviour is impossible to confirm, strong anecdotal reports suggest that the company is adhering to Washington-directed countries suffering economic sanctions. It remains unclear whether Google is forced to comply with these rules or is acting pre-emptively to avoid investigation. 'US sanctions preventing Cubans, Syrians from downloading Google Earth?', Ogle Earth, 1 October 2007. Reporters Without Borders claimed in 2004 that Telecom's Italia had signed a deal with Cuba's telecommunications operator ETECSA and was assisting internet censorship. 'Reporters Without Borders seeks meeting with Marco Tronchetti Provera, chairman of Telecom Italia's board of directors', 25 March 2004.

70 'Journalist on hunger strike to demand unrestricted internet access', Reporters Without Borders, 2 February 2006.

71 Doreen Hemlock, 'Dissident: "Down with corruption, I'm on a hunger strike"', *South Florida Sun-Sentinel*, 11 February 2007.

72 A number of paramilitary style groups, including Alpha 66, have been linked to assassinations and terror attacks against Castro's power in Miami and Cuba itself, but Washington ignores these elements primarily because the individuals are exhibiting behaviour it condones.

Tristram Korten and Kirk Nielsen, 'The coddled "terrorists" of South Florida', Salon, 14 January 2008. A key anti-Castro terrorist, Luis Posada Carriles, now lives openly in Miami, despite vast evidence of his violence against the Cuban people. Carol J Williams, 'Luis Posada Carriles, A terror suspect abroad, enjoys a "coming out" in Miami', *Los Angeles Times*, 7 May 2008. A book released in 2002 alleged that members of the Bush family were instrumental in releasing militant Cubans convicted of terrorist offences, in exchange for political and financial support. Duncan Campbell, 'The Bush dynasty and the Cuban criminals', *Guardian*, 2 December 2002.

73 'Castro's health—a Cuban blogger's view', BBC News online, 25 January 2007.

74 Wayne S Smith, 'The danger of doing as Bush does', *Guardian* Comment is Free, 3 December 2006.

75 Esteban Israel, 'Blogging from Havana, secretly', *International Herald Tribune*, 10 October 2007.

76 'Blocked blogger Yoani Sanchez receives prestigious award', Global Voices, 8 April 2008.

77 'Cubans should be free to travel, says Castro daughter', AFP, 11 May 2008.

78 'Cuba delays access to top Cuban blog', Reuters, 25 March 2008.

79 'Cuba: blocking bloggers', Global Voices, 26 March 2008.

80 Israel, ibid.

81 Tom Gjelten, 'Cuban newspaper pushes beyond party line', National Public Radio, 1 June 2008.

82 'Cuba's long black spring, Committee to protect journalists', 18 March 2008.

83 Email interview with the author, 2 February 2007.

84 Jean-Guy Allard, 'Mercenary NGOs meet in Washington: USAID reveals its plans for subversion in Cuba', *Granma International*, 3 June 2008.

85 Cuba: issues for Congress, Congressional Research Library, 20 November 2001.

86 Cuba: issues for the 110th Congress, Congressional Research Library, 21 August 2007.

87 'Abby Goodnough, US paid 10 journalists for anti-Castro reports', *New York Times*, 9 September 2006.

88 The Government Accountability Office found that nearly US$74 million of funds designed to promote democracy had been used by Miami groups, in the most extreme examples to purchase 'a gas chainsaw, a computer gaming equipment and software (including Nintendo Game Boys and Sony PlayStations), a mountain bike, leather coats, cashmere sweaters, crab meat and Godiva chocolates.' Karen DeYoung,

'GAO audit finds waste in Cuban aid program', *Washington Post*, 16 November 2006.

89 Interview with the author, Havana, 21 April 2007

90 The Cuban regime alleged that a leading member of Ladies in White, Laura Pollan, received US funds from the head of the US interests section in Havana and the money was split among members of the group. Rory Carroll, 'Cuban sting shows US diplomat handing cash to dissidents', *Guardian*, 24 May 2008.

91 Message by the Ladies in White to the European Parliament, 7 June 2007, translated by Rodrigo Acunã.

92 The head of Cuba's labour union told tens of thousands of workers on 1 May 2008 that 'inefficiencies and weaknesses' in Cuba needed to be overcome for the country to advance past the Fidel Castro era. Marc Lacey, 'Cubans urged to work toward change', *New York Times*, 2 May 2008.

93 Fidel Castro, after stepping down in early 2008, defended his 2003 crackdown on dissidents and claimed they were working for the American Government. 'Fidel Castro defends crackdown', United Press International, 25 March 2008.

94 Oscar Espinosa Chepe, 'Anatomy of the Cuban information apartheid', 17 November 2005, translated by Rodrigo Acunã.

95 Andrew Gumbel, 'Cuba's new Castro shows little patience with "Women in White"', *Independent*, 23 April 2008.

96 Miriam Leiva, 'Whose country is it, anyway?', Salon, 24 May 2004.

97 'Cuban youths pose tough questions in surprising video', AFP, 7 February 2008.

98 'Cuban student denies arrest after government criticism', CNN.com, 12 February 2008.

99 Aviva Chomsky, 'Pragmatic Raul, irrational Fidel: media distortions on Cuba', North American Congress on Latin America, 7 March 2008.

100 'Departure of a dictator who had outlived his times', *Independent*, 20 February 2008.

101 'Cuba to open up media to Vatican: report', Reuters, 27 February 2008.

102 'Cuba signs human rights accords', Al-Jazeera.net, 29 February 2008.

103 James C McKinley Jr, 'Raul Castro hints at change, but Cuba remains wary', *New York Times*, 27 February 2008.

104 'More reactions to Castro's retirement', Global Voices, 24 February 2008.

105 Rory Carroll, 'To save communism, Raul experiments with consumerism', *Guardian*, 7 April 2008.

106 Tony Karon, 'The guilty pleasure of Fidel Castro', Rootless Cosmopolitan, 20 February 2008.

107 Nathan Guttman, 'Community finds new life in Castro-less Cuba', *Forward*, 19 September 2007.

108 JTA, 29 February 2008.
109 Larry Luxner, 'Castro quits, but his policies remain', JTA, 19 February 2008.
110 Guttman, ibid.
111 Caren Osten Gerszberg, 'In Cuba, finding a tiny corner of Jewish life', *New York Times*, 4 February 2007.
112 Interview with the author, Havana, 23 April 2007.
113 Israel is the only country with which Cuba has cut off official diplomatic relations, probably because of its closeness to Washington. Caren Osten Gerszberg, 'In Cuba, finding a tiny corner of Jewish life', *New York Times*, 4 February 2007.
114 Guttman, ibid.
115 'How satisfied are Cubans? Gallup surveys two cities', *South Florida Sun-Sentinel*, 15 December 2006.
116 Chinese assistance given in 2008 to the brutal Zimbabwean dictatorship of Robert Mugabe—including weapons and troops on the ground—indicated that non-democratic states, including Cuba, would increasingly find willing supporters in Beijing. Cuba is not immune to similar issues. The new colonial masters, *Independent*, 19 April 2008.
117 Like many other more technologically connected countries, Cuban dissidents have started using email campaigns to push for change. One widely circulated email, written by a leading Cuban film critic, listed 30 Cuban-made films that had never been screened on state television. Gary Marx, 'Cuban intellectuals begin to question government', *Chicago Tribune*, 19 February 2007.
118 Patrick Symmes, 'Che is dead', *Wired*, February 1998.

China: Punching through the Great Firewall

1 Rowan Callick, 'China's great firewall', *Australian*, 12 March 2007.
2 Wuer Kaixi features in the 1995 documentary, The Gate of Heavenly Peace (http://www.tsquare.tv/film/transcript.html).
3 'China to step up "re-education" of Tibetans', AFP, 5 April 2008.
4 The London *Independent* editorialised that the torch relay, 'essentially a fashion accessory revived for the purpose of the 1936 Berlin Olympics', should be extinguished because it could not claim to represent harmony. 'Fanning the flame?', *Independent*, 7 April 2008. Some Chinese bloggers called for a boycott of French goods and contracts after protestors disrupted the torch relay in Paris in April 2008. John Lichfield, 'Chinese bloggers call for blacklist of French goods', *Independent*, 12 April 2008.
5 'If the games fail, human rights suffer', Spiegel online, 7 April 2008.

6   A popular Chinese website launched an online campaign for citizens to 'sign up' and protest anti-Chinese media coverage. It received more than one million signatures in its first twenty-four hours. 'People "sign up" to slam media bias', *China Daily*, 5 April 2008. Reporters Without Borders obtained a 2007 memo that outlined directives for government officials in dealing with the foreign media before and during the Beijing Games. 'Positive propaganda must be reinforced' was a key passage. 'Classified memo reveals government strategy for 'managing' foreign journalists', Reporters Without Borders, 30 March 2008.

7   'Bloggers declare war on Western media's Tibet', Global Voices, 24 March 2008. A Chinese primary school teacher and beautician launched a US$1.3 billion lawsuit against CNN for allegedly insulting the Chinese people. Clifford Coonan, 'Chinese sue for $1.3bn over CNN commentator's "goons" remark', *Independent*, 25 April 2008.

8   Rebecca MacKinnon, 'Anti-CNN and the Tibet information war', RConversation, 26 March 2008.

9   Kathleen E McLaughlin, 'China delays the news of Olympic torch relay', *San Francisco Chronicle*, 9 April 2008.

10   Despite massive support within China for the country's tough line on Tibet, a global poll conducted by WorldPublicOpinion.org found widespread criticism of Chinese policies towards Tibet and a majority belief that autonomy should be granted to Tibet. Poll of Western and Asian publics finds criticism of Chinese policy on Tibet, WorldPublicOpinion.org, 18 March 2008.

11   A number of Western bloggers encouraged greater engagement between Chinese and Western bloggers to try and better the other's perspectives on Tibet. Rebecca MacKinnon, 'Tibet … is discussion possible?', RConversation, 16 March 2008. The International Olympic Committee told China that it expected an unfiltered internet during the Beijing Games, but the regime was likely to uncensor the net only for foreign journalists and visitors. 'IOC pushes China on internet access', BBC, 2 April 2008.

12   'Patriotism triggered, though under censorship', Global Voices, 19 March 2008.

13   'Dalai Lama has "never done anything good"', Xinhua, 4 April 2008. One Tibetan blogger, based in Beijing, defied authorities and continued to write about the trauma in her homeland. Woeser told the *Washington Post* that she wanted to 'record all of the history and to be a witness to what is happening now'. Jill Drew, 'A lone Tibetan voice, intent on speaking out', *Washington Post*, 6 May 2008. A student at Columbia University met the Dalai Lama in April 2008 and in a widely circulated essay in China and in the Diaspora wrote that he was ' deeply impressed by his sincerity and hospitality'. 'A Chinese student's

interview with the Dalai Lama', China Digital Times, 3 May 2008. Aside from repression against the Tibetan people, the Uighur people, mainly Muslim and residing in the northwest part of China, also face discrimination. A popular online forum serving to bridge the gap between Han Chinese, the Uighur people and other minority groups was closed down in May 2008. Authorities wanted to suppress any public voice of these groups.

14 Protests across China, possibly part-organised by government officials, were launched in early 2008, especially against Western media companies and French supermarket chain Carrefour, for their supposed anti-Chinese bias. Newspaper editorials, web postings and text message spread the sentiment like wildfire. Andrew Jacobs, 'Protests of the West spread in China', *New York Times*, 21 April 2008. One Western company, Adidas, was keen to remain above politics. Its CEO, Herbert Hainer, told *Spiegel* that he was against any boycott of the Beijing Olympic Games and refused to make any criticism of China's human rights abuses. 'Our commitment to the Olympics is not a political commitment', Hainer said. 'It is a commitment to sport.' Lothar Gorris and Thomas Tuna, 'Interview with Adidas CEO Herbert Hainer', *Spiegel*, 7 May 2008.

15 Cheng Yizhong, an editor who tracks China's Olympic preparations and is the deputy publisher of *Sports Illustrated China*, said: 'The government is suffering from its own propaganda system, which has been rigid for a long time. China is lifting a rock only to drop it on its own feet.' Jill Drew and Maureen Fan, 'China falls short on vows for Olympics', *Washington Post*, 21 April 2008.

16 Ching-Ching Ni, 'China saw new freedoms with TV quake coverage', *Los Angeles Times*, 23 May 2008

17 Daniel A Bell, 'China's class divide', *New York Times*, 21 May 2008

18 John Garnaut and Hamish McDonald, 'China: the wall comes down', *Age*, 17 May 2008

19 I visited China in July 2007.

20 The Foreign Correspondents Club of China announced in early 2008 that a survey of its members found 180 journalists had been obstructed in their work since more 'liberal' rules came into play in late 2007. It was acknowledged, however, that the authorities were improving the situation for journalists. Rowan Callick, 'A little bit of transparency', *Australian*, 12–13 January 2008.

21 Edward Cody, 'Before Olympics, a call for change', *Washington Post*, 8 August 2007. Reporters Without Borders, at a Beijing press conference on 6 August 2007, issued a number of demands for the Chinese government to be implemented before the August 2008 Olympics, including the release of all imprisoned journalists and web users. Reporters Without Borders, Beijing 2008, 6 August 2007. The British

Olympic Association reviewed its athletes' contracts after a storm of criticism revealed that it prevented competitors from making political comments during the Beijing Games. It was yet another example of a Western government not wanting to offend China. Paul Kelso, 'Officials to review gag on Olympic athletes', *Guardian*, 11 February 2008.

22 Alexandri, ibid.
23 By September 2007, Chinese netizens requested more than 10 billion searches per month, for the first time beating America's monthly amount of 9.4 billion in the same period. *China Tech News*, 30 November 2007. A Chinese actress and director, Xu Jinglei, became the world's most widely read blogger in mid-2007 after attracting 100 million page views within 600 days. 'Actress scores hit with blog', *Shanghai Daily*, 20 July 2007.
24 'China: pollution map of China released', Global Voices, 17 December 2007.
25 Geremie R Barme and Sang Ye, 'The great firewall of China', *Wired*, June 1997.
26 Barme and Sang, ibid.
27 CNNC releases 2007 survey report on China weblog market: number of blog writers reaches 47 equalling one fourth of total netizens, 26 December 2007.
28 Jeremy Goldkorn, 'China becomes top internet user?', Danwei.org, 14 March 2008.
29 The Internet Society of China released a draft Voluntary Blogging Service Code of Conduct in 2007 that 'encouraged' bloggers to register their real names, but it was acknowledged to be technically impossible to track every user. Rowan Callick, 'China's bloggers beat Great Firewall', *Australian*, 26 May 2007.
30 Ji Shaoting, Li Huaiyan and Wang Pan, 'Internet becomes new medium for govt to collect public opinion', Xinhua, 4 March 2008.
31 Barme and Sang, ibid.
32 'China bloggers really are edgy', *Wall Street Journal China Journal*, 14 June 2008.
33 Barme and Jaivin, *New Ghosts, Old Dreams*, p. xxvi.
34 The Committee to Protect Journalists reported that 127 journalists were behind bars on 1 December 2007. Anna Schecter and Rehab El-Buri, 'New report: China is top journalist jailer', ABC News: The blotter, 6 December 2007.
35 Rowan Callick, 'China on slow boat to democracy', *Australian*, 28 February 2007.
36 Matt Rosenberg, 'China population', About.com, 19 August 2007.
37 Simon Usborne, 'China: in numbers', *Independent*, 10 May 2008.

38 Rowan Callick, 'The China model', *The American*, November/December 2007.

39 The news in early 2008 that China was reportedly providing military arms and troops to Robert Mugabe's Zimbabwe caused critics to worry that China was becoming a new colonial master around the world, allegedly not caring about human rights or good governance in its endless quest for resources. *The Independent* editorialised: 'As for Mr Mugabe, he marked Zimbabwean Independence Day yesterday by complaining of neo-colonialism and how Britain wants to retake control of Zimbabwe. He and other African leaders should think more carefully. There is a danger of their countries becoming a victim of a re-colonisation. But the threat is not from the West. It comes from the East.' 'The new colonial masters', *Independent*, 19 April 2008.

40 'Internet censor's latest "working instructions"', China Digital Times, 20 January 2008, http://chinadigitaltimes.net/2008/01/internet_censors_latest_working_instructions_1.php

41 A *New York Times* story reported in early December 2007, weeks before the assassination of Pakistani politician Benazir Bhutto, that China's state media was reporting turmoil in Pakistan with 'dry, narrowly drawn and sometimes inaccurate accounts of the events'. It was noted that local media was far bolder when reporting China-related stories. Howard W French, 'China media less aggressive in foreign coverage', *New York Times*, 7 December 2007.

42 'Journey to the heart of internet censorship', Reporters Without Borders, October 2007.

43 'How cyber-censors blocked dissemination of report on internet censorship', Reporters Without borders, 1 February 2008.

44 'Chinese ministries jointly regulating online order', ChinaTechNews.com, 19 February 2008.

45 '210 million Internet users in China', People's Daily Online, 21 January 2008.

46 Yao Yonghe of 51.com, a social networking site popular in smaller centres, argues that these less globally connected users are now driving the market. Rebecca MacKinnon, 'My web 2.0 week in Beijing', 12 November 2007. Users across the country spent nearly double the amount of money online in 2006 than 2005. In 2006, users spent a monthly average of US$21.79 for internet access, online shopping and games. 'Hu Jintao asks Chinese officials to better cope with internet', Xinhau, 25 January 2007. Despite the vast growth in wealth, the World Bank estimated in early 2008 that 300 million Chinese remained poor and excluded from the country's development. Howard W French, 'Lives of poverty, untouched by China's boom', *New York Times*, 13 January 2008. China's peasants remain largely ignored and exploited

in the rush for global supremacy. In the cities, QQ, an instant messaging service that has shades of Facebook, YouTube and MySpace, has become a massive craze with China's connected populace. More than 100 million Chinese are addicted to staring at their mobile phone screens after creating online personalities, or avatars—users can even choose clothes or buy pets—and sharing them with friends. One small business owner, Yu Cunyi, said that he used QQ 'to do all sorts of things: chatting, archiving photos, writing diaries, meeting new friends, shopping and playing games … I spend two to three hours every day on QQ.' Clifford Coonan, 'QQ craze holds key to China's internet market, *Independent*, 9 January 2008. Chinese mobile phone users sent 429 billion text messages in 2006. China out-texts rest of world', *Reuters*, 12 December 2007. Mobile phone users suffer spam attacks on a regular basis. According to a survey by the China Internet Society in 2006, 6.25 per cent of respondents received more than 40 spam messages per week. 'Spam text messages a headache for all', *China Daily*, 27 November 2006.

47 Tom Doctoroff, 'Chinese youth and their internet: deep love', Huffington Post, 31 January 2008.

48 Cameras were installed in internet cafes in Beijing 2006 to monitor the spread of 'unhealthy information' and enforce internet laws. 'Video cameras to monitor all Beijing's internet cafes', China Digital Times, 24 November 2006. Surveillance cameras have also been installed in other cities, such as Shanghai.

49 'Chinese cartoon cops patrolling websites', Global Voices advocacy, 30 August 2007.

50 The English language version of Wikipedia was initially available in China, but the Chinese version of Wikipedia was soon seen as a threat to the regime's control over information. The concept of objective content was relatively new for many Chinese. Philip P Pan, 'Reference tool on web finds fans, censors', *Washington Post*, 20 February 2006.

51 Wikipedia, in both its Chinese and English versions, remains intermittently available but the authorities block and then unblock the sites on a regular basis. Hiawatha Bray, 'Chinese cut off from Wikipedia', *Boston Globe*, 18 November 2006.

52 Gillian Wong, 'China: web censorship report groundless', Associated Press, 8 November 2006.

53 'Hu Jintao asks Chinese officials to better cope with internet', Xinhua, 25 January 2007.

54 Christopher Bodeen, 'China calls for stepped-up propaganda', Associated Press, 23 January 2008.

55 Researchers at UC Davis and the University of New Mexico discovered that the Chinese filtering system is a 'panopticon' that encourages

self-censorship through the belief that users are being monitored. The technology employed by the Chinese was in fact 'porous' and blocking was 'particularly erratic' when many users were online. 'Chinese web filtering "erratic"', BBC News online, 12 September 2007.

56 Jonathan Watts, 'China's secret internet police target critics with web of propaganda', *Guardian*, 14 June 2005.

57 Fons Tuinstra, 'Internet democracy with Chinese characteristics', Poynteronline, 25 June 2007.

58 'China: tough blogging the Communist Congress', Global Voices, 16 October 2007.

59 'China pulls plug on internet data centres ahead of party congress', Radio Free Asia, 13 September 2007.

60 Lindsay Beck, 'China press can criticise, but limits—watchdog', *Guardian*, 11 March 2008.

61 Mark Sweeney, 'China sidesteps internet criticism', *Guardian*, 20 March 2008

62 Adam J Schokora, 'Why do Chinese internet users like government controls?', Danwei.org, 31 March 2008.

63 A leading Communist Party journal published a scathing article in mid 2007 that acknowledged the price the party had paid for not addressing social injustice and corruption and worried that reforms had stalled. Mary-Anne Toy, 'China "going backwards" on reforms', *Age*, 17 July 2007.

64 Jane Macartney, 'Web censorship is failing, says Chinese official', *The Times*, 17 July 2007.

65 Many contributors to the site complained about the wealth accumulated by officials and lack of care in local services. Edward Cody, 'Chinese assail official misconduct with fervour', *Washington Post*, 20 December 2007. A massively popular computer game, *The Incorruptible Warrior*, was released by the authorities in 2007 and allowed players to kill corrupt officials, though only ones based in history and not the present day. Tim Johnson, 'Fighting corruption—online', China Rises, 2 August 2007.

66 Interview with the author, Shanghai, 7 July 2007.

67 Interview with the author, Beijing, 17 July 2007.

68 Interview with the author, Beijing, 17 July 2007.

69 Edward Cody, For China's journalism students, censorship is a core concept, *Washington Post*, 31 December 2007. China introduced a version of freedom of information on 1 May 2008 in a supposed attempt to add transparency to government at every level. A 2004 pilot program in Shanghai saw little success. Rowan Callick, Chinese FOI act tied by red tape, *Australian*, 1 May 2008.

70 Skype's chief executive, Niklas Zennstrom, admitted in 2006 that its Chinese partner was filtering text messages. Alison Maitland, 'Skype says texts are censored', *Financial Times*, 18 April 2006.

71 In the run-up to the 2008 Beijing Olympic Games, advocacy group Dream for Darfur, led by actress Mia Farrow, accused Western multinationals such as Coca-Cola, Kodak, BHP Billiton and Microsoft of failing to speak out and condemn China's support for the Sudanese regime. Stephen Hutcheon, 'Darfur group brands BHP moral cowards', Sydney Morning Herald online, 25 April 2008. Reporters Without Borders spoke at the Adidas shareholder meeting in May 2008 to inform a corporate sponsor of the Beijing Games about China's human rights abuses. Adidas CEO Herbert Hainer told German magazine *Der Spiegel* that he had no guilty conscience about his company's involvement. 'But one thing should be clear,' he said. 'Our involvement is not a recognition of any policy, society or culture, it is a recognition of sport. I fear these Olympics are now only about politics,' *Der Spiegel*, 7 May 2008.

72 Adi Ignatius, 'In search of the real Google', *Time*, 12 February 2006.

73 Rick Justice, Senior Vice President, Worldwide Field Operations, discusses how Cisco products are marketed and sold globally, 25 July 2005.

74 A senior Chinese official admitted in 2006 that torture was regularly used to obtain convictions. It was a rare moment of honesty on an issue that is rarely discussed publicly. 'China official admits to torture', BBC News, 20 November 2006.

75 Rebecca MacKinnon, 'My conversation with Cisco', RConversation, 22 July 2005.

76 Anne Applebaum, 'Let a thousand filters bloom', *Washington Post*, 20 July 2005.

77 Tamara Renee Shie, 'The tangled web: does the internet offer promise or peril for the Chinese Communist Party?', Journal of Contemporary China, August 2004.

78 Keith Bradsher, 'At trade show, China's police shop for the West's latest', *New York Times*, 26 April 2008.

79 Bill Gertz, 'China gets US Olympics help', *The Washington Times*, 5 June 2008.

80 Naomi Klein, 'China's all-seeing eye', *Rolling Stone*, 15 May 2008

81 James Fallows, 'The connection has been reset', *Atlantic*, March 2008.

82 Fallows, ibid.

83 Glenn Kessler, 'Cisco file raises censorship concerns', *Washington Post*, 20 May 2008.

84 Xeni Jardin, co-editor of the popular site http://boingboing.net/, has argued that companies that sell filtering technologies to repressive

regimes should be forced to declare these to the United States Munitions List (where American companies that sell bombs and guns to non-democratic nations must disclose their sales). Xeni Jardin, 'Exporting censorship', *New York Times*, 9 March 2006.

85   MSN and Yahoo China signed a 'self-discipline' pledge in August 2007 that agreed to encourage bloggers to use their real names and not post anonymously. Rebecca MacKinnon, 'Chinese bloggers thumb their noses at "self discipline"', RConversation, 28 August 2007.

86   Jonathan Watts, 'Microsoft helps China to censor bloggers', *Guardian*, 15 June 2005.

87   Microsoft issued a statement on 16 May 2006 in response to a statement by Amnesty International. The company pledged not to remove information from its Chinese-hosted sites unless it received 'a legally binding notice from the government indicating that the material violates local laws, or if the content violates MSN's terms of use'.

88   Todd Bishop, 'Microsoft answers shareholders', Seattle Post-Intelligence, 15 November 2006.

89   The Committee to Protect Journalists issued a press release in August 2007 to express concern over a decision by MSN China and Yahoo China and other blogging services to demand a pledge that 'encourages' real-name registration for bloggers and commits companies to deleting 'illegal or inappropriate information'. 'Committee to Protect Journalists, Yahoo, MSN affiliates agree to blogging controls in China', 27 August 2007.

90   Peter Singer, 'Fear and freedom on the internet', Global Envision, 14 February 2006.

91   A statement from Beijing blogger Michael Anti on 14 January 2006.

92   Western internet companies are often beaten to technological developments by Chinese firms. Using home-grown technology, a Chinese company designed a mapping service in late 2007 that featured 360 degree street-level imaging of amazing quality. Stephen Hutcheon, 'Online mapmakers get down to earth', *Sydney Morning Herald*, 30 October 2007. Another company, Ruzuo.com, allows users to vote for movies and when enough people select a particular film the company sources a print and arranges a screening. Jeremy Goldkorn, 'Cinema meets Web 2.0 in Beijing', Danwei.org, 28 December 2007. A Chinese version of the popular virtual world game Second Life was unleashed in 2007. Chief executive of Beijing-based partner CRD claimed that the game would generate around 10 000 jobs in the country and be able to handle seven million users at the same time. Vic Keegan, 'Watch out Second Life: China launches virtual universe with seven million souls', *Guardian*, 2 June 2007.

93 Paul Marks, 'New software can identity you from your online habits', *New Scientist*, 16 May 2007.

94 'Concern about Microsoft's research in China into "profiling" internet users', Reporters Without Borders, 1 June 2007.

95 Paul Dixon, 'Patriotic web users defend China', *Guardian*, 18 April 2008.

96 Tim Anderson, 'WordPress makes a stand for open source morality', *Guardian*, 11 October 2007.

97 Testing by Human Rights Watch in 2006 found that Google's Chinese search engine censored far less content than similar services provided by Yahoo and Microsoft. Rebecca MacKinnon, 'Asia's fight for web rights', *Far Eastern Economic Review*, April 2008.

98 David Drummond, a senior vice president for corporate development, said that, 'this proposal would prevent us from operating Google.cn' and was 'not the right thing to do at this point and is not the answer to the internet censorship problem'. Elinor Mills, 'Google shareholders vote down proposal on censorship', ZDNet News, 10 May 2007. Erik Larkin, 'Google shareholders vote against anti-censorship proposal', PC World, 10 May 2007.

99 Jane Martinson, 'China censorship damaged us, Google founders admit', *Guardian*, 27 January 2007.

100 Joseph Weisenthal, 'Google annual meeting: shareholder proposals fail, but Brin abstains; board re-elected', paidContent.org, 8 May 2008. Google announced in April 2008 that it would greatly expand its Chinese workforce in an attempt to unseat its main rival, Baidu. George Chen, 'Google to add China staff, promote products', Reuters, 19 April 2008. The company also said it was introducing an online directory to translate Chinese into other languages to compete with Baidu. 'Google, trailing Baidu in China, to offer translation service', Bloomberg News, 6 May 2008.

101 Nart Villeneuve, 'Toward a measure of transparency', 18 June 2008.

102 Andrew McLaughlin, 'Google in China', Google blog, 27 January 2006.

103 Elliot Schrage, Committee on international relations, United States House of Representatives, Google blog, 15 February 2006.

104 CNNIC reports Baidu with 74.5% Market Share, China Tech Stories, 25 September 2007.

105 Google opened a research and development centre in China in 2005 to tap into the growing internet market. 'Google to open research centre in China', *Agence France-Presse*, 20 July 2005. Google invested in the popular YouTube-style site Xunlei in early 2007 in an attempt to compete with the country's largest competitor, Baidu. Jonathan Richards, 'Google gains edge in Baidu fight', *The Times*, 5 January 2007. Google acknowledged the differences in the Chinese technology market in late 2007 by announcing an aggressive push to develop products for users

who go online via mobile devices, rather than from a PC. Google's China President Lee Kai-Fu said that 'most Chinese users who touch mobile internet will have no PC at all'. Sophie Taylor, 'Google to focus on mobile internet in China', Reuters, 25 October 2007.

106 Isaac Mao, 'An open letter to Google founders—to save Google in China and save internet in China', Isaacmao.com, 9 February 2007. Despite Google appeasing the Chinese regime on any number of occasions, the regime announced in May 2008 that it was investigating whether the company, along with other local web firms, had breached state security laws by displaying 'illegal' maps of the country. Richard Spencer, 'Google "breaching China's state secrecy laws"', *Telegraph*, 7 May 2008.

107 Peter Goodman, 'Yahoo Says It Gave China Internet Data', *Washington Post*, 11 September 2005.

108 Reporters Without Borders reported that three Chinese cyber-dissidents were serving various terms of imprisonment and Yahoo was reluctant to acknowledge its complicity in the sentences. 'Yahoo implicated in third cyberdissident trial', Reporters Without Borders, 19 April 2006. A Hong Kong legislator unsuccessfully tried to convince authorities in the Chinese-controlled province that Yahoo Hong Kong had provided information to the Chinese authorities in the jailing of Shi Tao. Authorities claimed there was insufficient evidence to move forward with an investigation. 'Yahoo dissident case is abandoned', Times Online, 14 March 2007. Former US President Bill Clinton addressed a conference for Alibaba in 2005 and boldly stated: 'The political system's limits on freedom of speech ... have not seemed to have had adverse consequences on e-commerce.' Danny Rosen, 'Online curbs in China', *Australian*, 4 October 2005.

109 Luke O'Brien, 'Yahoo betrayed my husband', *Wired*, 15 March 2007.

110 Britain's National Union of Journalists called on its 40 000 members in 2006 to boycott Yahoo over its behaviour in China. Jason Deans, 'NUJ urges Yahoo boycott', *Guardian*, 2 June 2006.

111 David Teather, 'Yahoo appeals for support in censorship row', *Guardian*, 14 February 2006. Michael Callahan, Yahoo's senior vice-president and general counsel, wrote to Amnesty's secretary general, Irene Khan, defending his company's actions and pleading ignorance about the Shi Tao case; he claimed Amnesty had no information about the regime's investigation. 'Until we read the distressing facts about Shi Tao in the news,' he wrote, 'we did not know the particular information about which Chinese authorities issued a lawful demand for information from Yahoo China.' Letter from Michael Callihan to Irene Khan, 27 January 2006.

112 Juan Carlos Perez, 'Yahoo stockholders vote against anticensorship', IDG News Service, 12 June 2007.

113 David Bandurski, 'Pulling the strings of China's internet', *Far Eastern Economic Review*, December 2007.

114 The wife of imprisoned writer Wang Xiaoning, Yu Ling, travelled to America to advocate for her husband's release and pressure Yahoo. She wanted the internet company to pay damages and agitate for her husband's release. 'Without my husband, I never have a whole meal. I don't feel whole.' Luke O'Brien, 'Yahoo betrayed my husband', *Wired*, 15 March 2007.

115 Miguel Helft, 'Chinese political prisoner sues Yahoo', *International Herald Tribune*, 19 April 2007.

116 'Calling for lawsuit's dismissal, Yahoo says it is "political and diplomatic issue"', Reporters Without Borders, 29 August 2007.

117 'Yahoo, subject of suit, scolds China on rights', Associated Press, 12 June 2007.

118 Yahoo chief executive Jerry Yang pledged to create a human rights fund to assist imprisoned cyber-dissidents and their families. 'Yahoo settles lawsuit by families of jailed Chinese cyber-dissidents', Reporters Without Borders, 14 November 2007.

119 Jim Puzzanghera, 'Yahoo taken to task over China', *Los Angeles Times*, 7 November 2007. China's surveillance boom is also proving to be attractive to Western investors and a number of prominent American companies are now assisting the regime in jails, banks and police agencies. Keith Bradsher, 'An opportunity for Wall St. in China's surveillance boom', *New York Times*, 11 September 2007. The *New York Times* reported in August 2007 that an American-financed company had provided at least 20 000 police surveillance cameras for the streets of Shenzhen. Keith Bradsher, 'China enacting a high-tech plan to track people', *New York Times*, 12 August 2007.

120 Dibya Sarkar, 'Yahoo asks US govt to help dissidents', Associated Press, 22 February 2008.

121 'Yahoo lobbied on China, foreign control', Associated Press, 22 February 2008.

122 'Holding "One World, One Web' conference in Beijing condemned as a provocation', Reporters Without Borders, 25 April 2008.

123 Tom Zeller Jr, 'Web firms are grilled on dealings in China', *New York Times*, 16 February 2006.

124 *The Financial Times* reported in September 2007 that, according to American officials, Chinese military hackers broke into the Pentagon computer in June. China denied the report. Demetri Sevastopuloin and Richard McGregor, 'China "hacked" into Pentagon defence system', *Financial Times*, 4 September 2007. China's vice-minister of information industry,

Lou Qinjian, claimed in response to the allegation that his country had suffered 'massive' and 'shocking' losses of state and military secrets on the internet from spies. Gareth Powell, 'China says it suffers 'massive' internet spy damage', *China Economic Review*, 17 September 2007. In the days after US President George W Bush met the Dalai Lama in Washington in October 2007, many American websites in China were re-directed to Chinese sites. It was suggested that Chinese authorities were retaliating against US warmth shown to the Tibetan leader. 'US websites "hijacked" by Chinese hackers', *The Telegraph*, 19 October 2007. After the anti-Chinese protests in San Francisco in April 2008 following the Olympic torch relay, US intelligence reported that pro-China protest groups had jammed mobile phone networks and collected photos of demonstrators. Anne Hyland and David Crowe, 'Chinese filming torch protestors, says US report', *Australian Financial Review*, 22 April 2008.

125 Guy Newey, 'China hits back at US on rights, says Iraq war a disaster', AFP, 13 March 2008.

126 The US State Department established the Global Internet Freedom Task Force (GIFT) in 2006 to 'monitor and respond to threats to internet freedom and to advance the frontiers of internet freedom by expanding access to the internet'. Global internet freedom task force (GIFT) strategy: a blueprint for action, US Department of State, 28 December 2006.

127 'EU: towards a European Global Online Freedom Act', Global Voices Advocacy, 6 March 2008.

128 Frank Davies, Senators grill tech companies on aiding Chinese censorship, *The Mercury News*, 21 May 2008

129 Phone interview with the author, 13 September 2007.

130 The last few years have seen discussions between Yahoo, Google, Microsoft, France Telecom, Swedish telecoms company TeliaSonera and a host of human rights group in a 'multistakeholder process' designed to find meaningful ways in which companies can behave responsibly across the world. The aim is to implement a system by which companies can be judged on their actions and investors and users can then determine where to invest their money. Rebecca MacKinnon, 'Asia's fight for web rights', *Far Eastern Economic Review*, April 2008.

131 Peter Navarro, 'Yahoo isn't the only villain', *Los Angeles Times*, 8 November 2007. The *New York Times* editorialised that Yahoo was not alone in cosying up to the Chinese regime and its desire for censorship, but chastised the internet giant. 'Yahoo betrays free speech', *New York Times*, 2 December 2007.

132 Rebecca MacKinnon, 'Yahoo settles with victims' families: the big picture', RConversation, 15 November 2007.

133 A reporter on Murdoch's *New York Post*, Ian Spiegelman, claimed that he 'was ordered to kill a Page Six story about a Chinese diplomat and strip club that would have angered the communist regime and endangered Murdoch's broadcasting privileges' in China. Ken Auletta, 'Promises, promises', *New Yorker*, 2 July 2007. Murdoch's HarperCollins publishing house has shelved projects that were likely to upset Beijing. Murdoch expressed his frustration that the Chinese regime wasn't bending to his will by stating in 2005 that authorities were paranoid and plans to develop his empire there had 'hit a brick wall'. 'Murdoch hits "brick wall" in China', *Agence France-Presse*, 19 September 2005. During a 1993 speech in London, Murdoch said that modern technology communications 'proved an unambiguous threat to totalitarian regimes everywhere' and spent the following years making up for his honesty by kow-towing to Beijing. Joseph Kahn, 'Murdoch's dealings in China: it's business, and it's personal', *New York Times*, 26 June 2007.
134 Tunku Varadarajan, 'Bad Company', *Wall Street Journal*, 26 March 2001.
135 Dover, *Rupert's Adventures in China*.
136 Bobbie Johnson, 'Roadblocks on the superhighway', *Guardian* Comment is Free, 14 November 2007.
137 Yahoo China and Microsoft (briefly) were caught assisting the regime in the hunt for suspected Tibetans in early 2008. Rebecca MacKinnon, 'France24 catches Yahoo and MSN (briefly) aiding Chinese police hunt for Tibetans', RConversation, 22 March 2008. All the major Chinese online news portals featured photographs of Tibetans wanted by the Lhasa public security bureau for allegedly violent acts. The accompanying text read: 'Welcome the broad masses to actively make reports to the public security apparatus. Confidentiality and rewards are offered to tipsters …' 'Most wanted in Tibet', EastSouthWestNorth, 22 March 2008. Yahoo denied posting photos on its website, though only the American arm of the company issued the statement. In China, internet portals are not allowed to run original news reporting and can only run stories from approved news sources. Rebecca MacKinnon, 'Caught in a culture war: Yahoo's sticky China situation', RConversation, 23 March 2008.
138 Tom Malinowski, 'China's willing censors', *Washington Post*, 20 April 2001. Sina.com launched an English language version of its website in May 2008 to meet the global demand for information about the Sichuan earthquake. It claimed then to have 800 million page views per day.
139 Malinowski, ibid.
140 Tim Johnson, 'As internet censorship tightens in China, private firms pitch in', *McClatchy Newspapers*, 5 October 2007.
141 Interview with the author, Shanghai, 7 July 2007.

142 Richard Lea, 'A new cultural revolution', *Guardian*, 16 January 2008.

143 Lea, ibid. There are an estimated 540 mobile phone users in China, with around 44 million new ones every six months. Simon Usborne, 'China: in numbers', *Independent*, 10 May 2008.

144 Aditya Chakrabortty, 'Is this the Indian century?', *Guardian*, 29 March 2008.

145 Interview with the author, Shanghai, 10 July 2007.

146 In *Time Magazine*'s 2007 '100 people who shape our world' edition, Arianna Huffington interviewed Zeng Jinyan, a famous blogger and activist whose husband, Hu Jia, was imprisoned by state security. Huffington's article couldn't help but mention the Tiananmen Square massacre even though there was no direct relevance to her short piece. Arianna Huffington, Zeng Jinyan, 30 April 2007. Her husband was arrested and released a number of times in 2007 and 2008. Reporters Without Borders awarded him and his wife its 'China' human rights prize in November 2007. Hu Jia was imprisoned in early 2008 for three and a half years for 'subverting state power'. Authorities were incensed with his online claims that the International Olympic Committee hadn't pushed Beijing to improve its human rights record. Clifford Coonan, 'Hu Jia: China's enemy within', *Independent*, 4 April 2008. Hu Jia's wife was able to continue posting on her blog after his imprisonment. She wrote in late March 2008: 'The brutal, irrational nature of the actual situation fills me with dread. Were it not for the support of friends and family, I might not have made it this far.' Zeng Jinyan, China Digital Times, 29 March 2008.

147 Geremie R Barme and Sang Ye, 'The great firewall of China', *Wired*, June 1997.

148 The massive growth of 'crowdsourcing' in China, the gathering of online crowds via chat rooms, instant messaging and bulletin boards, is the sign of things to come.

149 Unnati Gandhi, 'Tech-savvy Pro-Tibet protestors get message across', *Globe and Mail*, 8 August 2007.

150 Hong Kong based academic Rebecca MacKinnon argues it is likely that Chinese bloggers will further challenge hosting firms. 'The more these companies institute terms of service, and the more their censorship can't be explained by those terms of services, [the more] I predict we will see even more lawsuits.' Rebecca MacKinnon, 'Chinese bloggers thumb their noses at "self discipline"', RConversation, 28 August 2007.

151 A telling example of the kind of internet stories that generate huge interest in the Chinese online community is this story from early 2008 that features spoofing and parodying of a young girl and her comments about 'very yellow, very violent' images on TV: http://www.zonaeu

ropa.com/20080107_1.htm. Internet bulletin boards have also become extremely popular, allowing users to discuss unsolved crimes or the lives of husbands or wives allegedly committing adultery. Howard W French, 'Mob rule on China's internet: the keyboard as weapon', *International Herald Tribune*, 1 June 2006. When sexually explicit images of some of Asia's best-known pop stars started to appear online in early 2008, a furious debate ensued about the rights and responsibilities of websites. Hong Kong authorities arrested many people for publishing the photos but protestors argued that freedom of speech was being infringed. Keith Bradsher, 'Internet sex case stirs free-speech issues in Hong Kong', *New York Times*, 13 February 2008.

152 Jonathan Watts, 'Behind the great firewall', *Guardian*, 9 February 2008.

153 Despite the massive growth, China-based analyst Fons Tuinstra reported attending Tudou's New Year's Party in early 2007 to celebrate its passing the threshold of 10 million downloads per day. But the company was losing money despite being the market leader in China. Fons Tuinstra, 'China: very few making money online', Poynteronline, 13 January 2007.

154 Chinese authorities announced in early 2008 that any company showing online videos must have a licence but only state-owned outfits would qualify. Bruce Einhorn, 'New fears for China's YouTube wannabes', *Business Week*, 9 January 2008. The Ministry of Information clarified the rules soon after by stating that companies that had already uploaded audio and video content before the regulations came into effect could continue to operate as before but any new companies would have to comply. 'Ministry of information eases new rules on online video and audio sharing', Reporters Without Borders, 5 February 2008. Authorities added another level of censorship in early 2008 by including ghosts, monsters and supernatural figures to a list of banned items for video and audio content. 'Horror' had to be excised. 'Ghosts, monsters now banned in China', Reuters, 14 February 2008.

155 Rebecca MacKinnon, 'Tudou survives with a spanking', RConversation, 20 March 2008.

156 Facebook entered into a partnership with a Chinese company in late 2007 and hoped to avoid the pitfalls of previous Western internet companies by creating 'silos' of information that could more easily comply with Chinese regulations. Jane Macartney, 'Facebook's hopes to enter the tangled web of China gain momentum', *The Times*, 19 November 2007. Rebecca MacKinnon, 'Facebook goes to China … will it censor too?' RConversation, 31 October 2007.

157 David Smith, 'Murdoch his net to China', *Observer*, 20 May 2007.

158 Despite the prejudices many Western journalists bring to China, they are increasingly reading Chinese blogs to understand the country

beyond the regime's official line. Hong Kong based academic Rebecca MacKinnon writes that one of the key reasons for this is because 'the China story is not generally a 'breaking story' but rather a 'process story' about how this complex and geo-politically important country is changing, and what that change means for the rest of the world'. Fons Tuinstra, 'China: foreign correspondents rely more on blogs', Poynteronline, 27 June 2007.

159 'Officials enter China's blogosphere', *Australian*, 27 November 2006.
160 Thomas Friedman, *The World Is Flat: A Brief History of the Twenty-First Century*, Farrar, Strauss and Giroux, New York, 2005, pp. 512–14.
161 Mure Dickie, 'China city to tighten internet controls', *Financial Times Asia*, 9 July 2007.
162 Bruce Pedroletti, 'People power halts chemical factory plan', *Guardian Weekly*, 15 June 2007.
163 Colleen Ryan, 'Grim discovery opens a nation's eyes', *Australian Financial Review*, 19 June 2007. In early 2008, with many parents still searching for their children working as slaves in brick kilns, Chinese bloggers launched an online campaign to raise funds for the parents to support them. 'A net campaign for the parents of slaves', Global Voices, 25 January 2008.
164 'Citizen journos battle China's censors', *Agence France-Presse*, 25 June 2007.
165 Fons Tuinstra, 'Goodbye Gutenberg', Nieman Reports, Winter 2006.
166 Tuinstra, ibid.
167 Lev Grossman, 'Wang Xiaofeng', *Time*, 16 December 2006.
168 Yongnian Zheng and Guoguang Wu, 'Information technology, public space and collective action in China', *Comparative Political Studies*, 2005.
169 Interview with the author, Beijing, 11 July 2007.
170 Barbara Demick, 'China cracks down on irreverent websites', *Los Angeles Times*, 5 February 2008.

Afterword

1   Leonard Doyle, 'Tough-talking Clinton vows to "obliterate" Iran if it ever dares to attack US ally Israel', *Independent*, 23 April 2008.
2   'The world according to newspapers', Online journalism blog, 23 March 2008.
3   Jay Rosen, professor of journalism at New York University, argues that greater empowerment of citizens will inevitably lead to journalism with higher social value and worth. Whether this will assist the financial bottom line remains to be seen. Roy Gleenslade, 'How do we fund

journalism in future?' *Guardian*, 1 May 2008. Leading British commentator Roy Greenslade writes that journalists in the future will have to share information with readers to create more participatory media. 'Public service journalism' will allow, he says, the possibility of democratising a process that has been kept elitist for too long. Roy Greenslade, 'Move over: journalists will have to share their space', *Sydney Morning Herald*, 1 May 2008. User-generated content filled nearly the entire edition of *Budget Travel* magazine in early 2008, with over 300 people contributing writing and photography. Dylan Stableford, 'Magazine publishes 100 per cent user-generated issue', Foliomag.com, 12 May 2008.

4   A Zogby International poll of newspaper editors around the world in 2008 found that a majority believed that both online and print news would soon be free and they remained optimistic about the media business. The biggest threat to newspapers, they said, came from the web and young people. Katie Allen, 'Editors upbeat despite rise of free titles', *Guardian*, 6 May 2008.

5   'Fouad's blog, FreeFouad.com Blocked', Saudi Jeans, 3 April 2008.

6   Daniel H Pink, 'Why the world is flat', *Wired*, May 2005.

7   In early 2008, mainstream media commentators and economists started questioning Friedman's 'World is Flat' thesis, principally because of the stormy economic conditions and how a 'backlash against economic integration'—namely IMF—and World Bank-imposed policies—'has pressured governments to retreat from multilateralism'. National borders on the internet, with the increasing use of language-specific characters, is also leading to a Balkanisation of the technology. Bob Davies, 'World no longer flat: globalisation challenged', *Wall Street Journal*, 28 April 2008.

8   A study, published in *The International Journal of Press/Politics* in July 2008, found that although many journalists in the Arab world are favourable towards American people, they simply don't trust its government to assist in the movement towards democracy in the region. Lawrence Pintak, Jeremy Ginges and Nicholas Felton, 'Misreading the Arab media', *New York Times*, 25 May 2008.

9   Fareez Zakaria, 'The rise of the rest', *Newsweek International*, 3 May 2008.

10   Published by Public Affairs, New York, 2008.

11   Ian Buruma, 'After America', *New Yorker*, 21 April 2008.

12   Ibid.

13   The poll, conducted by WorldPublicOpinion.org, in a host of countries (including the US, Mexico, Ukraine, Britain, France, China, the Palestinian territories and Nigeria), recorded encouraging signs of a global consensus over media freedom and a desire for greater

openness. Interestingly, only citizens in Iran and Jordan strongly endorsed governmental regulation of the internet. Another study by WorldPublicOpinion.org, released in May 2008, found that publics across the world wanted more responsive governments and remained disappointed with many of their current representatives. 'World publics say governments should be more responsive to the will of the people', 12 May 2008.

14 Eric Alterman, 'Out of print', *New Yorker*, 31 March 2008.

15 Darren Waters, 'Web in infancy, says Berners-Lee', BBC News, 30 April 2008.

16 Circulation figures for the major American papers remain in free-fall, though *USA Today* and the *Wall Street Journal* are challenging this trend. In many other regions around the world, however, newspapers are thriving in popularity, including the Middle East. The *National*, an English-language daily based in Abu Dhabi, launched in early 2008 as an example of a Western-friendly publication with journalists poached from some of the world's finest papers. Its independence and success will be tested only in time. Heather Timmons, 'High hopes for English-language paper in Abu Dhabi', *International Herald Tribune*, 28 April 2008.